GOURMET LIGHT

"Greer Underwood wrote *Gourmet Light* not as a weight-loss manual
but as a collection of techniques and recipes aimed at *prevention*
of weight gain for lovers of fine food."
—*Woman's Day*

"(The recipes) call for French cooking techniques but are 'lightened'
with special cooking methods that cut in half the calorie content of
traditional gourmet meals."
—*Tufts University Diet & Nutrition Letter*

"At last—a book that shows how to take a basic recipe and cut down its calories
by reducing fattening ingredients without totally changing its taste."
—*ALA Booklist*

"For lots more tips and recipes on cooking leaner, we like
Greer Underwood's *Gourmet Light.*"
—*Mademoiselle*

"A guide to cutting the calories without cutting the good taste. . . .
The food is lighter, but definitely not short on taste."
—*Richmond (VA) Times-Dispatch*

---

*Winner of the Duncan Hines/IACP 1985 Best Cookbook of the Year award
in the special diet catagory*

GOURMET LIGHT

Simple and Sophisticated Recipes for the Health-Conscious Cook

SECOND EDITION

BY GREER UNDERWOOD

ILLUSTRATED BY FRANK WESTERBERG

The Globe Pequot Press

OLD SAYBROOK, CONNECTICUT

Nutrition analysis by Nutrition and Diet Services, Portland, Oregon

Cover and text design by Nancy Freeborn

Library of Congress Cataloging-in-Publication Data

Underwood, Greer.

    Gourmet light: simple and sophisticated recipes for the health-conscious cook/ by Greer Underwood: illustrated by Frank Westerberg.—2nd ed.

       p. cm.

    Includes index.

    ISBN 1-56440-232-0

    1. Reducing diets—recipes. I. Title.

RM222.2.U54 1993

641.5'635—dc20   93-9727

                                           CIP

Manufactured in the United States of America

Second Edition/First Printing

CONTENTS

ACKNOWLEDGMENTS

This book is hardly the work of a single person despite the credit on the cover. The know-how of a lot of people is bound between these covers; were it not for them it would never be done. Thanks to all, and to Cary Hull for her enthusiastic guidance. And for their contributions of another sort, thanks to my three guys.

INTRODUCTION

The Health-Conscious Cook

These are exercise-crazed yet food-happy times. Never have so many Americans panted and pumped their way to visions of physical perfection. And never have so many been interested in food and its paraphernalia—an irony peculiar to this athletic-shoe era. The culinary consciousness of the last decade, like the national devotion to exercise, has grown more rapidly than a croissant can rise. The challenge of the times is to enjoy the one without compromising the other.

Fitness is more than physical; it's a healthy psyche as well as a strong body. It's a vitality of body and spirit that can't be nurtured on an inadequate diet. One too rich in calories and fats or too poor in nutrients defeats all that hard work. As eaters one and all, we have our homework to do. The basics of nutrition are as foreign to most of us as the intricacies of a silicon chip. While we wouldn't try to build a computer without knowing how one works, we often try to build our bodies on a similar lack of knowledge. Of the three classifications of food, proteins, carbohydrates, and fats, which do you think nutritionists recommend should make up the bulk of our daily diet? And the second? Most experts agree carbohydrates should account for more than half (60 to 65 percent), fats for a bit less than a third (25 to 30 percent), and the proteins the remaining 10 to 15 percent.

You may think your daily fat intake is decidedly below that 30 percent figure. Yet in this century, according to the Food and Nutrition Board of the National Academy of Sciences, fat intake has risen from 32 percent to 42 percent of our daily intake, probably due to the excessive use of fats, oils, and to some degree, meat. We have one of the highest fat-content diets in the world. It lurks in most everything we eat, from avocados to zweiback, making a 100 percent fat-free diet as impossible as it is unhealthful. With our burgeoning culinary curiosity and fat intake, it makes sense to cut calorie corners where we can—without diluting our pleasure or endangering our health.

Voicing a concern about calories, fats, and vitamins was once the province of health food faddists, the type who would forage for wild nuts and berries rather than eat anything a machine had touched. Today, the cook who is unconcerned with overprocessed foodstuffs, nutritionally empty foods, and fats is the rarity. We're learning about the foods we eat even as we begin to hanker for pasta instead of spaghetti. Many are finding it difficult to indulge their love of fine food and maintain a healthy respect for the body. This book will point the way.

Thinking Thin

Is your life a revolving cycle of Spartan restraint followed by hedonistic indulgence? Do you diet successfully for a week or two, denying all pleasures, then binge on goodies? Is a hot fudge sundae your idea of a reward for losing weight?

If you answered yes to all the above, you're probably still looking for a way to lose weight. Yo-yo dieting, the starvation-binge route, is ineffective because the body's metabolic rate slows during times of calorie restriction. As you eat less, the body adjusts to function on less calories. Unfortunately, as you resume more normal eating habits, the body continues to prepare for times of "starvation" and the pounds start packing back on. Now you're eating a fairly normal diet, but actually gaining weight, instead of just maintaining. Nobody ever said life was fair. But there is a bright side; if you learn to eat in the most healthy way possible, you can enjoy delicious foods without ever being hungry and manage to maintain your ideal weight.

The most successful dieters are those who don't. Don't binge diet, that is. They enjoy good food, in moderation, every day. They are aware of calorie counts in common foods. They know there is no such thing as a skinny food, that only water is calorie-free. And they are active people, not necessarily marathon runners, but people who stand when they can sit, walk instead of ride, climb stairs, and shun elevators. Successful dieters know, at least intuitively, that taking fat off via exercise and semi-starvation is much harder than not eating to begin with.

Consider this: A 120-pound person running an eight-minute mile expends about 82 calories per mile; a 160-pounder will use about 110 calories. That's the equivalent of an apple for the lighter runner or a glass of low-fat milk for the heavier one. Nutritionists estimate that a pound of fat represents about 3,500 calories your body didn't use. Assuming you can exercise off 100 calories for every mile run, it would take 11 or 12 days to lose a pound of fat running 3 miles every day. Disheartening, isn't it? In light of these figures (and your own), thinking thin is more than a state of mind, it must be a mode of life.

What Gourmet Light Is

To be a winner at the weight-loss game means educating yourself about the basics of metabolism and nutrition. It means learning how to eat to satisfy your hunger and learning how to cook to satisfy your appetite. This is a cookbook, an everyday guide to good, healthful eating habits. Many of you don't need to lose a pound, but you are looking for ways to eat well and maintain your happy weight state.

Gourmet Light is for those who enjoy fine food but keep a health-conscious eye peeled. This is a cookbook for people who exercise not only for the sport of it but also because it feels good. This is also a cookbook for people who plan to exercise but can never quite fit it in, people who are looking for viable ways to trim extra calories and fat from their daily meals. This is for those who like to keep abreast of food trends, from sun-dried tomatoes to shiitake mushrooms, and for people who relish a meal not only for what it is, but also for what it is not.

Herein the reader will find information on nutrition, metabolism, and the role of fats, proteins, and carbohydrates. You'll find out what pot to buy for which task, how to store foods, and where to find hard-to-come-by ingredients. There are tips on cooking techniques, and short soliloquies on nutritional concerns. Because not everyone is a seasoned cook, the recipes are thorough and detailed. If you already know your way around the kitchen, this book will teach you how to reduce calories in many of the dishes you now prepare, as well as give you some new and delicious ideas. When the ten techniques of *Gourmet Light* cooking become as natural to you as boiling water, you'll be able to pare calories from many of your favorite dishes.

This is not meant to be the only cookbook you'll ever need, for there are decidedly occasions when a no-stops, full-calorie-ahead, four-star dinner is in order. This is a way of cooking for everyday sort of use that you can live with happily, for a lifetime. Learn to cut a few superfluous calories from your daily "bread" and those strident days of diet may become a thing of the past.

What It Is Not

This is not a diet manual. No promise here of pounds lost in two easy weeks and no ersatz ingredients.

It's tempting when writing a reduced-calorie cookbook to imply that all manner of foods can be prepared in such a way as to render them skinny. Not so. You'll find a Mimosa Sherbet but not ice creams. You'll enjoy Pork Cutlet in Cider Cream Sauce, but without unhealthy amounts of saturated fats. Many dishes can be rewritten to remove excessive calories; those that cannot simply aren't here. The aim was not to make do but to do well, and if that couldn't be done the recipe wasn't included. Indulge in Sole and Crab Peppers, Chilled Tomato Soup with Basil Cream, Turkey Cutlet with Cranberried Apple Sauce, and finish with a smooth Mango Mousse. Here are the techniques of good cooking without excessive use of highly fatty, cholesterol-choked foods.

How It Came to Be

Internationally, the French have always been acclaimed for turning out the world's best chefs, and it is to them we have turned for decades to decree what's new. When they threw away the flour bin, reaching instead for the stockpot and mounds of butter, we followed (or at least au courant restaurants did). When they threw the vegetables into the food processor creating smooth purees, we did too. When they started undercooking not only beef, but also lamb and fish, we at least agreed the beef should be very rare, and many started enjoying lamb that way, too. If they said "Pirouette!" we obliged like good students. They taught us haute cuisine, they brought us nouvelle cuisine, and they introduced cuisine minceur, the "skinny" cooking of Michel Guerard. One hears little of cuisine minceur these days, mostly because it is time-consuming and expensive to duplicate in the average kitchen, but I would be remiss not to mention what was a large inspiration for this book. I had long believed that good food didn't have to be fattening and that thin food didn't have to be boring, and had worked on ideas to that effect. But it was the international interest in Guerard's cuisine minceur that led me to believe others were looking for good, but not fattening, food. Guerard's cuisine minceur is not for the single-person kitchen or even for the American kitchen, calling for such delicacies as squab and spiny lobster. But it is a volume to which I still go to browse.

Food today in France and the United States has been strongly influenced by nouvelle cuisine as outlined by Guerard, Paul Bocuse, and other French chefs as well as an innovative crop of American chefs, primarily from California, who have come to enjoy international prominence. Now there are fewer red meats; fish and poultry predominate. There is a greater emphasis on vegetables and how food looks. Sauces are lighter. The grill is in. Pastas, grains, beans, and "peasant" foods are dished up at tony restaurants right beside precious and often hard-to-find ingredients such as radicchio, yellow and eggplant-hued peppers, and bonsai (miniaturized) vegetables.

In the United States the newfound pride in our native foods and chefs has meant less dependence on the grand masters—and a surge of independence. Everyone is talking about American cuisine, its dedication to simplicity, home-grown ingredients, and the hometown talent responsible for it. Although when one sees a recipe that typifies the new cuisine, such as Chèvre-Stuffed Chicken Breast with Wild Mushroom Sauce, I sometimes wonder just who redefined simplicity. Perhaps the crux of the matter is best explained by the French gastronome and cook, Raymond Oliver, who wrote, "To innovate in cooking it is more difficult to attack a boiled egg than a pheasant mousse." Cooks have long known it is easier to elaborate than delineate, easier to pile luxury on excess than improve on the ordinary. Nevertheless, the new American cuisine remains true to its indigenous roots—namely plain food, in the sense of native products such as corn, grits, buckwheat, and maple syrup that are coming into their own again. Our chefs have become the trendsetters in a field heretofore dominated by Europeans.

Gourmet Light cooking includes a bit of all these trends, for it is a product of our times. Its soul lies in gourmet techniques, lightened in the spirit of the day and using the very freshest and best our native seas and lands have to offer—but always with an eye on the scale. So enjoy!

Substitutes for Fatty Foods

Fatty Foods	Skinny Foods
DAIRY	**DAIRY**
whole milk	skim milk
cream, half and half	skimmed evaporated milk
sour cream	nonfat sour cream, yogurt, crème blanc
ice cream	nonfat sugarless frozen desserts
butter	reduced-calorie margarine
cheese	fat-free cheese, goat cheese (in small amounts), Parmesan cheese, homemade yogurt cheese
MEATS and EGGS	**MEATS, EGGS, and OTHER PROTEIN SOURCES**
sirloin, porterhouse, and chuck steak, ground beef, ribs	eye of the round, top round, ground poultry without skin, rice and beans, vegetables, fish
beef bologna and most cold cuts	lean ham and turkey or chicken breast
fatty pork cuts including ribs	pork tenderloin
sausage, bacon	Canadian bacon, bacon bits made from soy
dark poultry with skin	white meat poultry with no skin
hot dogs	low-fat hot dogs
egg yolks	substitute 2 whites for each yolk in cooking, egg substitute
BREADS, FLOUR PRODUCTS, and GRAINS	**BREADS, FLOUR PRODUCTS, and GRAINS**
granola	fat-free granola
muffins, biscuits, scones, cookies, cakes	reduced-fat and -sugar muffins and cookies and cakes, angel food cake, graham crackers, breads and rolls
COOKING FATS and FLAVORINGS	**COOKING FATS and FLAVORINGS**
butter, margarine	reduced-fat margarine in small amounts
oils	vinegars, broth, wine, lemon juice or water, nonstick cooking spray, nonstick pans, parchment paper, microwave, grill, broil
salad dressings	reduced-fat salad dressings, pureed fruits, lemon juice, yogurt, tofu, crème blanc, broth, vinegars, herbs
marinades	vinegars, broth, wine, or water, herbs, fruit juices, mustards, salsa
mayonnaise	fat-free mayonnaise, homemade reduced-fat mayonnaise–type dressings
SNACKS	**SNACKS**
nuts	roasted chestnuts
potato chips	pretzels, air-popped unbuttered popcorn
crackers	reduced- or fat-free crackers
candy	dried and fresh fruits, hard candies in moderation
MISCELLANEOUS	**MISCELLANEOUS**
sesame seeds	use sesame seeds sparingly, bread crumbs, poppy and caraway seeds, water chestnuts, chestnuts
avocado	basil-pesto sauce, salsa, minced cucumber

CHAPTER 1

THE PRIMER

The Primer

The Primer is perhaps the most important chapter in this book, for here are the ten techniques of *Gourmet Light* cooking. Once you've mastered them, paring calories and fat from most any recipe will become automatic. Nothing here is tricky or requires culinary expertise; anyone who can separate an egg can cook—deliciously—the thin way. Success rests on your resolve to think thin, always looking for ways to cheat a dish of excessive calories but not at the expense of flavor.

This Primer will teach you how to cut down on the overuse of butter, fats, oils, and calorie-heavy flour thickenings. You'll discover how some readily available and inexpensive kitchen equipment can make you a winner at the calorie game. And you can have some fun testing your calorie and fat IQ.

So hone up those knives, and fill your kitchen with appetizing aromas fat only with flavor and happy cooking!

Getting Started

Not convinced? Think the only way to watch your weight is to go on a celery and water regime for a few days? Perhaps the following tallies will give you pause. The same meal, one prepared the traditional way and one the *Gourmet Light* way. Both are good, but which would you choose?

The Traditional Meal

Gazpacho, made with oil and croutons	157 calories/cup
Sauteed sole (6 oz) with Hollandaise	425 calories
Asparagus Mimosa (1 cup)	115 calories
Mixed-Green Salad with Vinaigrette	135 calories
Apple Pie	404 calories
TOTAL	1236 calories

The Gourmet Light Meal

Gazpacho (limited oil, no croutons)	64 calories/cup
Steamed sole (6 oz), Reduced-Calorie Hollandaise	205 calories
Asparagus Mimosa (1 cup)	46 calories
Mixed-Green Salad with Herbed French Vinaigrette	47 calories
Hot Apple Tart	144 calories
TOTAL	506 calories

Cooking the *Gourmet Light* way is no more difficult than any other. It takes only the resolve to want to change a few habits, the knowledge of what to change, and a nodding acquaintance with calorie and fat counts. Why not test your Calorie IQ right now with the quiz below? And then on to the stove! (Or do you have to exercise first?)

Check Your Calorie and Fat IQ

You can't play the game until you know how to score. Calorie and fat awareness is the key to weight control. While it's not necessary to carry a pocket calorie guide, it is sensible to have a working knowledge of some basic calorie and fat facts. Check your nutritional IQ here.

TRUE or FALSE

1. A calorie is a calorie is a calorie. All calories, being units of energy, are treated the same in the body, which cannot distinguish between a carrot calorie and a brownie calorie.

2. If you're watching your fat intake but find yourself at a fast food restaurant, you'd be better off with a regular hamburger than a garden salad (without meat and cheese) and a packet of dressing.

3. There's no fat in skim milk.

4. Baked goods, snack foods, and breads that boast "No Cholesterol" and

"100% vegetable oil" can still be high in unhealthy fats and contribute to blood cholesterol levels.

5. A 4-ounce serving of poached salmon has fewer calories than a 4-ounce serving of lean broiled steak.

6. You can enjoy any food in moderation.

7. A tablespoon of honey has more nutrients and is lower in calories than a tablespoon of sugar.

CIRCLE THE FOOD LOWER IN CALORIES AND FAT

8. A 5-ounce piece of steamed haddock seasoned with parsley, dill, and lemon or 1 deviled egg.

9. A tablespoon of vegetable oil, margarine, or butter.

10. A cup of cottage cheese or a chocolate-coated ice cream bar.

11. A McDonald's Fillet o'Fish sandwich or a McDonald's hamburger.

12. A piece of pepperoni pizza (from a 10-inch pie) or a McLean hamburger.

13. A half-cup serving of chocolate pudding, a cup of New England–style clam chowder, or 1 cup of fruited yogurt.

THE ANSWERS

1. False. All calories are not created equal. Calories from fat are not only twice as fattening as those from carbohydrates and proteins (a gram of fat supplies 9 calories compared to 4 for proteins and carbohydrates) but also tend to be stored as body fat. Two factors contribute to this. One, because fats are easily digested, the body uses only about 3 percent of their calories to process them. On the other hand, digestion of carbohydrates and proteins, with more complex molecules, uses up about 20 percent of their calories. Second, the body prefers to store fat calories as fat, rather than use them for fuel. So eating a low-fat diet is more important than calorie counting alone.

2. True. A hamburger has 9 grams of fat. The salad contains 20 grams of fat if you use the whole packet of dressing, and that's without a serving of croutons or bacon bits.

3. False. Skim milk gets 5 percent of its calories from fat.

4. True. If the products are made with a highly saturated fat (for example, an oil that is hydrogenated, or a tropical oil) they may lead to higher blood cholesterol levels.

5. True. But the difference is much smaller than you might think. The salmon, a relatively fatty fish, has about 246 calories and 8 grams of fat for 4 ounces; the beef, with visible fat removed, about 272 calories and 9 grams of fat.

6. False. Despite the conventional wisdom that any and all foods can be enjoyed in moderation, if you truly want to experience weight loss without hunger and enjoy a healthy diet, foods high in saturated fat should be avoided nearly to the point of abstinence. These foods include butter; full-fat dairy products like whole milk, cream, and sour cream; fatty meats such as bacon and sausage; and desserts such as cakes and premium ice cream.

7. False. a tablespoon of honey has 61 calories; a tablespoon of sugar has 46. Honey does supply a very small amount of potassium.

8. The haddock has about 112 calories and ½ gram fat in 5 ounces; the egg, made with mayonnaise, has 180 calories and 8 grams of fat.

9. All the same, approximately 100 calories and 12 to 14 grams of fat per tablespoon.

10. Although the ice cream bar is lower in calories (150) than the cottage cheese (240), the ice cream bar is higher in fat. In this case then, the cottage cheese, in spite of its higher calories, is the better choice, because it is lower in fat.

11. The McDonald's burger has 257 calories and 9 grams of fat; the fish sandwich, 370 calories and 18 grams of fat. Although raw fish is generally lower in calories than raw beef, the frying and the mayonnaise used in the sandwich make up the extra 113 calories and added fat grams.

12. A McLean hamburger has 10 grams of fat and 320 calories. The slice of pizza has 6 grams of fat and 140 calories.

13. The pudding has 247 calories and 9 grams of fat; the chowder has 271 calories and 14 grams of fat; the fruited yogurt has 260 calories and 7 grams of fat.

11–13 correct	highest honors
8–10 correct	honor roll
5–7 correct	passing grade
0–4 correct	it's study time

This is not to suggest that those interested in losing pounds or maintaining their weight should opt for a chocolate-coated ice cream bar instead of cottage cheese, or pudding instead of chowder. Its intent is to point out some commonly held misconceptions and myths; fish is *not* automatically low in calories; how it's prepared is essential. Butter is not more fattening than margarine, honey isn't much better for you than sugar, and a well-dressed salad may wreak havoc with your daily fat tally. A paperback calorie and fat gram guide is good reading for anyone interested in weight control.

Here are the ten techniques of *Gourmet Light* cooking. Digest them and say good-bye to diets forever.

THE TEN TECHNIQUES OF GOURMET LIGHT COOKING

1. "Sauteing" in stocks, broths, and wine instead of fats and oils

When a recipe calls for butter and/or oil for the sauteing of onions, garlic, shallots, and so on, substitute stock, broth, or wine or a combination for calorie- and fat-free cooking. Add enough liquid to cover the bottom of the pan by about one-eighth inch, bring to a boil, add food to be "sauteed," cover, and reduce heat to medium. Stir frequently, adding more liquid if it evaporates before the food is cooked.

2. Replacing heavy cream with skim or low-fat milk

The importance of using milk, either whole, low-fat, or skim, is best stressed by the figures (pun intended):

Skim milk	90 calories/.5 gram fat/cup
Low-fat (1%) milk	100 calories/3 grams fat/cup
Low-fat (2%) milk	120 calories/5 grams fat/cup
Whole (3.5%) milk	150 calories/8 grams fat/cup
Half-and-half	300 calories/32 grams fat/cup
Light cream	480 calories/48 grams fat/cup
Heavy cream	800 calories/72 grams fat/cup

How many calories and fat grams you want to save will determine which of these dairy products you use. A nutritional aside: Cooking with skim milk supplies almost twice the amount of protein found in cream.

3. Reducing and replacing oil in salad dressings

When a skinny bowl of greens is lavished with 2 tablespoons of regular dressing, the result is a caloric avalanche of at least 200 calories and 12 to 14 grams of fat. If you eat but 5 salads a week, it will only take 3½ weeks for that dressing to be a pound of fat. Why not reduce or even eliminate much of the oil used in dressings with a skinny alternative? The unlikely but excellent surrogate is chicken stock (the kind you make yourself) or canned beef consomme. Why homemade? Why the consomme and not just canned broth? Both the canned consomme and your own homemade stock contain enough gelatin—one occurring naturally as the collagen in the bones melts, the other added—to somewhat duplicate the natural viscosity of oil. Another very acceptable alternative is enriched commercial broth: instructions may be found on page 21. Stock-based salad dressings are light, flavorful, and nutritious.

4. Thickening with cornstarch and arrowroot instead of flour

Although a recent culinary trend, popularized by nouvelle cuisine, is to thicken sauces by reduction (that is, boiling down), it is occasionally necessary to thicken a soup, stew, or sauce by means of a starch—either flour, arrowroot, or cornstarch. Note these measures for the *same* thickening ability:

3 teaspoons flour (1 tablespoon)	50 calories
2 teaspoons cornstarch	20 calories
1 teaspoon arrowroot	15 calories

Arrowroot and cornstarch (you may also use potato starch) give a shiny, translucent quality to a sauce, while flour gives a more opaque look. Both arrowroot and cornstarch must be dissolved in a little cold water before using; if heated too long or brought to a boil, a sauce thickened with arrowroot or cornstarch may liquefy, a process called hydrolyzing. To avoid this problem, always keep foods with these starches added to them on moderate heat.

5. The magic of crème blanc

Sometime in my early twenties I became aware of the omnipotent presence of the calorie god. Now every morsel I ate and drank seemed to get counted whereas before it had gone unnoticed. As a child I yearned for the independence of adulthood, only to find it came harnessed with responsibility. Mother didn't make me finish eating liver anymore, but that didn't mean I was free to eat potato chips for dinner either. To escape the calorie god's ever-watchful eye, I became a constant calorie counter, being careful not to overindulge. To avoid the boredom of diet foods, I experimented in the kitchen a great deal, developing the cooking style you find here. One wonderful way I found to cheat the calorie god at her own game was crème blanc, a mixture of cottage cheese and yogurt used in place of sour cream and sometimes butter, which adds a touch of finesse and variety. You'll find out how to make it on page 34. If, like me, you are often pressed for time, substitute nonfat sour cream or plain nonfat yogurt.

6. Retaining the natural moisture in foods

It may seem redundant to stress the importance of buying fresh foods in a day when overly processed foods are as "in" as a beehive hairdo, but natural flavors are so vital to the success of *Gourmet Light* cooking that it can't be stressed enough. Second only to buying the best is to select the cooking method that most retains the natural moisture in foods, reducing, even eliminating, the need for fats, oils, and rich sauces. Here are suggestions in no particular order of importance.

a. *Parchment paper, aluminum foil, and waxed paper*—By encasing the food in an envelope, evaporation is greatly reduced and the food stews in its own juices, creating a natural sauce. Lettuce, cabbage leaves, and cornhusks may also be used.

b. *Salt-encased cooking*—This very old method of cooking is excellent for roasting large pieces of meat, fish, or poultry to juicy perfection. The food is encased in a paste of coarse salt and water, forming an inedible crust that is cracked open and discarded after roasting. Oddly, the salt doesn't permeate the food; because of the salt, the moisture in the food isn't lost.

c. *Poaching*—The term means to immerse a food in a simmering liquid. Poaching is generally reserved for poultry, but lamb and even beef can be deliciously poached. For oven poaching the food is placed in a film of liquid, covered with aluminum foil or waxed paper, and roasted; it's excellent for chicken breasts.

d. *Steaming*—Using either a cake rack, Chinese bamboo steamer, or metal basket with folding sides, the steaming of fish, poultry, and vegetables is much used in *Gourmet Light* cooking.

e. *Grilling*—This watchword of the new American cooking is ideal for our purposes, for foods pick up the added flavor of the smoke and cook with a minimum of added fats.

f. *Microwaving*—Ideal for today's fat-conscious cooking style, microwaving allows foods to be cooked with little to no fat and with maximum retention of vitamins and minerals.

Note: The recipes in this book were tested in a 650-watt microwave oven. Because cooking times vary considerably depending on wattage and oven size, you may need to adjust the suggested cooking times.

7. Pureeing vegetables

This darling of nouvelle cuisine, which like so many trends is really a revival more than a discovery, is an excellent way to add variety and create a richly satisfying dish without butter. Pureeing vegetables, either alone or in creative combinations, is best accomplished in a food processor, but it can be done using a food mill or ricer.

8. Desserts

Because *Gourmet Light* cooking doesn't use saccharin or other ersatz substitutions, most of the desserts in this book rely on the natural sweetness of fruits. You will find recipes for them poached in wine, iced, or pureed. There are also recipes that use reduced amounts of sugar. But taste was always the deciding factor: If a reduced-sugar recipe tasted like something was missing, it wasn't included here.

9. Presentation

Presentation is important because I've always felt cooking is a little bit of art; its visual appeal is nearly as important to me as its taste. But spending precious time carving radish roses and lemon baskets is best left to well-staffed kitchens. Mine, as I suspect yours, is most often a one-person show. So presentation for me has come to mean simple garnishes, minced fresh parsley, twisted lemon slices, a grating of carrot, or a snippet of chive. It means taking care to wipe away a dribble of sauce and arranging the food on the plate or platter with an eye toward color and order. Nor is presentation an afterthought. It rightly belongs up-front during menu planning when you consider not just what tastes good together but what looks good together as well. And while considering color contrasts, don't overlook texture, what I call "toothsomeness." Pair something hard with something soft, something crisp with something creamy. The art of cooking doesn't stop at the stove; it is part of both the conception and the presentation, and all the workings in between. Cooking is a pragmatic art, a personal expression that brings pleasure and satisfaction. Do with these recipes as *you* will; your creative input will make them work for you.

10. Equipment for reduced-calorie and fat-free cooking

The cook who wants to incorporate the *Gourmet Light* way into his or her cooking style may like to investigate the following:

a. *Cooking sprays*—There are a few nonstick sprays on the market that grease a pan while adding only minimal calories. You could probably accomplish the same by dipping a pastry brush or paper towel in oil and rubbing it on the pan surface. Naturally, you won't achieve perfect browning, but foods won't stick if cooked at moderate heat.

b. *Teflon and other nonstick pans*—Although it is sometimes difficult to brown foods in these pots and pans, they do allow high heat searing and cooking without sticking. I recommend owning at least an 8-inch skillet of excellent quality.

c. *Degreaser*—Looking like a measuring cup with the spout coming off the bottom, degreasers have become widely available of late. They are excellent for separating fats from soups, broths, and sauces.

d. *Ice cream maker*—A luxury item useful for creating fruit ices and sherbets.

e. *Parchment paper*—Covered in Technique 6, parchment and waxed papers allow food to cook without losing precious juices to evaporation.

f. *Chinese bamboo steamer*—Also covered in Technique 6, this inexpensive and useful contraption allows you to cook a whole meal in one pot.

g. *Immersion blenders*—Immersion blenders are like mechanically powered whisks. They make it possible to whip milk and are advantageous for persons with arthritis.

h. *Grill*—Also listed under Technique 6, indoor or outdoor grills allow for fat-free cooking with maximum flavor.

A Note about Nutrition Analysis

The nutrition information that appears with each recipe shows you at a glance how light and healthy the dish is. It tells the number of calories in the dish as well as the amount of protein, fat, cholesterol, carbohydrates, sodium, and fiber. The saturated fat is broken out so you can see how much of the total fat content is made up of the unhealthy kind.

When a choice of ingredients is given in a recipe, the analysis has been based on the choice that's the lowest in calories, fat, and sodium. Optional ingredients are not included in the nutrition analysis.

Recipes that call for beef broth have been analyzed using *Gourmet Light* beef stock unless the recipe specifically calls for a canned product. All egg substitute products are basically created equal, except regarding their sodium content. Recipes calling for egg substitute have been analyzed using the brand that is lowest in sodium. Similarly, the analysis for recipes that call for rice wine vinegar or Chinese cooking wine is based on a reduced-sugar and -sodium product. Skim milk was used for the analysis of all recipes that call for milk.

The Foundations: Stocks and Sauces

The Recipes

THE FOUNDATIONS

We've covered the ten techniques that can help you to lose or maintain weight loss without depriving yourself the enjoyment of good food. The following are the foundations upon which this cooking style is built: the stocks, or enriched commercial products, reduced-calorie and -fat egg sauces—Hollandaise and Béarnaise—Mexican cheese sauce, basil salsa, and more.

TAKING STOCK

Because stocks and broths are used extensively in *Gourmet Light* cooking, you might like to make your own. The microwave makes this otherwise time-consuming process infinitely quicker. If you do make stock on the stovetop, I'd suggest doing it in large quantities and freezing the stock in various size containers. Canned broths may be used or enriched with additional bones and/or vegetables if added flavor or thickness is desired. Commercially prepared consomme is an excellent alternative, because the added gelatin nicely equates the natural thickness of a homemade stock.

BEEF STOCK

8 pounds uncooked beef bones, marrow bones highly recommended

3 carrots, sliced (no need to peel)

3 small to medium onions, sliced (no need to peel, the skins add color)

3 celery stalks, sliced

7 quarts water

1 cup red wine (optional)

a small handful fresh parsley stems, chopped

freshly ground pepper to taste

1 bay leaf

1 garlic clove, halved

Yield: 4 quarts

Calories per cup: 17

Protein per cup: 2g

Fat per cup: 1g

  Saturated per cup: trace

Cholesterol per cup: 4mg

Carbohydrates per cup: 1g

Sodium per cup: 18mg

Fiber per cup: trace

1. Put the bones and vegetables in a 12-quart stockpot, cover with the water, add the wine, and bring to a full boil.

2. Reduce heat to a simmer and scrape the scum that rises to the surface with a slotted spoon. Repeat scrapings two or three times until most of the scum is removed.

3. Add parsley, pepper, bay leaf, and garlic. Half cover the pan and simmer about 8 hours, adding more water if the volume falls more than a quart below the original.

4. Wring out an old kitchen towel or a piece of cheesecloth in cold water and line a strainer with it. Pour or ladle the stock through the strainer.

5. If using the stock immediately, pour what you need into a degreaser to complete the defatting, or refrigerate the stock. A pancake of fat will form that is easily scraped off. Freeze stock in plastic containers of various sizes.

MICROWAVE BEEF STOCK

The microwave makes quick work of homemade stock. Stock may be frozen with no flavor loss up to 6 months.

8 cups water

5–6 pounds beef marrow bones

1 cup red wine (optional)

3 carrots, roughly chopped

2 stalks celery, roughly chopped

2 cloves garlic, halved, unpeeled

1 teaspoon fresh thyme leaves or $^1/_2$ teaspoon dried thyme

1 teaspoon liquid beef bouillon

4–5 parsley sprigs

Yield: 4 cups

Calories per cup: 9

Protein per cup: trace

Fat per cup: trace

   Saturated fat per cup: trace

Cholesterol per cup: 0

Carbohydrates per cup: 2g

Sodium per cup: 125mg

Fiber per cup: 0

1. Combine all ingredients in a gallon microwave-safe container. Cover and microwave at high (100 percent power) for 90 minutes.

2. Strain into a bowl. Discard bones. Press vegetables with the back of a spoon to extract juices. Discard contents of strainer.

3. Refrigerate stock until fat coagulates on the surface, about 6 hours.

4. Discard fat. If desired, strain stock through a double thickness of moistened cheesecloth or a moistened coffee filter. You may find it necessary to heat the last cup or so of stock to facilitate straining, because it will be so thick from the naturally occurring gelatin. Stirring the stock as it strains will also speed the process.

Meat Glaze (Glacé de Viande)

Like an expensive perfume, meat glaze is used sparingly—a little goes a long way. Half a teaspoon stirred into sauces or soups boosts the flavor without making its presence known. It is truly a chef's secret. A commercial alternative is meat extract or concentrated beef-flavored broth, usually available in the gourmet section of the supermarket or at specialty food shops. Use half the amount of the commercial as you would the homemade; it tends to be salty.

Reduce any quantity of homemade or bone-enriched commercial beef stock down to one half its original volume. You will have an iridescent, deep brown syrup. It should be thick enough to coat a metal spoon.

Meat glaze will keep in the refrigerator in a sterile glass container for about two weeks. After that a harmless mold may form that can be scraped away. Or freeze the glaze in ice cube trays and pop them into plastic bags when frozen. Thaw the cubes in a small, covered saucepan with a tablespoon of water.

Yield: 1 1/2 cups

Calories per tablespoon: 3

Protein per tablespoon: trace

Fat per tablespoon: trace

Saturated fat per tablespoon: trace

Cholesterol per tablespoon: 1 mg

Carbohydrates per tablespoon: trace

Sodium per tablespoon: 2 mg

Fiber per tablespoon: trace

Thinking Thin Tip

How many fat grams can you eat a day? Divide your ideal weight by two, and remember, only 10 percent should come from saturated sources like those found in some meats and dairy products.

CHICKEN STOCK

5–6 pounds uncooked chicken bones (saved from boning breasts, or buy
  wings and backs)
2–3 carrots, sliced (no need to peel)
2 medium onions, sliced
2 celery stalks, sliced
4 quarts water
1 cup dry white wine (optional)
a small handful fresh parsley stems, chopped
freshly ground pepper to taste
1 bay leaf
1 garlic clove, halved

Yield: 3 quarts
Calories per cup: 6
Protein per cup: 1g
Fat per cup: trace
  Saturated fat per cup: trace
Cholesterol per cup: 3mg
Carbohydrates per cup: 0
Sodium per cup: 9mg
Fiber per cup: 0

1. Place bones and vegetables in a 12-quart stockpot, cover with the water, and add the wine. Bring to a boil.

2. Reduce heat to a simmer and scrape the scum that rises to the surface with a slotted spoon. Repeat scrapings two or three times until most of the scum is removed.

3. Add the parsley, pepper, bay leaf, and garlic. Half cover the pan and simmer about 4 hours, adding more water if the volume falls more than a quart below the original.

4. Wring out an old kitchen towel or a piece of cheesecloth in water and line a strainer with it. Pour or ladle the stock through the strainer.

5. If using the stock immediately, pour what you need into a degreaser to complete the defatting, or refrigerate until a pancake of fat forms. Scrape off the fat and freeze the stock in plastic containers of varying sizes.

MICROWAVE CHICKEN STOCK

The microwave makes quick work of homemade chicken stock. Freeze the stock without flavor loss for up to 6 months. There's no need to peel the onion, as the skins lend color.

2 pounds uncooked chicken bones

10 cups water

3 stalks celery, roughly chopped

2 or 3 carrots, roughly chopped

1 small yellow onion, unpeeled and quartered

1 clove garlic, unpeeled and halved

a few sprigs fresh thyme or $1/2$ teaspoon dried thyme

3–4 sprigs fresh parsley

$1/2$ teaspoon salt

Yield: 2 quarts

Calories per cup: 6

Protein per cup: trace

Fat per cup: trace

  Saturated fat per cup: trace

Cholesterol per cup: 0

Carbohydrates per cup: 1g

Sodium per cup: 148mg

Fiber per cup: trace

1. Combine all ingredients in a gallon microwave-safe container. Cover and microwave at high (100 percent) power for 90 minutes.

2. Strain into a bowl. Discard bones. Press vegetables with the back of a spoon to extract juices. Discard contents of strainer.

3. Refrigerate stock until fat coagulates on the surface, about 6 hours.

4. Discard fat. If desired, strain stock through a double thickness of moistened cheesecloth or a moistened coffee filter. You may find it necessary to heat the last cup or so of stock to facilitate straining, because it will be so thick from the naturally occurring gelatin. Stirring the stock as it strains will also speed the process.

Enriched Quick Commercial Beef or Chicken Broth

¹/₂ pound uncooked beef or chicken bones

3 unpeeled carrots, sliced

1 onion, chopped

1 quart canned beef or chicken broth

¹/₂ cup red or white wine (optional)

1 bay leaf

1 clove garlic, halved

freshly ground pepper to taste

a small handful fresh parsley stems, chopped

Yield: 3¹/₂ cups

Calories per cup: 23

Protein per cup: 4g

Fat per cup: 1g

  Saturated fat per cup: trace

Cholesterol per cup: 4mg

Carbohydrates per cup: 0

Sodium per cup: 104mg

Fiber per cup: 0

1. Put all ingredients in a 2¹/₂-quart saucepan, half cover, and simmer 30 minutes.

2. It may be used immediately after straining and discarding bones, vegetables, and herbs.

Chill canned broth before opening. The fat will coagulate for easy removal.

Ice Cube Stock

Freeze homemade stock in ice cube trays and pop the frozen cubes into a plastic bag. Use when a few tablespoons of broth are called for to "saute" an ingredient.

FISH STOCK

This delicate stock must be frozen if not used within 24 hours.

1 fish rack (skeleton) weighing about 1 1/2 pounds from a white-fleshed,
   nonoily fish such as haddock or cod, innards removed and rack
   rinsed
6 cups water
2 cups dry white wine (optional)
1 small onion, chopped
1 small carrot, chopped
1 bay leaf

Yield: 1 quart
Calories per cup: 9
Protein per cup: 1g
Fat per cup: trace
  Saturated fat per cup: trace
Cholesterol per cup: 3mg
Carbohydrates per cup: trace
Sodium per cup: 12mg
Fiber per cup: trace

1. Put the fish rack (don't shy away from using the head, as it contains lots of collagen, which melts into gelatin) in a heavy pot, preferably nonaluminum if using the wine, and add the water and wine.

2. Bring to a boil, reduce heat so liquid just simmers, and scrape the scum away with a slotted spoon. When most of the scum is removed, add the remaining ingredients and half cover pot. Simmer 40 minutes.

3. Rinse out an old kitchen towel or a piece of cheesecloth in water, line a strainer with it, and pour or ladle stock through. Refrigerate or freeze.

Note: Bottled clam juice is a very acceptable substitute in recipes calling for fish stock. Dilute the bottled product with 1/4 cup dry white wine or vermouth to 8 ounces clam juice, and omit salt from the recipe.

THE TRADEMARKS OF CLASSIC COOKING—SAUCES

The cynosures of fine cooking are frequently the sauces: lemony Hollandaise ribboning asparagus, rich and pungent Béarnaise complementing a flavorfully steamed fish, the cool richness of crème blanc offsetting a steamy bowl of beet soup. *Gourmet Light* cooking doesn't deny the lover of good food the pleasures of the table. Here are the reduced-calorie and -fat versions of such classic recipes.

Egg-Based Sauces

Egg-based sauces owe their creamy richness to the emulsion that forms when egg yolks poach in butter and an acid such as lemon juice (Hollandaise), vinegar (Béarnaise), or wine. You'll find my thin versions of these sauces packed with flavor that belies their lightness. You'll be happy to note that they may be prepared ahead and gently reheated with little danger of curdling or separating.

The *Gourmet Light* version of the classic Hollandaise is a great favorite in my kitchen, because it is much less fattening (10 calories per tablespoon and 1 fat gram compared to 67 calories and 7 fat grams for the traditional recipe), tastes lighter, holds better than the traditional sauce, and may even be gently reheated. It is wonderful on eggs, poultry, fish, and vegetables, and with the addition of a bit of mustard, terrific with lamb as well. Note the range of uses with a slight variation in ingredients.

Remember Hollandaise and its cousin Béarnaise were never meant to be served hot, just warmed. Should you accidentally heat the sauce beyond 140 degrees, causing it to separate or break, put a teaspoon of acid (lemon for Hollandaise, vinegar for Béarnaise) in a food processor or blender and slowly dribble in the sauce. It will form the emulsion again.

HOLLANDAISE SAUCE

How good could a low-fat Hollandaise be? You won't believe it until you try this one. Your test can be ready in about the time it takes to steam a bunch of broccoli. If needed, reheat the sauce in a microwave oven at medium (50 percent power) for about 30 seconds, or over very low heat on the stove top.

4 tablespoons lemon juice (the juice from 1 lemon)
³/₄ cup chicken broth
¹/₃ cup egg substitute, shaken vigorously
2 tablespoons reduced-calorie margarine, melted
a dash each salt and pepper

Yield: 1 cup
Calories per tablespoon: 10
Protein per tablespoon: trace
Fat per tablespoon: 1gm
  Saturated fat per tablespoon: trace
Cholesterol per tablespoon: trace
Carbohydrates per tablespoon: trace
Sodium per tablespoon: 38mg
Fiber per tablespoon: trace

1. In a small saucepan, combine the lemon juice and broth. Boil until reduced to a little more than ¹/₂ cup, about 3 minutes.

2. Meanwhile, beat or whisk the egg substitute in a 1-quart or smaller heavy-bottomed saucepan for 30 seconds. Place on low heat and dribble in the hot broth, whisking vigorously until the sauce thickens, about 4 minutes. Gradually increase heat to medium as more broth is added, but be careful not to curdle the eggs.

3. When sauce is the consistency of melted ice cream, whisk in the melted margarine. Season with salt and pepper. The sauce will thicken more on standing.

Variations:

1. Maltaise Sauce is a classic accompaniment for asparagus. Using the Hollandaise recipe, substitute orange juice for the lemon juice, adding 1 teaspoon lemon juice and a bit of grated orange rind to the finished sauce.

2. A fabulous sauce for fish, cauliflower, asparagus, and broccoli, a classic Mousseline Sauce is made by folding ¹/₄ cup heavy cream, which has already been whipped, into a finished Hollandaise. If you have an immersion blender, you can whip skim milk and fold it into our thin version of Hollandaise for a cloudlike sauce just this side of heaven.

BÉARNAISE SAUCE

Much less finicky than a traditional Béarnaise sauce, this recipe may well become a staple at your house as it has at mine. It can be gently reheated in a microwave oven at medium (50 percent power) for about 30 seconds. It is excellent with fish, chicken, beef, or vegetables. Cold Béarnaise makes an excellent dip for crudités, or mix it with mustard for a pretzel dip.

> 4 tablespoons red wine vinegar
>
> 1 tablespoon minced shallot
>
> 1 tablespoon minced fresh tarragon or 1 teaspoon dried tarragon
>
> 1/2 cup egg substitute
>
> 1/4 cup chicken broth
>
> 2 tablespoons reduced-calorie margarine
>
> salt and pepper to taste

Yield: 1/2 cup

Calories per tablespoon: 21

Protein per tablespoon: 1g

Fat per tablespoon: 1g

   Saturated fat per tablespoon: trace

Cholesterol per tablespoon: trace

Carbohydrates per tablespoon: 1g

Sodium per tablespoon: 68mg

Fiber per tablespoon: trace

1. Combine the vinegar, shallot, and tarragon in a 3-cup heavy-bottomed saucepan. Boil over high heat until reduced by half to about 2 tablespoons liquid.

2. Meanwhile, process the egg substitute in a food processor for about 30 seconds on full power.

3. Add the chicken broth and margarine to the vinegar mixture. Heat over high heat until the margarine is melted.

4. Dribble the vinegar/broth mixture into the egg substitute with the food processor on high.

5. Return mixture to 3-cup saucepan. Whisk continually over high heat, reducing if necessary to prevent mixture from curdling. Sauce will thicken in about 4 minutes and continue to thicken as it cools. It may be made ahead and gently reheated on the stove top or in the microwave. It keeps, chilled, up to one week.

Variations:

1. Add 1 tablespoon tomato paste to the finished Béarnaise to make Sauce Robert. This is an excellent sauce with meats.

2. Horseradish Béarnaise is delicious as a spread for cold roast beef. Add 2 teaspoons prepared horseradish to the finished Béarnaise.

MAYONNAISE VARIATIONS

To 1¼ cups fat-free mayonnaise, add any of the following:

2 tablespoons chopped fresh dill for use with fish salads.

2 tablespoons chopped fresh basil for use with tomatoes (or use 1 teaspoon dried basil).

1 tablespoon chopped dill pickles, 1 tablespoon capers, 1 tablespoon fresh tarragon (or 1 teaspoon dried), and 1 tablespoon chopped chives for a Gribiche Sauce for steamed or poached fish.

1 tablespoon horseradish and 1 tablespoon minced fresh parsley for use with cold roast beef.

3 tablespoons tomato paste, 3 tablespoons minced green pepper, and 1 teaspoon snipped chives for use with hamburgers or as a dip for raw vegetables.

Flour-Based Sauces

Flour-based sauces, what Mother called white sauce and the French term Béchamel (made with milk) or Velouté (made with milk and stock), have fallen out of favor. Instead of being thickened with flour, sauces are now thickened with reduced cream or mounds of butter, or by reducing naturally gelatinous homemade stocks to a syrupy stage and then enriching them with butter. Naturally, with the exception of the reduced stock, none of these are appropriate for reduced-calorie and -fat cooking. Therefore for the rare, but nonetheless real occasion when a dish would benefit from a "cream" sauce, here is a recipe for *Gourmet Light* Velouté, with less than half the calories of a traditional Velouté, as well as a reduced-calorie Mexican Cheese Sauce.

VELOUTÉ SAUCE

2 cups stock, use whatever will complement the dish: fish, beef, or
   chicken
1 tablespoon grated onion
2 teaspoons cornstarch or arrowroot dissolved in 2 tablespoons skim milk
1 1/2 tablespoons reduced-fat margarine
1/4 teaspoon salt
a dash of white pepper to taste
a few gratings fresh nutmeg

Yield: 2 cups
Calories per tablespoon: 4
Protein per tablespoon: trace
Fat per tablespoon: trace
   Saturated fat per tablespoon: trace
Cholesterol per tablespoon: trace
Carbohydrates per tablespoon: trace
Sodium per tablespoon: 21 mg
Fiber per tablespoon: trace

1. Combine the stock and onion in a saucepan and bring to a boil.

2. Reduce the heat to medium, whisk in the cornstarch or arrowroot, and cook, stirring, about 5 minutes or until the sauce is smooth and thick.

3. Whisk in margarine. Taste and season with salt, pepper, and a bit of nutmeg.

MEXICAN CHEESE SAUCE

Use this on bobolis or pizzettas (see pages 67, 68, and 70), as a hot dip for crudités or oil-free taco chips, as a sauce for broccoli or cauliflower, or eat it straight from the pan! The sauce will keep in the fridge up to one week.

Yield: 1 1/2 cups

Calories per tablespoon: 21

Protein per tablespoon: 2g

Fat per tablespoon: trace

   Saturated fat per tablespoon: trace

Cholesterol per tablespoon: 1mg

Carbohydrates per tablespoon: 2g

Sodium per tablespoon: 41mg

Fiber per tablespoon: trace

1 small yellow onion

2 cloves garlic

1/2 green pepper

2 tablespoons instant-blending flour

1 12-ounce beer or nonalcoholic beer

1 cup shredded fat-free or reduced-fat cheese such as cheddar, about
    4 ounces

3 tablespoons "recipe ready" tomatoes or 1 small fresh tomato, chopped

2 tablespoons hot salsa

1 tablespoon minced fresh coriander

1 teaspoon cumin

1/2 teaspoon Adobo seasoning (available in Spanish section of market)
    or salt

1/4 teaspoon powdered mustard

1. Mince the onion, garlic, and green pepper together in the bowl of a food processor or by hand. Saute in a 2 1/2-quart heavy-bottom saucepan sprayed with nonstick cooking spray over medium-high heat, stirring occasionally, for 4 to 5 minutes or until the mixture is softened but not browned.

2. Sprinkle with the flour and cook another minute, stirring constantly.

3. Reduce heat to medium and drizzle in the beer, stirring constantly.

4. Reduce heat to low and stir in all remaining ingredients. Cover and adjust heat so mixture just simmers. Simmer 1 hour, stirring occasionally. If mixture is not smooth and creamy (some fat-free cheeses don't melt well), puree in a food processor.

Herb-Based Sauces

Fresh herbs combined with stock, a hint of oil, and nuts or cheese make wonderful sauces for pasta, salads, and poached chicken or fish. They are a snap to make with the aid of a food processor and keep up to a week when refrigerated.

Recipe-Ready Tomatoes

If you're tired of peeling and seeding fresh tomatoes or can't find a winter tomato even worth the effort, search out "Recipe-ready Tomatoes" on the supermarket shelf next to other canned tomato products. Currently, several manufacturers are producing these time-savers in two styles; one with a bit of oil and basil which is labelled "Pasta-ready" and the other with no added seasoning or fat, labeled "Recipe-ready." Unlike crushed tomatoes, tomato puree, or whole tomatoes, both of these products more closely resemble fresh peeled and seeded tomatoes in texture and taste.

LEMON PARSLEY SAUCE

Try this sauce smeared on thick, fresh tomato slices, then broil just until heated through or brush it on grilling chicken or fish. Thin it with a few tablespoons broth and serve it as a delightfully different dip for crudités. Toss it with pasta, add a few cooked shrimp, cool to room temperature, and serve as a hot-weather meal.

Yield: ⅔ cup
Calories per tablespoon: 6
Protein per tablespoon: trace
Fat per tablespoon: trace
  Saturated fat per tablespoon: trace
Cholesterol per tablespoon: trace
Carbohydrates per tablespoon: 1g
Sodium per tablespoon: 9mg
Fiber per tablespoon: trace

½ cup fresh parsley, snipped
½ cup fresh watercress, snipped
3 tablespoons dried bread crumbs
½ teaspoon prepared mustard
juice of half a lemon
1 tablespoon chicken broth or consomme
freshly ground pepper to taste
1 teaspoon sugar

1. Combine all the ingredients in a food processor or blender. Use as described above.

Thinking Thin Tip

Beware of "no" or "low cholesterol" claims. If the food is still high in saturated fat (which could happen in no-cholesterol foods such as baked goods and snack foods), it can still raise your blood cholesterol count.

BASIL SALSA

This Basil Salsa is reminiscent of the ever-popular pesto minus the oil and with the added sparkle of balsamic vinegar. It has one-fourth the calories of a traditional pesto sauce. Its uses go far beyond a simple and delicious toss with pastas (a wonderful hot-weather dinner). Brush it on grilling chicken or fish the last few minutes of cooking, dab it on sun-warmed tomatoes, or stir it into a cool bowl of fresh Tomato Soup (page 74).

1/2 cup fresh parsley, snipped and loosely packed
1/2 cup fresh basil, snipped and loosely packed
1 tablespoon balsamic or malt vinegar
2 tablespoons grated Parmesan cheese
1 teaspoon sugar
2 tablespoons chicken broth, more if a thinner sauce is desired
1 clove garlic, minced
1 tablespoon finely chopped walnuts
freshly ground pepper to taste

1. Combine and process all the ingredients in a food processor or blender. Use as described above.

Variation

For Basil-Walnut Cream, combine in a food processor or blender until smooth equal amounts of Basil Salsa and nonfat cream cheese, nonfat sour cream, or yogurt cheese (page 54).

Yield: ¾ cup

Calories per tablespoon: 11

Protein per tablespoon: 1g

Fat per tablespoon: 1g

  Saturated fat per tablespoon: trace

Cholesterol per tablespoon: 1mg

Carbohydrates per tablespoon: 1g

Sodium per tablespoon: 17mg

Fiber per tablespoon: trace

Acid-Based Sauces

The most popular sauces in today's au courant restaurants are those made by emulsifying (blending) large amounts of butter in small amounts of acid, such as lemon juice or wine. Since no magician's wand can render 8 tablespoons of butter calorie- or fat-free, *Gourmet Light* cooking will forgo any attempt to produce a beurre blanc. Here, however, is an acid-based sauce that will fend off the boredom associated with reduced-calorie cooking.

LEMON BUTTER SAUCE

When you've eaten all the dry green beans you can, try this. Simple and delicious

1 tablespoon reduced-fat margarine

2–3 tablespoons freshly squeezed lemon juice

½ teaspoon salt

freshly ground pepper to taste

1 clove garlic, minced

1 teaspoon minced fresh parsley

½ teaspoon minced shallot or scallion

Yield: 4 servings

Calories per tablespoon: 16

Protein per tablespoon: trace

Fat per tablespoon: 1g

  Saturated fat per tablespoon: trace

Cholesterol per tablespoon: 0

Carbohydrates per tablespoon: 1g

Sodium per tablespoon: 300mg

Fiber per tablespoon: trace

1. Combine all the ingredients in a small skillet or saucepan and heat until margarine melts. Pour over cooked, drained vegetables.

TOMATO SAUCE

Tomato-based sauces are used extensively in *Gourmet Light* cooking, for they score high on flavor and low in calorie tally. Although many will opt to purchase tomato puree to make the sauce recipes called for in this book, here is a homemade version for those with gardens and/or the inclination to prepare their own.

Yield: approximately 3 cups

Calories per tablespoon: 6

Protein per tablespoon: trace

Fat per tablespoon: trace

  Saturated fat per tablespoon: trace

Cholesterol per tablespoon: trace

Carbohydrates per tablespoon: 1g

Sodium per tablespoon: 110mg

Fiber per tablespoon: trace

> *2 pounds tomatoes, roughly chopped or 44 ounces canned tomatoes*
>   *(2 large cans)*
> *1 small onion, chopped*
> *1 clove garlic, minced*
> *1 tablespoon tomato paste*
> *2 cups chicken stock (1 cup if using canned tomatoes)*
> *4 leaves fresh basil, snipped, or 1 teaspoon dried basil*
> *²/₃ teaspoon sugar*
> *¹/₂ teaspoon salt if using fresh tomatoes (omit if using canned)*

1. Combine all the ingredients in a medium-size saucepan and boil, uncovered, until reduced by half.

2. Puree the mixture in a food processor or blender, and strain to remove the seeds and skins if desired.

Discolored Sauces

Although aluminum is one of the best, meaning fastest, conductors of heat, an unlined aluminum pot may discolor a sauce if there is acid present, such as tomato, wine, vinegar, or lemon juice. The discoloration is caused by a reaction of the acid with the pot. Unlined aluminum pans become stained when washed with a high-alkali cleanser or used for cooking high-alkali foods such as potatoes. The acid in the sauce removes some of that stain, transferring it to the sauce, causing a grayish tint that is unappetizing but fortunately, not a health hazard.

CRÈME BLANC

This simple mixture of cottage cheese and yogurt is to this book what butter, sour cream, and heavy cream are to others. It is a flavor enhancer, while contributing to good nutrition as well. Cookbook readers will note its similarity to fromage blanc. It will keep in the refrigerator for up to one week, and its flavor and texture will improve if allowed to sit for a few hours.

4 ounces nonfat cottage cheese

4 tablespoons plain nonfat yogurt

2 tablespoons skim milk

1. Combine the ingredients in a food processor or blender, and mix until perfectly smooth. The sauce will thicken after being chilled about 6 hours.

Note: Two teaspoons of cornstarch (20 calories) added to this mixture will prevent it from separating during high heat cooking. You may then disregard my notes to cook crème blanc over low heat.

Yield: approximately 1 cup

Calories per tablespoon: 19

Protein per tablespoon: 2g

Fat per tablespoon: trace

  Saturated fat per tablespoon: trace

Cholesterol per tablespoon: 1mg

Carbohydrates per tablespoon: 2g

Sodium per tablespoon: 21mg

Fiber per tablespoon: 0

GINGERED ORANGE SAUCE

This simple sauce is very versatile. It will enhance a poached, grilled, or microwaved chicken or turkey breast; is delicious on grilled chops; keeps swordfish from drying out on the grill; and is very tasty on white fish fillets, such as broiled sole. I also like it on steamed green beans or drizzled over steamed peapods. The recipe makes enough for 2–3 servings of meat, fish, or vegetables. Double the recipe if you like; leftovers keep up to one week. Some specialty food stores sell prechopped ginger in a jar.

⅔ cup orange juice
2 teaspoons minced fresh ginger root
2 teaspoons honey

1. Combine the ingredients in a small saucepan. Bring to a boil over high heat, reduce heat to medium, and boil gently until reduced to about ⅓ cup, about 12–15 minutes.

Yield: ⅓ cup
Calories per tablespoon: 125
Protein per tablespoon: 1g
Fat per tablespoon: trace
  Saturated fat per tablespoon: trace
Cholesterol per tablespoon: 0
Carbohydrates per tablespoon: 31g
Sodium per tablespoon: 3mg
Fiber per tablespoon: trace

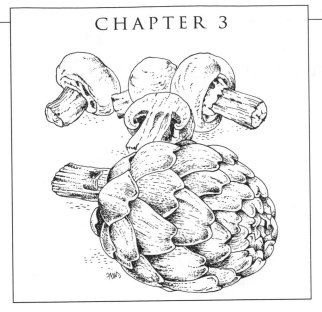

SAVORY LITTLE
SOMETHINGS

THE RECIPES

Note: Asterisked dishes may be served as entrees.

SAVORY LITTLE SOMETHINGS

By any name—smorgasbord, *tapas,* antipasto, *zakuska,* or hors d'oeuvres—appetizers are often pound packers. A 2-inch square of cheddar cheese, a mere ¼-inch thick (about ½ ounce), atop a cracker is an astounding 75 calories and 5 grams of fat. Typical cocktail fare is generally high in fat, such as cheese, or fried in fat, such as chips, so that a few bites can really wreak havoc with the day's total intake. Just 10 potato chips will bulk you up with 114 calories and 8 grams of fat; an ounce of peanuts contains 160 calories along with about 11 grams of fat; and a tablespoon of cream cheese dip for a little celery stick has at least 50 calories and as much as 5 grams of fat.

In a cookbook dedicated to slimming meals, the emphasis on appetizers is understandably minimal; the chief ingredients are on the slender side, with vegetables and seafood predominating. But if you offer your guests the sort of trim but tempting foods found here, they'll still be able to appreciate and enjoy your dinner.

Most of the nibbles that follow are small tasty bites. Some, such as the Chèvre-Stuffed Artichokes, would make a lovely first course if nestled on a tangle of mixed greens dressed with a light mustard vinaigrette. Others would do well in the light supper or lunch slot, such as the Fresh Mozzarella and Tomato Pizzetta, and others, like the Creamy Chicken Enchiladas, are special enough for a casual company meal.

Presentation is particularly important when serving appetizers. The mind must feast while the stomach yet waits. Mushroom caps on a white cloth napkin on a dark tray, crudités arranged attractively in baskets, chicken and pork skewers circled in spoke fashion with a tomato rose at the center—this attention to detail is key. Cooking without garnishing, no matter how simple, is like not lacing your running shoes before a run.

CHÈVRE-STUFFED ARTICHOKES

This recipe may be prepared with either frozen artichoke hearts or fresh baby artichokes, an easy size for cocktail fare. For larger servings, suitable for a salad, prepare the bottoms from fresh artichokes. The larger cheese-stuffed artichoke bottoms make a delicious salad or appetizer when placed in a tangle of greens and dressed with a mustardy *Gourmet Light* vinaigrette. The recipe may be made through Step 6 as much as a day before serving.

Yield: 12 artichoke hearts
Calories per heart: 27
Protein per heart: 2g
Fat per heart: 2g
  Saturated fat per heart: 1g
Cholesterol per heart: 2mg
Carbohydrates per heart: 2g
Sodium per heart: 41mg
Fiber per heart: trace

For the Artichokes

1 package frozen artichoke hearts, thawed, or 6 baby artichokes or
  4 large artichokes
4 tablespoons lemon juice
4 tablespoons flour
1/2 cup cold water

For the Marinade

4 tablespoons chicken broth
2 tablespoons red wine vinegar
1 tablespoon lemon juice
a few sprigs fresh thyme or 1/4 teaspoon dried thyme
freshly ground black pepper to taste

For the Stuffing

2 ounces chèvre (goat cheese), such as Montrachet, or a spiced
  fat-free cream cheese
2 tablespoons skim milk
1 tablespoon reduced-calorie margarine
1/2 clove garlic, minced
1 tablespoon dried bread crumbs

To Prepare the Artichoke Bottoms

1. Lay an artichoke on its side and slice off the top third with a stainless-steel knife. With scissors cut the spiny tips off the leaves. Cut away the tougher outer leaves with the knife as if peeling an orange. You'll now have an inner core of pale green leaves. Slice this off, leaving the bottom. Trim it to remove tough green fibers. As you finish each one, cut into thirds, and drop the pieces into a bowl of water with 2 tablespoons of the lemon juice added to help keep the artichoke from turning brown.

To prepare baby artichokes, follow the preceding instructions until you get to the inner core of pale leaves. Cut the artichoke in half the long way, and scrape away the fuzzy center.

To Cook

1. Make a paste with about 4 tablespoons flour in a half cup of cold water. Stir this into a quart of water with the remaining tablespoons lemon juice. Bring to a simmer, stirring occasionally. Add the artichoke bottoms and simmer until tender, about 10 minutes for the larger bottoms and 6 minutes for the baby ones. Drain, and when cool enough to handle, scrape away the fuzzy center.

2. Marinate the bottoms or thawed artichoke hearts in the chicken broth, vinegar, lemon juice, thyme, and pepper at least 4 hours or overnight.

3. Preheat oven to 350 degrees. Drain and discard the marinade.

4. Mix the goat cheese with the milk until smooth and creamy. Fill a pastry bag with the mixture or spoon the mixture on the artichoke hearts or bottoms.

5. Spray a baking sheet with cooking spray. Arrange filled hearts on it.

6. Melt the margarine in an 8-inch skillet. When foamy, cook the garlic over medium-low heat 1 minute. Add the bread crumbs and stir until lightly browned.

7. Divide the bread crumb mixture over the cheese. Bake 10 minutes in the preheated 350-degree oven until heated through.

Chèvre

Goat cheeses, collectively known as chèvres, have long been popular in Europe. In America they have become the darling of the upbeat food world and the star in many a recipe. Creatively turned out in various guises from stuffing for pasta to soufflés, the import and local manufacture of these distinctive handmade cheeses have grown greatly.

The flavor of chèvre is best described as clear, tangy, and fresh. Banon (wrapped in chestnut or grape leaves) is the mildest; Cortin de Chazignol is the sharpest; and Bucheron and Montrachet perhaps the best known.

MUSHROOMS À LA GRECQUE

The phrase "à la Grecque" means to blanch vegetables (though only mushrooms have been used here) in a pickling brine of oil, wine, and herbs (a court bouillon) and then to macerate and finally serve them in the cooking liquid. It's a pleasing change from crudités and needs no further dressing. Serve the mushrooms at room temperature or only slightly chilled for best flavor. Mushrooms and vegetables prepared this way will keep up to 4 days chilled.

Yield: 8 servings

Calories per serving: 20

Protein per serving: 1g

Fat per serving: trace

   Saturated fat per serving: trace

Cholesterol per serving: trace

Carbohydrates per serving: 2g

Sodium per serving: 142mg

Fiber per serving: trace

8 ounces mushrooms, caps and stems or just caps (as you please)

1 cup water

1 cup chicken broth

$1/2$ cup dry white wine

$1/2$ teaspoon salt

1 tablespoon balsamic or red wine vinegar

juice of half a lemon

1 teaspoon fresh tarragon leaves or $1/2$ teaspoon dried tarragon

1 tablespoon minced fresh parsley

1 clove garlic, sliced in 3 pieces

a few sprigs fresh thyme or $1/4$ teaspoon dried thyme

$1/4$ teaspoon dried oregano

1. Wipe the mushrooms clean with a towel and set aside for use in Step 3.

2. In a nonaluminum saucepan, combine the water, broth, wine, salt, vinegar, and lemon juice to make a court bouillon. Make a bouquet garni of the tarragon, parsley, garlic, thyme, and oregano by placing the herbs on a double-thick 3-inch square of cheesecloth. Roll the cloth in jelly-roll fashion, bring the ends together, and tie in a knot. Add this herb bundle to the liquid and bring to a boil for 1 minute.

3. Add the cleaned mushrooms, boil 3 minutes. Transfer vegetables with a slotted spoon to a nonmetal bowl or glass jar.

4. Boil the court bouillon over high heat until only 1 cup remains. Remove and discard bouquet garni. Pour liquid over mushrooms, and chill 2–4 hours or up to 4 days. Serve at room temperature, or slightly chilled.

Garlic

Romans fed garlic to their slaves to make them strong, and to their warriors to make them brave, and then forbade anyone having just eaten it to enter the temple of the Goddess of Nature. Perhaps the Romans didn't know that if the garlic had been simmered, long and slow, it wouldn't have been so offensive. Pureed garlic on French bread and Chicken with 40 Cloves of Garlic are popular dishes with many, the pungency of the bulb subdued thanks to long, slow cooking.

To mince garlic, cut the clove (one of the tissue paper–like wrapped crescents in the bulb) in half the long way. There's no need to peel it. Cut off the tiny brown nub at the tip. Place the garlic, flat side down, on the cutting surface, position the flat side of the knife over the clove, and smash down (carefully, on the broad side of the knife) with the heel of your hand. The garlic skin will lift off easily and the clove may be minced. Sprinkling the garlic with a little salt may help soften it to speed mincing. Lemon juice will help remove the garlic scent from your fingers.

DUXELLE MELBA

A delicious way to use up aging mushrooms, these cocktail toasts may be made when the spirit strikes and then frozen.

1 tablespoon reduced-calorie margarine, melted
4 slices thin-sliced white bread
6 ounces mushrooms
2 tablespoons shallots, minced
2 tablespoons chicken broth
1 ounce semisoft mild reduced-fat cheese, such as Havarti or
    Muenster, grated
1 tablespoon minced fresh parsley
1 tablespoon pine nuts or almonds, chopped
1/8 teaspoon salt
freshly ground black pepper to taste
a few gratings fresh nutmeg

Yield: 16
Calories in each: 31
Protein in each: 1g
Fat in each: 1g
    Saturated fat in each: trace
Cholesterol in each: 1mg
Carbohydrates in each: 4g
Sodium in each: 62mg
Fiber in each: trace

1. Preheat the oven to 325 degrees while melting margarine in an 8-inch skillet. Spray a baking sheet with cooking spray.

2. Place the bread slices in a stack and slice twice on the diagonal, making 16 triangles. Arrange in a single layer on the baking sheet.

3. Dab each *croustade* (bread triangle) with melted margarine on one side. Bake 12 minutes or until slightly crisp, in the preheated oven.

4. Wipe the mushrooms clean and mince them by hand or in a food processor. Scrape onto a kitchen towel, gather into a ball, twist ends of towel, and squeeze the mushrooms over the sink, extracting as much water as you can.

5. "Saute" the shallots in the chicken broth in the now-empty skillet. When liquid is evaporated and shallots are softened, spray the skillet with cooking spray, add the mushrooms, and cook at medium-low heat, gradually increasing the heat, about 5 minutes.

6. Remove mushrooms from heat, stir in the grated cheese, parsley, and pine nuts making a *duxelle.* Season with salt, pepper, and nutmeg.

7. Divide *duxelle* over the *croustades,* being certain to cover the bread points or they will burn. The hors d'oeuvres may be broiled now until browned, about 2–3 minutes or baked at 325 degrees until browned, about 12 minutes. You also may freeze them, uncooked, for future use.

CRABMEAT EGG ROLLS

Homemade egg rolls are really quite easy to make. When baked or steamed, they are a perfect candidate for low-fat feasting. For cocktail fare, use wonton wrappers or cut egg roll wrappers in half. Use as they come if serving the rolls as a first course, lunch, or as part of a Chinese dinner. Leftovers can be resteamed or microwaved.

> *1 cup roughly chopped Spanish onion (about ¹/₂ a medium onion)*
> *2 cloves garlic*
> *1¹/₂ cups thinly sliced green beans*
> *1 stalk celery*
> *4 tablespoons reduced-sodium soy sauce*
> *1 carrot*
> *1 cup coarsely chopped bean sprouts*
> *2 tightly packed cups chopped bok choy*
> *1 tablespoon oyster sauce*
> *1 tablespoon sesame oil*
> *1 teaspoon minced fresh ginger root*
> *a few drops hot oil*
> *1 pound crabmeat or seafood flakes*
> *1 pound egg roll wrappers*
> *fresh coriander sprigs for garnish (optional)*

Yield: 15 egg rolls, 30 appetizer size
  rolls, 40 if wonton wrappers are
  used.

Calories per roll: 225

Protein per roll: 24g

Fat per roll: 3g
  Saturated fat per roll: trace

Cholesterol per roll: 90mg

Carbohydrates per roll: 27g

Sodium per roll: 803mg

Fiber per roll: 1g
  (Note: Nutrition analysis is for 15
  egg rolls.)

1. Mince the onion and garlic together in the bowl of a food processor. Scrape into 6-cup or larger microwave-safe bowl, cover with plastic wrap, and microwave on high (100 percent power) for 5 minutes.

2. Meanwhile, combine the green beans and celery in the food processor (no need to wash the bowl) and process until minced. Add the beans, celery, and soy sauce to the onion mixture. Stir to combine, cover, and microwave on high (100 percent power) for 3 minutes.

3. Mince the carrot in the bowl of the food processor. Stir the carrot, bean sprouts, bok choy, oyster sauce, sesame oil, ginger root, and hot oil into the green bean/bok choy mixture. Cover and microwave on high (100 percent power) for 2 minutes. Stir in the crab.

4. To assemble the egg rolls, lay a wrapper on the work surface so a corner points at you. Spread 3 rounded tablespoons of filling diagonally along the lower quarter of the wrapper, leaving a 1-inch margin on either end. Moisten the edges of the wrapper with water. Tightly fold the corner nearest you over the filling. Fold in both sides, snugly encasing the filling. Roll until the flap is completely wrapped around the roll. Place seam-side down on a sprayed cookie sheet or other ovenproof dish. Repeat with remaining wrappers and filling.

Thinking Thin Tip

If you eat very quickly and in large bites, eat with chopsticks. It will slow you down at least until you become proficient with them.

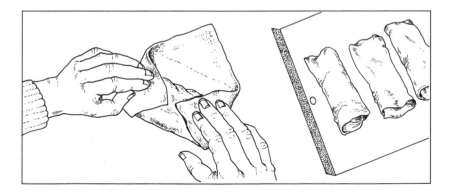

5. To bake, spray the rolls again with nonstick cooking spray. Place the cookie sheet in a 450-degree oven (no need to preheat) for 20 minutes or until the rolls are browned. Alternately, to steam, spray the rack of a Chinese bamboo steamer with cooking spray. Steam the rolls over a wok filled with 3 inches of water for 12–14 minutes. Garnish with coriander sprigs if desired and serve with soy-lime dipping sauce.

Soy-Lime Dipping Sauce

juice of ¹/₂ lime
6 tablespoons reduced-sodium soy sauce
3 tablespoons water
1 clove garlic, minced
1 teaspoon minced fresh ginger root
1 teaspoon sugar
2 scallions, minced

1. Combine all ingredients in a screw-top jar and shake to combine.

Yield of sauce: ³/₄ cup
Calories per tablespoon: 7
Protein per tablespoon: 1g
Fat per tablespoon: trace
    Saturated fat per tablespoon: trace
Cholesterol per tablespoon: 0
Carbohydrates per tablespoon: 2g
Sodium per tablespoon: 300mg
Fiber per tablespoon: trace

SEVICHE

Seviche is the Latin American cousin of Japan's sashimi. Unlike sashimi, which is strictly raw, seviche is prepared by marinating the fish several hours in lemon juice. This firms the flesh, turning it opaque; in essence, cooking it. Like sashimi, the freshness of the fish is imperative. Once it's marinated, however, seviche will keep for 2–3 days. Seviche makes a nice luncheon dish or first course as well as an appetizer. To give it a bit more body, do as a Peruvian friend of mine does: add a boiled, cubed sweet potato.

1¹/₂ pounds scallops or delicate white-fleshed fish, such as sole,
     cut into bite-size pieces
1 cup lemon juice
1 tablespoon finely chopped Bermuda or Spanish onion
¹/₄ green pepper, finely chopped
¹/₂ red pepper, finely chopped
¹/₂ blanched, skinned, and seeded tomato, cubed
¹/₃ cup lime juice (about 2 limes)
2 tablespoons orange juice, freshly squeezed preferred
3 tablespoons lemon juice
freshly ground pepper to taste
minced fresh parsley
lettuce

1. Marinate the seafood in the lemon juice in a nonmetallic container overnight.

2. Drain seafood, discarding marinade. Rinse with water.

3. Combine the onion, green pepper, red pepper, tomato, citrus juices, and fish. If desired, add the remaining halves of tomato and green pepper, also chopped. Season with pepper to taste. Garnish with a bit of parsley.

4. To serve, line individual plates or a platter with lettuce, mound mixture on top.

Yield: 10 appetizer servings
Calories for 1 appetizer serving: 89
Protein per appetizer: 12g
Fat per appetizer: 1g
   Saturated fat per appetizer: trace
Cholesterol per appetizer: 22mg
Carbohydrates per appetizer: 9g
Sodium per appetizer: 111mg
Fiber per appetizer: trace

or

Yield: 6 first-course servings
Calories per serving: 112
Protein per serving: 19g
Fat per serving: 1g
   Saturated fat per serving: trace
Cholesterol per serving: 36mg
Carbohydrates per serving: 7g
Sodium per serving: 179mg
Fiber per serving: trace

SOLE AND CRAB PEPPERS

These morsels may be made ahead and reheated, but for best flavor make them through Step 5, cooking just before serving. This recipe makes use of the seafood flakes (usually 35 percent crab–65 percent whitefish) now widely available. Or use 5 ounces uncooked shrimp or the real McCoy, of course. The sauce may be made ahead and reheated or omitted altogether if black bean or oyster sauce is unavailable.

For the Peppers

4 ounces sole or other whitefish fillets

1 scallion, minced

4 water chestnuts, fresh or canned, chopped

a pinch cayenne pepper

¹/₂ teaspoon red wine vinegar or rice wine vinegar

1 egg white

1 teaspoon cornstarch

5 ounces crabmeat or seafood flakes

2 medium red or green peppers

¹/₂ cup chicken broth

For the Sauce

1 tablespoon cornstarch

¹/₂ cup chicken broth

1 tablespoon black bean or oyster sauce (available at oriental or
    specialty food shops)

1 teaspoon sesame oil

Yield: 16 appetizers with sauce

Calories per appetizer: 24

Protein per appetizer: 3g

Fat per appetizer: trace

   Saturated fat per appetizer: trace

Cholesterol per appetizer: 11mg

Carbohydrates per appetizer: 2g

Sodium per appetizer: 70mg

Fiber per appetizer: trace

Note: Nutrition analysis includes
   sauce.

1. Put the fish in a food processor or through a meat grinder and process to a paste. Scrape into a bowl.

2. Add the scallion, water chestnuts, cayenne, vinegar, egg white, and cornstarch. Mix well.

3. Dice the crabmeat. Stir into the fish mixture.

4. Wash the peppers, cut in half, discard seeds, and cut each half in four pieces. (Don't wash the inside of the pepper or the filling won't adhere.)

5. Pack a heaping teaspoon of filling on each pepper.

6. Spray a 12-inch nonstick skillet with the cooking spray. Place filled peppers in skillet, pepper side down. Saute at high heat until peppers are just browned, add chicken broth, cover, and steam 3–4 minutes. Serve hot with black bean sauce dabbed on top or as a dip.

To Make the Sauce

1. Dissolve the cornstarch in the broth. Add black bean sauce and sesame oil. Stir over medium heat until thickened. Sauce may be reheated.

Baked Potato Chips

A slimming alternative to potato chips is to slice a baking potato as thinly as possible (a food processor works best, of course). Pat the slices dry. Spray one or two cookie sheets with nonstick cooking spray and spread out the potato slices in as close to a single layer as possible. Spray again with cooking spray, and sprinkle with seasoned salt. Bake in a 350-degree oven, no need to preheat, about 10 minutes; reduce heat to 300 degrees and bake another 15 minutes or until crisp and brown.

CLAM AND HAM APPETIZERS

These clam-and-ham–stuffed shells make a delicious hot cocktail nibble. The recipe may be prepared through Step 9 early in the day, and cooked at the last minute. The appetizers reheat nicely when covered with foil.

1/2 small onion, chopped

1 clove garlic, minced

1/2 cup chicken broth

3/4 cup dry white wine

12 hard-shell (littleneck) clams (about 2 pounds), well scrubbed

2 teaspoons cornstarch

3 ounces lean ham, chopped

3 tablespoons dried bread crumbs

1 tablespoon minced fresh parsley

Yield: 14

Calories in each: 20

Protein in each: 2g

Fat in each: trace

   Saturated fat in each: trace

Cholesterol in each: 6mg

Carbohydrates in each: 1g

Sodium in each: 78mg

Fiber in each: trace

1. "Saute" the onion and garlic in the chicken broth in a covered 2-quart saucepan until the vegetables are limp and almost transparent.

2. Add the wine (reserving 1 tablespoon for Step 3) and clams, cover pan, and steam over high heat until clams open, about 8 minutes.

3. Dissolve the cornstarch in the reserved tablespoon of wine.

4. Lift opened clams from the broth with a slotted spoon. Line a sieve with a piece of cheesecloth, coffee filter, or a heavy paper towel wrung out in water, and pour the broth through the sieve.

5. Pour 6 tablespoons strained broth back into the now-empty saucepan. Add dissolved cornstarch and cook, whisking, over medium heat until thickened. Set aside.

6. Pull clams from their shells, discard one half of shell. Chop clams roughly.

7. Combine chopped clams, ham, and thickened broth.

Thinking Thin Tip

A teaspoon of fat equals about 4 1/2 grams and has about 40 calories.

8. Spoon mixture into shells. Sprinkle ½ teaspoon bread crumbs on each stuffed shell.

9. Clams may now be baked in a 425-degree oven until bubbly and browned (about 12–14 minutes) or held, chilled, for baking later in the day. Broil briefly if the crumbs don't brown in the oven. Garnish the stuffed, baked clams with parsley.

SHRIMP-STUFFED MUSHROOMS

Stuffed mushroom caps are far from innovative, but their versatility and easy preparation make them enduringly popular. For variety, try filling the blanched caps with the Red or Yellow Pepper Puree (pages 260 or 77) or a *duxelle* (page 45) or chèvre mixed with a bit of milk. These may be made and assembled through Step 5, heating at the last moment.

Yield: 14 caps

Calories in each: 16

Protein in each: 1g

Fat in each: 1g

Saturated fat in each: trace

Cholesterol in each: 8mg

Carbohydrates in each: 2g

Sodium in each: 44mg

Fiber in each: trace

7–8 ounces mushrooms, chosen for broad caps

juice of ½ lemon or 2 tablespoons lemon juice

1 tablespoon reduced-calorie margarine

1 small rib celery, minced

2 ounces salad shrimp, chopped

additional few drops lemon juice

a few sprigs fresh thyme or ¼ teaspoon dried thyme

⅛ teaspoon salt

freshly ground pepper to taste

2 tablespoons dried bread crumbs

1. Wipe the mushrooms with a paper towel to remove dirt. Remove and mince the stems.

2. Bring a 2-quart saucepan half full of water with the lemon juice to a boil. Immerse cleaned mushroom caps and boil 2 minutes or just until softened. Drain on a towel, rounded-side up.

3. Meanwhile, melt the margarine in a 8-inch nonstick skillet over medium heat. When foamy, add the minced mushroom stems and celery and cook, covered, 2–3 minutes, stirring often.

4. Add the shrimp, lemon juice, thyme, salt, pepper, and bread crumbs. Turn heat to high, cook 30 seconds more, uncovered.

5. Remove shrimp mixture from heat. Place a heaping teaspoon on each mushroom cap. Place stuffed mushrooms on a baking sheet.

6. Broil until bubbly, 6–8 minutes.

Yogurt Cheese

Recipes for yogurt cheese have appeared in several books over these last few fat-restricted years. You'll find it a useful and remarkably easy basic to prepare. Simply turn a quart container of nonfat plain yogurt into a double thickness of cheesecloth. Gather the cloth into a ball and suspend over the kitchen sink tied to the faucet. Drain overnight. Refrigerate the resulting cheese for up to 5 days. The cheese may be frozen; although the texture will be grainy, it will be fine when cooked.

MUSSELS IN REMOULADE SAUCE

By popular demand, mussels are being cultivated, bringing a cleaner bivalve to the market. That means less scrubbing for the cook! Poach the mussels and make the sauce the day before, assemble them as much as two hours before serving this cold hors d'oeuvre.

Yield: 20 mussels in sauce

Calories in each: 36

Protein in each: 3g

Fat in each: 2g

　Saturated fat in each: trace

Cholesterol in each: 7mg

Carbohydrates in each: 1g

Sodium in each: 185mg

Fiber in each: trace

For the Mussels

1 pound mussels, about 15–20

3 tablespoons cornmeal

2 cups dry white wine

1 whole clove garlic

1 tablespoon minced fresh parsley

1 bay leaf

For the Sauce

$1/3$ cup egg substitute

5 drops lemon juice

$1/8$ teaspoon salt

2 tablespoons corn oil

$1/3$ cup reserved, strained mussel broth, boiling hot

$1/2$ teaspoon Dijon-style mustard

$1/2$ teaspoon capers

a pinch cayenne pepper

$1/2$ tablespoon minced fresh parsley

sprig of parsley for garnish (optional)

To Prepare the Shellfish

1. Discard any mussels that don't close when you poke the inside of the shell hinge with a sharp knife. Cut away the beards. Cover the mussels with water,

add the cornmeal, and let the mixture sit at least 30 minutes. The cornmeal is supposedly washed through the shellfish to carry out sand and grit.

2. Rinse the mussels thoroughly under running water.

3. Combine the wine, garlic, parsley, and bay leaf in a nonaluminum saucepan, cover, and bring to a boil. Add the mussels, cover, and boil until shells open, about 5 minutes.

4. Lift cooked mussels with a slotted spoon to a bowl. Chill the mussels. Discard the bay leaf from the broth.

5. Line a strainer with a double thickness of cheesecloth, a moistened coffee filter, or a heavy paper towel wrung out in water. Pour mussel cooking broth through strainer. Let liquid rest 5 minutes, then pour through again, discarding the sediment that sinks to the bottom of the pan. Set aside while preparing sauce.

To Prepare the Sauce

1. Put the egg substitute, lemon juice, and salt in a food processor and blend 20 seconds.

2. Dribble in the oil in a very fine, steady stream, almost drop by drop, while machine runs.

3. Meanwhile, heat strained mussel broth in a 1-quart nonaluminum saucepan. When boiling, dribble into the egg-oil mixture while machine runs.

4. Pour sauce into the now-empty saucepan and whisk until thickened over low heat, about 1 minute.

5. Remove from heat and stir in mustard, capers, cayenne, and parsley. Taste and adjust seasoning, add more lemon juice if sauce is too bland.

To Serve

1. Remove one half of mussel shell, discard. Free mussel from the other half, but leave in the shell, and arrange on a platter in a spoke fashion. Place a dab of sauce on each and garnish with a tiny sprig of parsley if desired.

Variation

Mussels may be served warm or cold, removed from the shell and tossed with the *remoulade* sauce, then mounded on a lettuce cup. Garnish with lemon slices dipped in parsley.

Thinking Thin Tip

Canola oil has the best fatty acid ratio; it is the highest of all oils in healthful polyunsaturated fats and the lowest in heart-damaging saturated fat.

CHICKEN AND PORK SKEWERS

This tasty combination of chicken and pork is for those who like it hot. If you prefer a milder flavor, reduce or omit the chili paste with garlic. Marinate the chicken and pork as much as two days before preparing. Soaking the wooden skewers 45 minutes before grilling will keep them from scorching.

Yield: 15 skewers
Calories per skewer: 47
Protein per skewer: 6g
Fat per skewer: 2g
  Saturated fat per skewer: 1g
Cholesterol per skewer: 16mg
Carbohydrates per skewer: 1g
Sodium per skewer: 253mg
Fiber per skewer: trace

1 whole chicken breast, boned and skinned

5 ounces boneless pork from chops or tenderloin, fat trimmed

6 tablespoons reduced-sodium soy sauce

1 tablespoon sesame oil, available at Chinese or specialty food shops

2 tablespoons chicken broth

1 scallion (white part only), chopped

a 1-inch piece of ginger root, peeled and minced

*2 teaspoons chili paste with garlic, available at Chinese or specialty
    food shops*

1. Put the pork in the freezer for 2 hours; place the chicken in the freezer about 10 minutes.

2. Slice the chicken in long, thin strips, slanting the knife slightly. Cut the pork so the strips are wide as well as long by placing what was the bone end flat on the cutting surface and slicing down.

3. Place the chicken and pork in a plastic or a glass bowl with the soy sauce, sesame oil, chicken broth, scallion, and ginger root. Marinate in refrigerator 2–4 hours.

4. Drain poultry and meat, reserving marinade. Thread the chicken and pork alternately on skewers. You may refrigerate assembled skewers up to 12 hours before cooking.

5. Mix the marinade with the chili paste. Bring marinade to a boil for 30 seconds. Grill or broil chicken skewers, brushing with chili paste marinade, 12–16 minutes or until done. The meat and poultry should be juicy, not overdone.

CREAMY CHICKEN ENCHILADAS

These "creamy" chicken enchiladas have universal appeal. Cooked layer-cake fashion, they are coveted family fare; assembled in tiny muffin tins, they make terrific hors d'oeuvres. Instructions for each follow. You might like to vary the chicken filling with the Beef Taco Sedona filling on page 142, the Black Bean and Beef Chili filling on page 140, or a minced vegetable mixture seasoned with coriander.

Red Chili Sauce

1 small yellow onion, minced

2 garlic cloves, minced

2 tablespoons instant-blending flour

2 teaspoons chili powder

1 teaspoon unsweetened cocoa powder

1 teaspoon dried oregano

1/2 teaspoon cumin powder

1/2 teaspoon salt

1 13³/₄-ounce can chicken broth

"Cream" Sauce

1 cup skim milk

2 tablespoons instant-blending flour or 1 tablespoon cornstarch

*2 ounces fat-free shredded, mild cheese such as Monterey Jack or
    light cheddar*

Yield: 6 servings

Calories per serving: 378

Protein per serving: 40g

Fat per serving: 9g

 Saturated fat per serving: 1g

Cholesterol per serving: 75mg

Carbohydrates per serving: 38g

Sodium per serving: 891mg

Fiber per serving: 2g

Yield: 36 hors d'oeuvres

Calories each: 65

Protein each: 7g

Fat each: 1g

 Saturated fat each: trace

Cholesterol each: 12mg

Carbohydrates each: 7g

Sodium each: 139mg

Fiber each: trace

Chicken Filling

3 cooked chicken breast quarters, skinned and shredded (about 4 cups)

4 ounces mushrooms, thinly sliced

3 or 4 scallions, chopped

2 teaspoons minced fresh coriander or to taste

1 teaspoon minced canned chipotle chili peppers and about 1 teaspoon
    sauce or minced jalapeño to taste

1 cup canned "recipe-ready" tomatoes with a little juice

1/2 teaspoon Adobo seasoning (available in Spanish section of market)
    or salt

5 or 6 8-inch or larger whole wheat or white flour tortillas (for layer cake
    presentation or 1 package 6-inch flour tortillas for hors d'oeuvres)

1/4 cup shredded fat-free mozzarella cheese

fresh coriander sprigs for garnish (optional)

1 minced scallion for garnish (optional)

To Prepare the Red Chili Sauce

1. Combine the onion and garlic in a 2½-quart heavy-bottom saucepan. Spray with cooking spray. Saute over medium heat 4 minutes or until the onion is softened but not browned. Sprinkle in the flour, chili powder, cocoa, oregano, cumin, and salt. Stir over medium-high heat about 1 minute. Reduce heat to medium and whisk in the chicken broth. Continue to whisk until sauce is smooth and starting to thicken. Adjust heat so sauce just simmers. Simmer 25–30 minutes until thickened.

To Prepare the Cream Sauce

1. Meanwhile, combine the milk and flour in a 2-cup glass measure or other microwave-safe container. Cover with plastic wrap. Microwave on high (100 percent power) for 4 minutes or until thickened. Stir in the cheese, cover, and microwave on high (100 percent power) for an additional minute. Set aside.

To Prepare the Filling

1. If preparing the dish as an hors d'oeuvre, mince the chicken in a food processor; if preparing as an entree, leave the chicken in shreds.

2. Spray an 8-inch nonstick skillet with cooking spray. Saute the mushrooms over high heat for 5 minutes or until lightly browned. Add the mushrooms to the chicken.

3. Stir the scallions, coriander, chili peppers with sauce, tomatoes, and Adobo seasoning or salt into the chicken/mushroom mixture along with the cream sauce.

To Assemble Layer-Cake Fashion

1. Film the bottom of a pie plate or other baking dish with 1-inch sides with a few tablespoons of red chili sauce.

2. Dip a tortilla in the chili sauce to coat both sides. Place in the baking dish. Spread chicken-cream mixture over as if making a peanut butter sandwich. Repeat with remaining tortillas and filling, ending with a tortilla. Pour any remaining sauce on top. Sprinkle with the remaining cheese. The dish may be assembled to this point and refrigerated, up to 6 hours before baking.

3. Place in the upper third of a 350-degree oven (no need to preheat) for 25–30 minutes, or slightly longer if the uncooked dish has been refrigerated. Garnish and let rest 5–8 minutes before slicing into wedges.

To Assemble as Hors D'Oeuvres

1. Spray 3 12-cup tiny muffin tins with nonstick cooking spray. Cut a package of tortillas into eighths, in wedges. Press 1 or 2 wedges into the muffin cups. Spoon in a rounded tablespoon of chicken mixture. Add a teaspoon or so of red chili sauce and top with a pinch of cheese. Press any errant tortilla tips into the filling. Bake 15 minutes in a 350-degree oven (no need to preheat) or until the cheese is lightly browned. Let the tiny tacos rest about 5 minutes before removing from the tin. If made ahead, reheat in the oven (not in the microwave—the tortillas will become too soggy).

Thinking Thin Tip

A good way to become aware of calorie counts in foods you commonly eat is to keep a diary of *everything* you consume for a few days, then tally the calories and fat grams with the help of a calorie listing.

CRUDITÉS AND SKINNY DIPS

Raw vegetables cut into bite-size pieces (crudités) have been a popular nibble for years. Obviously, they're just right for *Gourmet Light* cooking too, if the accompanying dip is on the slender side.

When choosing vegetables for a crudité basket, keep color and texture in mind. Mushrooms, a soft vegetable, need the crunch of a celery stick, for example, and radishes can be offset with cherry tomatoes. Choose any vegetable that can be eaten raw. Happily, most vegetables can be prepared in advance and held as long as two days in ice water, which keeps them crisp. Those that resemble a flower bud, such as a cauliflower and broccoli, are great timesavers, requiring no more preparation than the snap of a stalk.

Because most baskets are too deep for the vegetables to look attractive in, a false bottom will create the illusion of bounty. Layer crumbled-up wax paper in the bottom, and cover with a cloth napkin. Position the dip, in a bowl—perhaps one made from a vegetable—in the center and arrange prepared vegetables around it.

Another pretty presentation is to choose a rectangular tray. Arrange the vegetables in "ribbons" that run diagonally, a mirror image on either end of the tray, with small bowls of different dips (also on the diagonal) in the center.

Qué Salada!

Adobo seasoning, available in the Spanish section of many markets, is a blend of salt, oregano, and garlic that comes with or without pepper. I make frequent use of Adobo seasoning in my cooking because it heightens the flavor of and complements many savory dishes better than salt alone.

BASIL-WALNUT CREAM

My good friend Lissa paid this the highest compliment, "This tastes like calories!" Terrific with crudités or spread on sun-ripened tomatoes.

6 ounces fat-free cream cheese

2 ounces reduced-fat Havarti cheese, garden vegetable variety preferred

1/2 cup snipped fresh basil leaves

1 shallot

2 tablespoons Parmesan cheese

1 tablespoon balsamic vinegar

1 teaspoon fresh thyme leaves

1/2 teaspoon horseradish mustard or to taste

a dash seasoned salt

2 tablespoons chopped walnuts

Yield: 1 cup

Calories per tablespoon: 30

Protein per tablespoon: 3g

Fat per tablespoon: 1g

   Saturated fat per tablespoon: 1g

Cholesterol per tablespoon: 5mg

Carbohydrates per tablespoon: 1g

Sodium per tablespoon: 109mg

Fiber per tablespoon: trace

1. Combine all ingredients except the walnuts in the bowl of a food processor and process until smooth. Add walnuts and pulse machine just to mix. Will keep refrigerated up to 5 days.

CURRIED CREAM DIP

Raw vegetables are the perfect nibble for cocktail or anytime, but typical fat-laden dips are anything but. If you eat but 2 tablespoons of an ordinary dip, you may be padding your fat gram tally with as much as 22 grams, more than a third of an average person's daily allotment. Offer this dip next time. Your friends won't ask if it's low-fat, only if there's any more.

Yield: 1 1/2 cups

Calories per tablespoon: 23

Protein per tablespoon: 1g

Fat per tablespoon: trace

   Saturated fat per tablespoon: trace

Cholesterol per tablespoon: 1mg

Carbohydrates per tablespoon: 4g

Sodium per tablespoon: 79mg

Fiber per tablespoon: trace

1/2 small onion, cut into chunks

1 clove garlic

1/2 cup yogurt cheese (page 54)

1/4 cup nonfat sour cream

1/4 cup fat-free mayonnaise

1 tablespoon regular mayonnaise

1 tablespoon honey

1 tablespoon curry powder

2 teaspoons prepared horseradish

2 teaspoons white wine vinegar

1 teaspoon sugar

1/2 teaspoon seasoned salt

freshly ground pepper to taste

3 tablespoons golden raisins

1. Process the onion and garlic together in the bowl of a food processor until minced. Add all remaining ingredients except the raisins. Process until well combined. Taste and correct seasonings if necessary. Add raisins and process briefly just until they are mixed in. Mixture will keep in the refrigerator up to 3 days.

BLUE CHEESE AND HERB DIP

Substituting tarragon for the rosemary will produce an equally delicious dip. In the unlikely event of leftovers, try a spoonful or so on a baked potato. Keeps in the fridge about 5 days.

4 ounces fat-free cream cheese

1/4 cup fresh minced parsley

2 tablespoons reduced-fat margarine

2 tablespoons fresh basil leaves

2 teaspoons fresh rosemary or tarragon leaves

1 clove garlic

1 teaspoon fresh thyme leaves

2 teaspoons Worcestershire sauce

few drops lemon juice

1 1/2 ounces blue cheese

Yield: 1 cup

Calories per tablespoon: 22

Protein per tablespoon: 2g

Fat per tablespoon: 1g

 Saturated fat per tablespoon: 1g

Cholesterol per tablespoon: 3mg

Carbohydrates per tablespoon: trace

Sodium per tablespoon: 101mg

Fiber per tablespoon: trace

1. Combine all ingredients except the blue cheese in the bowl of food processor and process until smooth. Stir in the blue cheese. Refrigerate.

ROQUEFORT SKINNY DIP

If any of this is left over, it will make a romaine lettuce salad a great partner.

2 ounces Roquefort or blue cheese
¹/₂ cup crème blanc (page 34) or 2 ounces nonfat cottage cheese and
   2¹/₂ ounces plain nonfat yogurt
2 tablespoons fat-free cream cheese
¹/₄ teaspoon paprika
¹/₂ teaspoon sugar
freshly ground pepper to taste

Yield: 1 cup
Calories per tablespoon: 26
Protein per tablespoon: 2g
Fat per tablespoon: 1g
   Saturated fat per tablespoon: 1g
Cholesterol per tablespoon: 4mg
Carbohydrates per tablespoon: 2g
Sodium per tablespoon: 72mg
Fiber per tablespoon: trace

1. Combine all the ingredients in a food processor or blender and mix well.

BOBOLI WITH FRESH VEGETABLES AND HERBS

The boboli shells widely available at supermarkets make quick, custom piz-
zas a snap. I make a low-fat, multi-veggie version for the adults and a
traditional topping for the kids. Cut the circles into little squares for cocktail
fare. Flour tortillas make a good substitute for the bobolis.

Yield: 2 small bobolis (1 per serving)

Calories per serving: 589

Protein per serving: 35g

Fat per serving: 20g

  Saturated fat per serving: 2g

Cholesterol per serving: 31mg

Carbohydrates per serving: 65g

Sodium per serving: 1,346mg

Fiber per serving: 4g

1¹/₂ cups chopped mixed vegetables such as zucchini, summer squash,
  carrots, Spanish onion, broccoli, and mushrooms
¹/₂ cup Mexican Cheese Sauce, page 28 (optional)
2 small boboli shells
1 tablespoon olive or canola oil
1 tablespoon mixed fresh herbs (basil, tarragon, oregano and/or rose-
mary)
¹/₄ teaspoon Adobo seasoning (page 62) or salt
freshly ground pepper to taste
3 ounces reduced or fat-free cheese such as mozzarella or cheddar,
  shredded

1. *Place the vegetables in a microwave-safe container. Cover with plastic
wrap and microwave at high (100 percent power) for 5 minutes or until the
vegetables are tender but crisp. Drain off any accumulated water.* Alternately, spray a 10-inch nonstick skillet with nonstick cooking spray. Saute
the vegetables over medium-high heat, stirring frequently until vegetables
are tender but crisp.

2. Spread the cheese sauce over the shells. Cover with the vegetables. Drizzle with the oil and sprinkle with the herbs, salt, pepper, and cheese.

3. Bake in the upper third of a 425-degree oven (no need to preheat) for 10
to 15 minutes or until the cheese is lightly browned.

RED PEPPER AND GOAT CHEESE PIZZETTA

Treat this not so much as a recipe but as a starting point for your own cre-
ations. Pizzettas are simplicity itself; they are extraordinarily easy to prepare
and versatile. Serve them for snacks, cocktail fare, lunch, or casual supper.

1 clove garlic, minced

¹/₂ shallot, minced

1 teaspoon walnut oil or fine-quality olive oil

¹/₂ each yellow and red bell pepper, seeded and julienned

a few shakes Adobo seasoning (available in Spanish section of many
markets) or salt

2 6-inch flour tortillas

2 ounces goat cheese, crumbled

1 tablespoon shredded part-skim mozzarella cheese

¹/₂ teaspoon crushed or to taste fresh rosemary leaves

pepper to taste

¹/₂ teaspoon oil or nonstick cooking spray

Yield: 2 pizzettas (1 pizzetta per
 serving)

Calories per serving: 235

Protein per serving: 10g

Fat per serving: 12g

 Saturated fat per serving: 5g

Cholesterol per serving: 17mg

Carbohydrates per serving: 22g

Sodium per serving: 325mg

Fiber per serving: 2g

1. Saute the garlic and shallot in the walnut oil in an 8-inch nonstick skillet
over medium-low heat about 2 minutes. Add the peppers and Adobo seasoning. Saute, stirring often, about 4 to 5 minutes more or until the peppers are
softened. Do not let them brown excessively.

2. Place the tortillas on a cookie sheet or another ovenproof dish. Divide the
peppers between them. Top with the cheeses, rosemary, and pepper. Drizzle
with oil or spray with cooking spray. Place in the upper third of a 450-degree
oven (no need to preheat) for about 10 minutes or until the cheeses are bubbly and hot.

Variations

1. Saute Spanish and Bermuda onion with a few teaspoons of brown sugar; add a couple of dollops of part-skim ricotta cheese and a skimpy smattering of diced deli-style black or green olives; season with thyme.

2. Saute a couple tablespoons of minced Spanish onion with garlic and shallot. Mix with drained "recipe-ready" tomatoes; top with spears of asparagus arranged like spokes on a wheel. Sprinkle with fat-free shredded cheese and minced fresh basil.

3. Saute sun-dried tomato with a few tablespoons "recipe-ready" tomatoes, garlic, and shallot, seasoned with a few drops balsamic vinegar, freshly minced parsley, and oregano. Cover with sauteed mushrooms and grated Parmesan cheese.

Fresh Mozzarella and Tomato Pizzetta

Assemble this pizzetta no more than an hour before serving or the tortilla will get soggy. Fresh mozzarella, the kind sold in brine and available at some specialty food stores, makes a delicious change from the supermarket variety.

1 large, burrito style, flour tortilla (sold refrigerated in the supermarket dairy section)

1 large, fully ripe tomato, thinly sliced, slices cut in half

2 ounces fresh mozzarella cheese, cut into strips

4 or 5 fresh basil leaves, snipped, or ¹/₂ teaspoon dried basil

1 teaspoon extra-virgin olive oil

¹/₈ teaspoon salt and freshly ground pepper to taste

Yield: 4 servings

Calories per serving: 97

Protein per serving: 5g

Fat per serving: 4g

  Saturated fat per serving: 2g

Cholesterol per serving: 8mg

Carbohydrates per serving: 10g

Sodium per serving: 161mg

Fiber per serving: 1g

1. Preheat oven to 475 degrees. Place the tortilla on a baking sheet. Arrange the tomato slices, overlapping them spoke fashion, on the tortilla.

2. Cover the tomato with the cheese strips.

3. Sprinkle basil over cheese, dribble on oil, then season with salt and pepper.

4. Bake in a 475-degree oven about 6 minutes until cheese is melted. Then broil until lightly browned, about 3 minutes more. Cool slightly before cutting into quarters with a pizza cutter.

THE SOUP BOWL

THE RECIPES

THE SOUP BOWL

Of soup and love, the first is best.
—SPANISH PROVERB

Soup—what diversity in a single bowl! From the elegance of a sparkly clear consomme to an unpretentious potato soup, from a trendy blueberry bisque to a plain old clam chowder, soups come in a fashion for every taste and occasion. Whether you're looking for a meal in a bowl or just a tasty starter, even a dessert, soup fills the bill.

Many cooks today are rediscovering the natural goodness of homemade soups. Perhaps the food processor is partly responsible for the newfound popularity, maybe it's because most soups freeze so well—a boon for today's busy cook. Maybe it's just the down-home appeal of a good bowl of soup. Regardless, soups are a natural in *Gourmet Light* cooking, for a deliciously satisfying first course can be enjoyed for less than 100 calories, or a nutritionally balanced meal consumed for under 300 calories. Naturally, you won't find heavy cream soups here, but you will find their updated, lightened versions and more. Some of the soups are skinny by nature such as Gazpacho and Two-Mushroom Consomme; others have been run through the calorie reducer such as the New Wave Fish Chowder. Some are a snap to fix, others require a lengthier kitchen commitment.

CHILLED TOMATO SOUP WITH BASIL-WALNUT CREAM

This is one of my favorite summertime soups because of its delightful combination of flavors and colors. There's no need to buy perfect tomatoes for this recipe; the "seconds" or bruised tomatoes offered at many farm stands are ideal. The soup freezes well, too, making it possible to enjoy the flavor of summer in the dead of February. Garnish with a dollop of Basil-Walnut Cream, page 63, or Basil Salsa, page 31.

3 pounds ripe tomatoes, cored

8–10 fresh basil leaves, snipped, or 1 teaspoon dried basil

³/₄ teaspoon salt

2 medium onions, sliced

2 cloves garlic, minced

1–2 teaspoons sugar

1 tablespoon fresh tarragon, snipped, or 1 teaspoon dried tarragon

freshly ground pepper to taste

¹/₂–³/₄ cup chicken broth, if needed

Basil-Walnut Cream (page 63) or Basil Salsa (page 31) for garnish

1. Quarter the tomatoes. Put them in a large saucepan with the basil, onions, garlic, sugar, tarragon, salt, and pepper. Turn heat to medium high, cover, and simmer until tomatoes are completely soft and pulpy, about 20 minutes. Stir occasionally.

2. Uncover the pan, lower the heat to medium-low, and cook about 30 minutes or until reduced by ¹/₃.

3. In batches, process soup in a food processor, blender, or food mill. Strain if desired to remove the seeds and skins. Chill and serve the soup garnished with Basil-Walnut Cream or Basil Salsa.

Yield: 4 cups

Calories per cup: 106

Protein per cup: 4g

Fat per cup: 1g

   Saturated fat per cup: trace

Cholesterol per cup: 1mg

Carbohydrates per cup: 23g

Sodium per cup: 430mg

Fiber per cup: 5g

Note: Nutritional analysis does not include Basil-Walnut Cream.

GAZPACHO

This zesty bowl of garden goodies, which is really improved the second day, is naturally low in calories. For a special treat, serve with the Basil Salsa on page 31, or garnish with minced fresh cilantro leaves.

1³/₄ pounds ripe tomatoes

1 medium onion, chopped

1 cucumber, peeled, seeded, and chopped

1 green pepper, seeded and chopped

1 red pepper, seeded and chopped (optional)

1 clove garlic, minced

24 ounces tomato juice

4 tablespoons red wine vinegar

1 teaspoon salt

a few drops hot pepper sauce

2 tablespoons chopped chives (from scallion tops)

oven-dried croutons (optional)

cilantro leaves (optional)

Yield: 6 cups

Calories per cup: 64

Protein per cup: 2g

Fat per cup: 1g

   Saturated fat per cup: trace

Cholesterol per cup: 0

Carbohydrates per cup: 15g

Sodium per cup: 799mg

Fiber per cup: 3g

1. Core the tomatoes and cut a cross in each one's bottom. Immerse tomatoes in boiling water for 15 seconds. Cool them under running water and strip the skins. Quarter the tomatoes. Squeeze the tomatoes in a strainer supported over a bowl to remove the seeds. Press the seeds with the back of a spoon to extract the juice. Discard the seeds.

2. In a food processor or blender, combine half of the seeded tomatoes, all the juice from the same, the onion, half of the cucumber, green pepper, red pepper, all the garlic, and half the tomato juice. Process until somewhat smooth.

3. Stir in the remaining tomato juice, vinegar, salt, pepper sauce, the remaining tomato, cucumber, peppers, and all the chives. Chill at least 2 hours; also chill the soup bowls. Serve with oven-dried croutons and cilantro leaves if desired.

Oven-Dried Croutons

1. Dice 4 slices of bread. Place in a single layer on a cookie sheet in a 325-degree oven for 15 minutes; stir the cubes occasionally. To brown slightly, spray a frying pan with cooking spray and saute oven-dried cubes over medium heat until lightly browned.

Yield: 6 cups (¼ cup serving size)

Calories per serving: 13

Protein per serving: trace

Fat per serving: trace

   Saturated fat per serving: trace

Cholesterol per serving: 0

Carbohydrates per serving: 2g

Sodium per serving: 16mg

Fiber per serving: trace

CAULIFLOWER "CREAM" WITH YELLOW PEPPER PUREE

"Cauliflower is nothing but a cabbage with a college education."

—MARK TWAIN

In a class ahead of its cousin the cabbage or not, cauliflower is a calorie counter's dream, supplying only 28 calories a cup and a good supply of vitamin C. Here, it's pureed in a soup to be served hot or cold and garnished with a swirl of Yellow Pepper Puree, an economical way to serve delicious but rather dear yellow peppers. The puree also makes a delightful dip for vegetables at cocktail time. You may substitute red peppers for the yellow. Because commercially prepared cream soups can get as much as 60 percent of their calories from fat, it makes sense to create your own the *Gourmet Light* way when the urge for a good cream soup strikes.

3 small leeks, white part only
3 cups blanched cauliflower (about ¹/₂ head)
1¹/₂ cups skim milk
¹/₂ cup skimmed evaporated milk
1 small potato, peeled and diced
³/₄ teaspoon salt
freshly ground pepper to taste
freshly grated nutmeg

For the Garnish

2 yellow peppers
1 cup loosely packed snipped fresh basil leaves or 2 tablespoons
    dried basil
4 tablespoons grated Parmesan or Romano cheese
1 tablespoon olive oil

Yield of soup: 4 cups
Calories per cup: 140
Protein per cup: 11g
Fat per cup: 1g
    Saturated fat per cup: trace
Cholesterol per cup: 4mg
Carbohydrates per cup: 24g
Sodium per cup: 534mg
Fiber per cup: 3g

Yield of puree: 1 cup
Calories per tablespoon: 80
Protein per tablespoon: 3g
Fat per tablespoon: 5g
    Saturated fat per tablespoon: 1g
Cholesterol per tablespoon: 4mg
Carbohydrates per tablespoon: 7g
Sodium per tablespoon: 94mg
Fiber per tablespoon: 2g

To Prepare the Soup

1. Slice the leeks and rinse thoroughly. Place the leeks in a 1-quart saucepan with enough water to half cover. Cover the pan, turn heat to high. When a boil is reached, reduce the heat so the liquid simmers. Uncover after 10 minutes and continue to cook until the leeks are soft, about 5 minutes more. Drain and reserve liquid.

2. Meanwhile, core the cauliflower and blanch the head in boiling water for about 5 minutes. Drain and chop it. Combine the cauliflower with both kinds of milk, potato, salt, pepper, and leeks in a 2-quart saucepan.

3. Cover the pan, bring to a boil, and reduce heat to a simmer. Simmer for 20 minutes.

4. Puree the mixture in a food processor or in batches in a blender. Thin if desired with the reserved liquid from Step 1, or milk. Add nutmeg and taste for seasoning adjustment. Overseason if serving the soup cold. Serve with a tablespoon of the yellow pepper puree swirled in.

To Prepare the Yellow Pepper Puree

1. Cut the peppers in half, flatten them with the heel of your hand, and place peppers on a baking sheet, skin side up, under a hot broiler. Broil until the peppers are completely blackened and charred, which can take as long as 10 minutes. Remove peppers to a plastic or paper bag rolled tightly shut and chill until cool enough to handle.

2. Peel the loosened skin from the peppers and discard. Chop the peppers and puree them in a food processor, blender, or food mill. See the illustrations on page 259.

3. Add the basil, cheese, and olive oil to the peppers. The puree will be thick and chunky. It will keep up to one week chilled, or it may be frozen.

"CREAM" OF LETTUCE SOUP

This cream soup owes its richness more to the vegetable itself than cream, making it as healthful as it is calorie conservative. Make it in quantity when garden lettuce is in season and freeze for a taste of summer in the chill of winter. The soup is good hot or cold and may be made as much as 24 hours in advance.

1 head lettuce, preferably romaine (about ³/₄ pound)

2¹/₂ quarts water

1 can (13³/₄ ounces) chicken broth

³/₄ cup fresh or frozen peas

2 scallions, roughly chopped

1 tablespoon minced fresh parsley

¹/₂ teaspoon salt

freshly ground pepper to taste

¹/₂ cup skimmed evaporated milk

4 tablespoons crème blanc, page 34 (optional)

Yield: 4 cups

Calories per cup: 64

Protein per cup: 6g

Fat per cup: trace

   Saturated fat per cup: trace

Cholesterol per cup: 1mg

Carbohydrates per cup: 10g

Sodium per cup: 373mg

Fiber per cup: 2g

1. Wash and core the lettuce, and tear the leaves in half. Bring the water to a boil. Add the lettuce leaves and boil, uncovered, for 3–4 minutes or until wilted and somewhat softened.

2. Drain the lettuce and place it in a food processor or blender in small batches, with the broth, peas, scallions, parsley, salt, and pepper. Process the mixture and leave it slightly coarse.

3. Pour the mixture into a saucepan, add milk, and simmer 15–20 minutes.

4. Before serving add a dollop of crème blanc to each serving.

Note: Overseason if serving soup cold.

"Cream" of Mushroom Soup

Use this recipe as an example of how to rewrite old favorites in the *Gourmet Light* way. To update, add a half ounce of sherry-soaked cepes or chanterelles at Step 8.

1 quart chicken broth plus an additional ¹/₂ cup

1 small onion, minced

1 tablespoon reduced-fat margarine

3 tablespoons flour, instant blending recommended

12 ounces mushrooms, wiped clean

juice of half a lemon or 1 tablespoon lemon juice

¹/₃ cup egg substitute

¹/₂ cup skimmed evaporated milk

1 tablespoon sherry

¹/₄ teaspoon salt

freshly ground pepper to taste

freshly ground nutmeg

Yield: approximately 4 cups

Calories per cup: 119

Protein per cup: 8g

Fat per cup: 2g

   Saturated fat per cup: trace

Cholesterol per cup: 5mg

Carbohydrates per cup: 17g

Sodium per cup: 265mg

Fiber per cup: 2g

1. Bring ¹/₄ cup broth to a boil in a 10-inch skillet. "Saute" the onion at high heat until it becomes limp and transparent.

2. Meanwhile, bring 1 cup of broth to a boil in a 2¹/₂-quart saucepan.

3. When the onion is limp and the broth almost evaporated, reduce the heat to medium. Add the margarine. When it's melted and foamy, stir in the flour. Stir with a wooden spoon for 1 minute over low heat.

4. Remove the skillet from the heat. Whisk in the hot broth. Whisk in an additional cup of cold broth. Transfer the ingredients to the now-empty saucepan. Add the remaining 2 cups broth.

5. Remove stems from the mushrooms. Mince the stems and slice caps. Add the stems to broth-onion mixture. Simmer, covered, for 20 minutes.

6. Place the caps in now-empty skillet, add lemon juice, and remaining ¼ cup broth, and "saute" at high heat until mushrooms are soft and liquid is evaporated. Set aside.

7. Strain the stems and onions from the broth-onion mixture. Press the vegetables with the back of a wooden spoon to extract their juices.

8. Beat the egg substitute with milk in a small bowl. Drizzle ½ cup strained hot soup base into egg mixture while beating with a fork. Slowly pour egg mixture into remaining soup base, and whisk over low heat until thickened, about 4 minutes.

9. Add mushroom caps to the soup. Add the sherry, season with salt, pepper, and nutmeg.

Note: Do not boil soup once the egg mixture has been added.

Nutmeg

Recipes in this book frequently specify using freshly grated nutmeg, as it is considerably more flavorful than the ground variety. Whole nutmegs—the pit of a West Indian peachlike fruit—are available at some supermarkets and specialty food shops. Mace, a similar but stronger taste than nutmeg, is the outside sheathing that covers the nutmeg. It is sold already ground. Nutmeg grinders (similar to small pepper mills) are available as are small, inexpensive graters that often have a hinged top to store the nutmeg.

Grilled Corn and Tomato Chowder with Fresh Herb Salsa

Thick and chunky, bursting with the smoky flavor of grilled corn and tomatoes, this chowder dishes out nowhere near the 15 grams of fat found in a traditional cup. Although a recipe is given here for fresh herb salsa, the Basil Salsa on page 31 would be equally as good. Leftover herb salsa will keep in the refrigerator up to 12 days.

For the Chowder

5 ears of corn, husks left on

1/2 head garlic

1/2 red onion

2 tomatoes, cored and quartered, seeds popped out with your thumb

1 teaspoon canola oil

3 cups chicken broth

1/2 teaspoon salt

pepper to taste

For the Herb Salsa

1 bunch fresh basil, stemmed, about 1 1/2 cups loosely packed

1/2 cup tightly packed fresh parsley, stemmed

3 tablespoons chicken broth

1 tablespoon plus 1 teaspoon balsamic vinegar

4 tablespoons grated Parmesan cheese

1 teaspoon sugar

2 teaspoons walnut oil

1/2 teaspoon salt

freshly ground pepper to taste

1/4 teaspoon crushed red pepper flakes

Yield: 6 cups chowder

Calories per cup: 111

Protein per cup: 4g

Fat per cup: 2g

  Saturated fat per cup: trace

Cholesterol per cup: 2mg

Carbohydrates per cup: 23g

Sodium per cup: 199mg

Fiber per cup: 4g

Yield: 3/4 cup herb salsa

Calories per tablespoon: 19

Protein per tablespoon: 1g

Fat per tablespoon: 1g

  Saturated fat per tablespoon: trace

Cholesterol per tablespoon: 1mg

Carbohydrates per tablespoon: 1g

Sodium per tablespoon: 111mg

Fiber per tablespoon: trace

To Prepare the Chowder

1. Soak the unhusked corn in a sink full of water for 5 minutes.

2. Grill the corn, turning to cook evenly, until the kernels are roasted, about 12 minutes. At the same time, grill the garlic for about 20 minutes, or until the cloves (not the papery outer layers) are very soft and mushy. Brush the onion and tomato with the oil. Grill the onion until lightly blackened and softened, about 10 minutes. Grill the tomato until the skin is blackened and the flesh is softened, about 10 minutes. Individual grill temperatures will vary and affect cooking times; err on the underdone side.

3. When the corn is cool enough to handle, husk it and cut the kernels from the cobs. Reserve about 1 cup kernels. Peel the garlic, discarding the papery outer covering.

4. In the bowl of a food processor, combine the remaining corn kernels, peeled garlic, onion, and chicken broth. Process until pureed, about 1 minute.

5. Add the tomato, salt, and pepper. Process just until combined. Chunks of tomato should remain. Stir in the reserved corn.

6. Place soup in a 2½-quart saucepan. Place over medium heat and simmer 10–12 minutes, stirring occasionally. Soup may be chilled and reheated or served immediately with herb salsa.

To Prepare the Herb Salsa

1. In the bowl of a food processor, combine all salsa ingredients. Process until pureed, about 1 minute.

2. To serve, place a heaping tablespoon of herb salsa on each cup of hot chowder. Let diners swirl it into the chowder themselves.

HARVEST SOUP

A hearty soup, perfect for chilly days. Any leftovers freeze nicely.

1 1-pound package yellow or green split peas

2 carrots

1 Spanish onion

1 parsnip, peeled

3 stalks celery, stringed

1/2 purple-top turnip

2 cloves garlic

1 cup chopped fresh flat-leaf parsley (about 1/2 bunch)

1 meaty ham bone, fat removed, or 2 or 3 ham hocks

1 tablespoon minced fresh thyme or 1 teaspoon dried thyme

2 teaspoons stone-ground mustard

2 teaspoons salt or to taste

1 teaspoon ground pepper

1 teaspoon cumin

Yield: about 4 quarts

Calories per cup: 141

Protein per cup: 10g

Fat per cup: 3g

   Saturated fat per cup: 1g

Cholesterol per cup: 9mg

Carbohydrates per cup: 20g

Sodium per cup: 469mg

Fiber per cup: 3g

1. *Place the split peas in a microwave-safe 4-quart container. Add 2 quarts water and microwave at high (100 percent power) for 30 minutes.* Alternately, soak the peas in water to cover overnight or for 8 hours. Drain.

2. Chop the carrots, onion, parsnip, celery, turnip, and garlic in batches in the bowl of a food processor or by hand.

3. *Combine the microwaved or soaked peas, chopped vegetables, and all remaining ingredients in a microwave-safe 4-quart container. Add 10 cups water. Cover and microwave at high (100% power) for 1 hour and 20 minutes.* Alternately, bring all ingredients to a simmer on the stove top and simmer 2 hours.

4. Remove and discard the bones. Puree the soup in batches in the food processor.

CURRIED ZUCCHINI SOUP

Omit the curry if it's a spice you'd rather live without. This recipe makes good use of baseball bat–size zucchini, but remove the seeds first. Because the soup freezes well, you might like to double the recipe.

2 large onions, diced

1 quart plus 6 tablespoons chicken broth

1 clove garlic, minced

3–4 pounds zucchini, diced

1 cup cooked rice

1 tablespoon curry powder

8–10 fresh basil leaves, snipped, or 1 teaspoon dried basil

5–6 fresh sage leaves, snipped, or 1/2 teaspoon dried sage

1 teaspoon fresh thyme leaves or 1/2 teaspoon dried thyme

1 teaspoon salt (less if using canned broth)

freshly ground pepper to taste

1/2 cup grated low-fat cheddar cheese

1 cup skim milk

Yield: approximately 6 cups

Calories per cup: 158

Protein per cup: 10g

Fat per cup: 2g

   Saturated fat per cup: trace

Cholesterol per cup: 8mg

Carbohydrates per cup: 26g

Sodium per cup: 447mg

Fiber per cup: 5g

2 pt.

1. "Saute" the onions in a 10-inch skillet in the 6 tablespoons of chicken broth until they're limp. Add the garlic and cook 1 minute more.

2. In a 4-quart or larger saucepan, combine the onions, garlic, zucchini, remaining broth, rice, spices, and herbs. Cover and simmer at least 1 hour or as long as two.

3. Puree the zucchini-onion mixture in a food processor or food mill in batches. Strain the soup if desired.

4. Stir in the grated cheese and milk. Heat to blend.

ROASTED THREE-ONION SOUP

Oven roasting some of the onions for this soup imparts a smoky, almost-sweet flavor. The onions, shallot, and garlic may be roasted early in the day.

2 Spanish onions

1 medium yellow onion

2 shallots

6 cloves garlic

2 13¾-ounce cans beef broth, plus an additional cup

¼ cup full-bodied red wine

1 teaspoon minced fresh thyme or ½ teaspoon dried thyme

1 bay leaf

1 teaspoon or to taste seasoned salt

½ teaspoon liquid beef bouillon

1 teaspoon sugar

2 tablespoons instant-blending flour

1 tablespoon cognac (optional)

freshly grated Parmesan cheese (optional)

Yield: about 2 quarts

Calories per cup: 55

Protein per cup: 2g

Fat per cup: trace

   Saturated fat per cup: trace

Cholesterol per cup: 0

Carbohydrates per cup: 11g

Sodium per cup: 226mg

Fiber per cup: 1g

1. Roast one Spanish onion and the yellow onion in a baking dish in a 350-degree oven for 30 minutes (no need to preheat). Add the shallots and roast 30 minutes more. Add the garlic and roast 30 minutes more. Let cool, then discard the skins.

2. Place the roasted onions, shallots, and garlic in the bowl of a food processor with 1 cup of the broth. Puree.

3. Turn the onion puree into a 2½-quart saucepan. Add all but 1 cup of the remaining broth, red wine, thyme, bay leaf, salt, and bouillon. Bring to a simmer.

4. Meanwhile, thinly slice the remaining onion in a food processor or by hand. Spray a nonstick 10-inch skillet with nonstick cooking spray. Saute the onion over medium-high heat, stirring often, until onion is browned and limp, about 10 minutes. Sprinkle with the sugar and flour and stir over medium-high heat, 1 minute.

5. Add the remaining broth and simmer, stirring occasionally, 4 minutes more. Add to the onion/broth mixture in the saucepan. Stir in the cognac and simmer 10 to 30 minutes. Remove the bay leaf before serving. Pass cheese at the table.

TWO-MUSHROOM CONSOMME

If consomme brings to mind images of Victorian ladies presiding over sherry parties, this version holds a surprise for you. It is updated with cepes, which are dried mushrooms imported from France. Their earthy scent perfumes this light soup. Although it is easily made with store-bought consomme, you might enjoy the satisfaction and rich flavor of making your own.

5 cups degreased homemade beef stock or 3 cans (10 1/2 ounces)
  beef consomme
2 egg whites and the eggshells
8 ounces mushrooms, wiped clean with a cloth
3 tablespoons beef broth
2 tablespoons lemon juice
1/2 ounce cepes (available at specialty food stores), soaked in sherry or
water to cover
1/3 cup Madeira or sherry
2 tablespoons finely minced chives

Yield: 6 servings

Calories per serving: 43

Protein per serving: 3g

Fat per serving: 1g
    Saturated fat per serving: trace

Cholesterol per serving: 4mg

Carbohydrates per serving: 4g

Sodium per serving: 47mg

Fiber per serving: 1g

To Clarify Homemade Stock

1. Beat 1 cup cold stock with the egg whites and eggshells (yes, shells!) in a large bowl. Meanwhile, bring remaining stock to a boil.

2. Gradually pour the hot stock into the egg whites, beating all the while. Pour the whites and stock back into the saucepan and set over moderate heat. As the stock regains a simmer, stir with a spoon. As soon as the simmer is regained, stop stirring.

3. Turn the heat to low. Move the pan very gently partially off the heat, as the liquid must not bubble or move too much. Let it rest for 15–20 minutes.

4. Line a colander with a double layer of cheesecloth that has been wrung out in water. Gently ladle stock-egg mixture through the cheesecloth. Discard the shells and whites. The resulting soup should be crystal clear.

For Canned Consomme or to Finish Soup

1. Slice the mushrooms. "Saute" them in a little broth and lemon juice in an 8-inch skillet.

2. Drain the cepes, mince them, and discard the wine or strain it through a double-thick, wrung-out piece of cheesecloth before adding it to soup. Add cepes to mushrooms and heat through.

3. Combine clarified stock (or canned consomme diluted according to directions) with the mushrooms, Madeira, and chives. Serve hot in small cups.

Thinking Thin Tip

There are times when it might be better to eat a little something fattening than a lot of something skinny.

SPIKED SQUASH SOUP WITH APPLE

Repeat "Oh, it was easy" several times while putting together this quick soup. It's an acceptably humble response for the sure compliments this velvety puree will earn you.

½ small Spanish onion, chopped (about ¾ cup)

1 cup cider

1 medium butternut squash, peeled, seeded, and roughly chopped

1 Granny Smith apple, peeled, cored, and roughly chopped

2 14½-ounce cans chicken broth

1 teaspoon brown sugar

1 teaspoon chopped fresh thyme or ½ teaspoon dried thyme

1 teaspoon salt

freshly ground pepper to taste

a few gratings fresh nutmeg

1 tablespoon bourbon

snipped chives for garnish (optional)

8–10 roasted, peeled, and chopped chestnuts (optional)

Yield: about 2 quarts

Calories per cup: 71

Protein per cup: 2g

Fat per cup: trace

  Saturated fat per cup: trace

Cholesterol per cup: 0

Carbohydrates per cup: 16g

Sodium per cup: 310mg

Fiber per cup: 2g

1. Combine the onion and cider in a microwave-safe container. Cover and microwave at high (100 percent power) for 8 minutes.

2. Meanwhile, combine the squash, apple, chicken broth, sugar, thyme, salt, pepper, and nutmeg in a 2½-quart saucepan. Cover and bring to a boil over high heat. Reduce heat to medium. Add the onion-cider mixture and simmer 30 minutes.

3. Puree the soup in batches and return to the saucepan. Stir in the bourbon. Ladle into bowls and garnish with chives and chestnuts if desired.

PUMPKIN MAPLE SOUP

Served in small pumpkins, this soup makes a festive start to a holiday meal. Of course, it is just as good ladled into soup dishes. Fortunately, the microwave makes easy work of cooking fresh pumpkin, for it is well worth the little extra effort. Adobo seasoning—a mixture of salt, oregano, and garlic—is available in the Spanish section of many markets.

1 pumpkin, about 3 pounds, halved and seeded, or 4 cups unsweetened
    pumpkin puree
¹/₂ small Spanish onion, chopped (about ³/₄ cup)
1 fresh jalapeño pepper, halved and seeded
1 13³/₄ ounce can chicken broth
¹/₃ cup orange juice
3 tablespoons maple syrup
1 tablespoon maple extract
1 teaspoon salt
¹/₂ teaspoon Adobo seasoning (optional)
¹/₄ teaspoon cayenne powder, or to taste
dash ground cloves
8 small (about ¹/₂ to ³/₄ pound each) pumpkins with attractive stems, lids
    cut into each, stringy pulp discarded (optional)

Yield: about 2 quarts

Calories per cup: 78

Protein per cup: 2g

Fat per cup: trace

   Saturated fat per cup: trace

Cholesterol per cup: 0

Carbohydrates per cup: 18g

Sodium per cup: 293mg

Fiber per cup: 2g

1. Reserve the pumpkin seeds if you wish to roast them for a garnish (instructions follow). Put the pumpkin halves (from the 3-pound pumpkin) in a plastic bag with about 2 tablespoons water. Tie the bag opening and microwave at high (100 percent power) for 30 minutes or until the flesh is soft when pierced with a fork. Drain. Scrape the flesh into the bowl of a food processor. Set aside while preparing the onion.

2. To roast the seeds, rinse them thoroughly and discard the stringy orange pulp. Spray a cookie sheet with nonstick cooking spray. Arrange pumpkin seeds in a single layer and spray again with cooking spray. Salt according to taste. Roast in a 350-degree oven about 30 minutes.

3. Combine the onion, jalapeño pepper, and 1 cup of the chicken broth in a microwave-safe container. Cover and microwave at high (100 percent power) for 8 minutes.

4. While the onion cooks, puree the pumpkin with the remaining chicken broth. Scrape into a 2½-quart saucepan. (If using canned pumpkin, simply scrape the puree into the saucepan. Add the remaining broth.)

5. Puree the cooked onion, jalapeño, and cooking broth in a food processor. Stir into the pumpkin puree with the remaining ingredients.

6. Simmer about 10 minutes at medium high; do not allow to boil. Serve in soup bowls, or ladle into prepared pumpkins and heat in a microwave for 5 minutes or until soup is warmed through. Pass roasted pumpkin seeds at the table if desired.

NEW WAVE FISH CHOWDER

Unlike traditional chowders, this new-wave version is low in fat. As an added bonus, clean-up is a snap, thanks to microwave cooking bags. The chowder is even better the second day.

4 small potatoes, peeled and cubed

3 medium onions, thinly sliced

celery leaves from 1 bunch of celery, minced (about 1 cup)

2 pounds boneless, skinless white fish fillets, such as cod, cut into
*   2-inch chunks*

1 8-ounce bottle clam juice

1 12-ounce can skimmed evaporated milk

2 cups skim milk

1 tablespoon reduced-fat margarine

1 clove garlic, minced

2 teaspoons salt

1 bay leaf

¼ teaspoon celery seed

1 tablespoon minced fresh dill or 1 teaspoon dried dill

1 teaspoon paprika

pepper to taste

1 cup skim milk

3 tablespoons instant-blending flour

Yield: about 3 quarts

Calories per cup: 171

Protein per cup: 20g

Fat per cup: 1g
    Saturated fat per cup: trace

Cholesterol per cup: 35mg

Carbohydrates per cup: 19g

Sodium per cup: 535mg

Fiber per cup: 1g

1. Line a 3-quart microwave-safe bowl with a 12-pound-size microwave cooking bag. Fold excess bag down over the bowl's rim. Place all ingredients except the last cup of milk and flour in the bag. Close bag with the tie provided or with a strip of the bag itself.

2. Microwave at medium-high (75 percent power) for 1 hour or until potatoes are tender. Lift bag and jostle ingredients 2 to 3 times during cooking.

3. Mix the remaining cup of milk and flour. Stir into the chowder. Microwave at medium-high (75 percent power) for 15 minutes more. Chowder may be served immediately or reheated.

BOUILLABAISSE OF SCALLOPS

This soup perfumes the air. Serve it with the Fire and Ice Salad, page 108, for a fine, light cold-weather meal, or serve it chilled in summer.

Yield: 4 servings

Calories per serving: 185

Protein per serving: 23g

Fat per serving: 3g

   Saturated fat per serving: 1g

Cholesterol per serving: 41mg

Carbohydrates per serving: 16g

Sodium per serving: 292mg

Fiber per serving: 3g

2 leeks, white part only, thinly sliced

1 medium onion, thinly sliced

4–5 tablespoons chicken broth or bottled clam juice

4 large tomatoes or 2 cups canned tomatoes

2 cloves garlic, minced

4 cups fish stock or 3 1/2 8-ounce bottles clam juice mixed with 3 ounces
   vermouth and 1 ounce water

2 tablespoons orange zest

2–3 tablespoons orange juice, freshly squeezed preferred

6–7 fresh basil leaves, snipped, or 1 teaspoon dried basil

a pinch of saffron

1 bay leaf

1/4 teaspoon dried thyme

1/2 teaspoon fennel seeds

1 pound scallops or white fish fillets, cut into chunks

2 tablespoons minced fresh parsley

a bowl of freshly grated Parmesan

1. "Saute" the leeks and onion in a 10-inch skillet with the broth. Cover the pan while cooking, adding more liquid if necessary. *Alternately, combine the leeks, onion, and broth in a microwave-safe container. Cover and microwave at high (100 percent power) for 8 minutes.*

2. To peel and seed the tomatoes, bring a 2 1/2-quart saucepan 3/4 full of water to a boil. Core the tomatoes, and cut a cross in each one's bottom. Immerse the tomatoes in boiling water for 15 seconds or until the skins loosen. Drain, cool under running water, and peel off the skins. Cut the tomatoes in quarters and squeeze over a strainer to remove seeds. Press the seeds with the back of a wooden spoon to extract the juice. Reserve the juice.

3. When the leeks and onion are limp, add the garlic, tomatoes, reserved juice, stock, orange zest, orange juice, basil, and saffron. Tie the bay leaf, thyme, and fennel in a cheesecloth bag (a bouquet garni) and add to the skillet. Simmer, covered, for 30–40 minutes.

4. Add the scallops, raise heat to medium, and cook covered, until they are opaque, about 4–5 minutes.

5. Remove the bouquet garni, stir in the parsley, and taste for seasoning. Ladle the finished soup into warmed bowls and pass grated Parmesan cheese at the table.

Bouquet Garni

To make a bouquet garni, cut a piece of cheesecloth about 6 inches by 4 inches. Place the herbs called for, generally thyme, garlic (no need to peel), fresh parsley stems, and peppercorns (crushed, please) in the center. Roll the cloth in jellyroll fashion, then bring the ends together and knot. The flavors suffuse the soup, stew, or broth, but the herbs can be easily removed before serving.

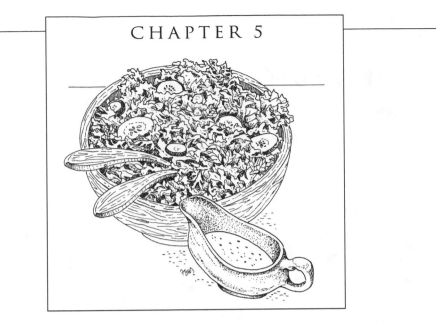

SALADS AND THEIR DRESSINGS

The Recipes

Note: Asterisked dishes may be served as meatless entrees.

SALADS

Salads have risen to new heights, both in popularity and design in recent years. Where once a few leaves of iceberg, chopped cucumber, and minced onion would suffice as a side dish, one now finds a range of rare goodies artfully presented as main-course meals. Radicchio, lamb's lettuce, and baked chèvre cheese are but a few of the salad items popular today. To support the demand, fancy green-grocers are popping up like mushrooms from coast to coast, offering an enormous selection of fresh produce from near and—thanks to modern transportation—far.

This chapter focuses on salads as a side course. The majority of the main-dish salads are found in the chapter of the predominant ingredient. For example Sole, Scallop, and Pea Pod Salad is found in the seafood chapter, and Chicken and Pasta Salad with Golden Raisins and Capers is found in the poultry chapter.

THE GREENS

A simple tossed salad is so much more interesting with two or three greens. Why limit yourself to one when there's such a big garden of salad things to choose from, everything from arugula to watercress. While iceberg is probably the most popular salad green, it is also probably one of the dullest. It has its place, keeping the bread from getting soggy in a tuna salad sandwich, but it is far outclassed by other varieties. Three other types of lettuces to consider are:

Cos or romaine—large, almost rectangular leaves, dark green at the tip, paler green at the base. This is the lettuce of choice for Caesar salad. It is also excellent torn into small pieces for a tossed green salad.

Butterhead—The lettuces of this group offer soft, velvety leaves that unfortunately bruise and rust quickly. This perishable type includes Boston, a medium-size, light green head, and Bibb, a smaller, more compact head. Limestone lettuce is another Butterhead variety. For longer storage life, rinse, dry, and chill these lettuces as soon after purchase as possible. These soft-leafed lettuces are excellent for simple salads composed of mixed greens, or even alone, tossed with a vinaigrette and possibly a scattering of freshly made croutons.

Leaf lettuces—The lettuces in this group grow as clumps of leaves rather than as heads. It is quite a hardy lot, ranging from red leaf (mostly green turning to red at the tip) to salad bowl, a tangle of curly, narrow leaves. Leaf lettuces are best in combination with other greens.

Less well known, but fun to experiment with, are beet, dandelion, and mustard greens; even nasturtium leaves lend a salad distinction. And there are watercress with its peppery crunch, chicory, endive, and of course spinach. Radicchio, a red "green," and lamb's lettuce are specialty items you'll find on trendy restaurant menus or in chic produce markets. With such a wealth of greens, most of which are available year-round, it seems sad to reach for the old standby every time.

Select greens with an eye for color and texture. An excellent combination is a salad of Bibb, red leaf, and watercress, the softness of the Bibb offset by the crunch of the watercress, and the red leaf adding vibrant color.

While my personal bias leans toward a salad of mixed greens graced only by a sprinkling of freshly made croutons, many enjoy other additions. Any vegetable in its prime that can be eaten raw is a candidate. Again, keep color, texture, and flavor in harmony.

There is no written rule that demands a tomato in every salad. When they are out of season, which sadly is most of the year, get color from other sources. Roasted, julienned red peppers (see page 258) are delicious; a bit of grated red cabbage or carrot will do the trick, as will a diced apple or a few leaves of red leaf lettuce. Put nothing in the salad that is tasteless, such as a winter tomato. For a change of pace, "saute" mushroom slices before adding them. I find the flavor enhanced when they're cooked.

Purchase greens that look perky, without yellow or rust spots, and if possible with most of the outer leaves intact, because these contain more nutrients than the delicate centers. Generally, the greener the leaf, the greater the source of vitamins A, C, and E as well as iron and calcium. A quarter of an average-size head contains a meager 15 calories.

Salad greens retain their nutrients best when held at near-freezing temperatures in high humidity. Head lettuce will keep in the vegetable crisper of the refrigerator for 3–4 days; some varieties will last even longer. Leaf lettuces are more perishable and keep best if rinsed, spun dry, and stored in a loose plastic bag with a few paper towels on every other layer to absorb moisture, a leading cause of rust and bad spots. Lacking a lettuce spinner, wash the lettuce, shake off excess moisture, lay leaves in a single layer on an old thick bath towel, roll loosely, and refrigerate. The lettuce will keep this way about 24 hours. Washing, drying, and chilling any lettuce about 4–5 hours before serving will make for a beautifully crisp salad. For those special occasions, don't forget to chill the plates, too.

Don't store lettuce near apples, melons, or avocados because the ethylene gas these fruits give off acts as a ripening agent, maturing the lettuce before its time and turning it brown.

THE SALAD SYNDROME OR THE INVISIBLE CALORIE

It's become common knowledge that the culprit is the butter not the potato, but the fats in salads remain invisible to many—that is, until they show up on the waistline. "All I ever have for lunch is a salad, and I still gain weight!" is a common lament. The demon is the salad dressing. Most dressings are very high in fat, contributing 150 to 200 calories and as much as 14 grams of fat in just 2 tablespoons to an otherwise skinny bowl of greens. *Gourmet Light* dressings are based mostly on stocks or consomme and contribute far fewer calories than commercial preparations. The recipes that follow are dressings for mixed-green salads; beyond that are recipes for specialty salads.

Vinaigrettes

Vinaigrette, a classic combination of oil and vinegar with or without additional seasonings, is the true French dressing. Following are several variations on the simple vinaigrette theme, all prepared the *Gourmet Light* way. (For more on skinny dressings, see the Primer, page 7.) First, these tips:

1. If you don't make your own naturally thick chicken or beef stock, use commercially prepared consomme or canned chicken broth. The former, because of its added gelatin, will give the best results.

2. When using homemade stock, double the amount called for in the recipe and boil it until reduced by half. This double-strength stock will give your dressings body. Don't reduce commercial broths though, for they will be too salty.

3. If you do not use canned consomme, you will need to add salt to taste.

4. If possible prepare the dressing at least 2 hours before serving, to let the flavors marry.

5. A dressing made with homemade stock or store-bought consomme will jell in the refrigerator. Remove it an hour before serving or heat briefly to liquefy.

HERBED FRENCH VINAIGRETTE

A true French dressing is not the mayonnaise/ketchup variety commonly called "French," but an emulsion of oil and vinegar. Here is a skinny version.

5 tablespoons double-strength homemade beef or chicken stock or
*   canned consomme*
2 tablespoons red wine vinegar
1 teaspoon sugar
½ teaspoon Dijon-style mustard
1 tablespoon extra-virgin olive oil
1 clove garlic, minced
2 teaspoons chives, minced
1 teaspoon paprika

Yield: ⅔ cup

Calories per tablespoon: 13

Protein per tablespoon: trace

Fat per tablespoon: 1g

   Saturated fat per tablespoon: trace

Cholesterol per tablespoon: trace

Carbohydrates per tablespoon: 1g

Sodium per tablespoon: 9mg

Fiber per tablespoon: trace

1. Combine all the ingredients in a jar, shake well, check for seasoning, and refrigerate.

Apple-Maple Vinaigrette

Try this vinaigrette on a winter salad of tossed greens, chopped apples, a handful of raisins, and just a smattering of chopped walnuts. Maggi seasoning is a soy-based product that you'll find in the supermarket with condiments such as Worcestershire sauce (which is an acceptable substitute).

1 McIntosh apple, peeled, cored, and roughly chopped

¹/₂ cup cider

2 tablespoons white vinegar

1 tablespoon walnut oil

2 teaspoons maple syrup

1 teaspoon Maggi seasoning (optional)

¹/₂ teaspoon stone-ground mustard

¹/₂ teaspoon salt

freshly ground pepper to taste

1. Combine all ingredients in the bowl of a food processor. Turn machine to full power until apple is pureed. Store in the refrigerator up to 1 week.

Yield: 1 cup

Calories per tablespoon: 26

Protein per tablespoon: trace

Fat per tablespoon: 2g

Saturated fat per tablespoon: trace

Cholesterol per tablespoon: 0

Carbohydrates per tablespoon: 3g

Sodium per tablespoon: 69mg

Fiber per tablespoon: trace

Thinking Thin Tip

Because *Gourmet Light* cooking uses so little oil, buy the best. Extra-virgin olive oil is the first pressing of the olives and the most flavorful. Virgin quality is the next, and so on until the final pressings, which rely on hot water poured over the pits to coax the final droplets of oil.

BALSAMIC-WALNUT OIL VINAIGRETTE

Balsamic vinegar, a malt vinegar aged in wooden casks, and walnut oil have become buzz words in culinary circles. Both are available at specialty food stores. Here they are combined to create a delicious dressing for mixed greens.

double-strength homemade beef or chicken stock or canned consomme

walnut oil (refrigerate after opening)

balsamic vinegar

1 tablespoon water

¹/₂ teaspoon prepared mustard

¹/₂ teaspoon sugar

freshly ground pepper to taste

Yield: ¹/₂ cup

Calories per tablespoon: 26

Protein per tablespoon: trace

Fat per tablespoon: 2g

  Saturated fat per tablespoon: trace

Cholesterol per tablespoon: trace

Carbohydrates per tablespoon: 2g

Sodium per tablespoon: 5mg

Fiber per tablespoon: trace

1. In a 1-cup glass measure, pour in the consomme until the liquid reaches the ¹/₄-cup mark. Add walnut oil until the liquid measures ¹/₃ cup. Add the balsamic vinegar until the liquid measures ¹/₂ cup. Add water, mustard, sugar, and pepper. Shake well, check for seasoning, and refrigerate.

Vinegars

Once used as a medicine or as a drink when heavily diluted with water, and often used as a preservative with salt, vinegars are the slightly aging darling of the growing gourmet food industry. Where most kitchen cabinets once stored pretty much your basic cider variety, many shelves are now crowded with enough labels and flavors to rival a modest wine cellar. Indeed, some vinegars carry a higher price tag than jug wines! Some vinegars, such as balsamic, are even aged like spirits in oak barrels. The added cost is offset by the wonderful flavor they impart.

CAESAR SALAD DRESSING

Make this salad with romaine lettuce, freshly grated Parmesan or Romano cheese, and, if you like, a handful of freshly made croutons. Arrange the lettuce leaves in spoke fashion around the plate, sprinkle cheese and croutons on top, and drizzle with the following dressing. To eat, pick up the leaves in your fingers, using them as scoops to hold the croutons and cheese. Delicious!

Yield: ⅔ cup

Calories per tablespoon: 23

Protein per tablespoon: 1g

Fat per tablespoon: 2g

   Saturated fat per tablespoon: trace

Cholesterol per tablespoon: 20mg

Carbohydrates per tablespoon: 1g

Sodium per tablespoon: 25mg

Fiber per tablespoon: trace

2 cups water

1 egg

5 tablespoons double-strength homemade beef or chicken stock or
    canned consomme

juice of ½ lemon

1 tablespoon extra-virgin olive oil

6 or 7 drops Worcestershire sauce

a few drops hot pepper sauce to taste

1 clove garlic, minced

freshly ground black pepper to taste

2 tablespoons freshly grated Parmesan cheese

1. To coddle the egg, bring 2 cups water to a boil. Add the egg, cover, and boil for 1 minute. Drain and cool under running water.

2. Crack open the coddled egg into a jar. Combine all the remaining ingredients, except the cheese. Sprinkle cheese over the salad greens, then drizzle with dressing.

Note: For instructions on making croutons, see page 76.

Sesame Seed Dressing

This dressing is the perfect partner for a spinach salad with shredded hard-cooked egg white and sliced "sauteed" mushrooms.

2 tablespoons sesame seeds

4 tablespoons double-strength homemade beef or chicken stock or
    canned consomme

2 teaspoons sesame oil, available at specialty food shops

2 tablespoons lemon juice

1 teaspoon sugar

freshly ground pepper to taste

Yield: ½ cup

Calories per tablespoon: 25

Protein per tablespoon: trace

Fat per tablespoon: 2g

  Saturated fat per tablespoon: trace

Cholesterol per tablespoon: trace

Carbohydrates per tablespoon: 1g

Sodium per tablespoon: 1mg

Fiber per tablespoon: trace

1. Spray a baking sheet with cooking spray. Sprinkle sesame seeds over sheet. Turn oven to 350 degrees, put baking sheet in oven, and remove 10 minutes later.

2. Combine sesame seeds in a jar with all the other ingredients. Shake well, check for seasoning, and refrigerate.

Fresh Herb Vinaigrette

This is the dressing of choice for herb gardeners looking for ways to preserve summer's fragrant gifts, for it freezes nicely. Delicious on vine-ripened tomatoes (which have twice the vitamin C of hothouse winter tomatoes) or cold fish salads tossed with leftover corn cut from the cob.

1 cup loosely packed fresh basil leaves

½ cup loosely packed fresh tarragon leaves

2 tablespoons homemade chicken or beef stock or canned consomme

1 tablespoon raspberry or red wine vinegar

1 tablespoon safflower oil

1 scant teaspoon sugar

freshly ground pepper to taste

1. Put the herbs in a bowl or measuring cup and snip repeatedly with scissors until they're reduced to about half the original volume.

2. Combine the herbs in a food processor or blender with the remaining ingredients. Blend until herbs are mostly minced and sauce is a lovely pale green. Check for seasoning. May be frozen.

Yield: ¾ cup

Calories per tablespoon: 12

Protein per tablespoon: trace

Fat per tablespoon: 1g

  Saturated fat per tablespoon: trace

Cholesterol per tablespoon: trace

Carbohydrates per tablespoon: 1g

Sodium per tablespoon: 2mg

Fiber per tablespoon: trace

Thinking Thin Tip

All oils contain three types of fats: polyunsaturates, considered to be beneficial fats for their ability to help rid the body of cholesterol; monosaturates, considered neutral; and saturated fats, which are linked to elevated blood cholesterol levels.

OAK CREEK ORANGE-WALNUT DRESSING

I'd love to take credit for this delicious combination of flavors, but in truth, this is another of my attempts to replicate a restaurant's offering. I love this on a winter salad of red leaf lettuce with mandarin oranges and homemade fat-free croutons. While walnut oil is expensive, its flavor makes a small bottle worth the price; keep it in the fridge for longer shelf life.

¼ cup egg substitute

½ cup plus 1 tablespoon orange juice, freshly squeezed recommended

2 tablespoons walnut oil

2 tablespoons rice wine vinegar

2 tablespoons Chinese cooking wine

1 teaspoon sugar

½ teaspoon salt

freshly ground pepper to taste

zest of 1 orange

1. Place the egg substitute in the bowl of a food processor and turn to full power. Drizzle in remaining ingredients. Store in refrigerator up to 1 week.

Yield: 19 tablespoons

Calories per tablespoon: 21

Protein per tablespoon: trace

Fat per tablespoon: 1g

    Saturated fat per tablespoon: trace

Cholesterol per tablespoon: 0

Carbohydrates per tablespoon: 1g

Sodium per tablespoon: 57mg

Fiber per tablespoon: trace

JAPANESE DRESSING FOR SNOW PEAS

Yet another alternative to a mayonnaise dressing is tofu, a soybean product. The following recipe is excellent tossed with blanched snow peas or broccoli.

4 ounces tofu

5 tablespoons double-strength homemade chicken stock or canned consomme

1 tablespoon sesame oil

1 tablespoon walnut oil

2 tablespoons rice wine vinegar, available at oriental or specialty food stores

1 teaspoon reduced-sodium soy sauce

1 quarter-size piece of fresh ginger, peeled and minced.

1. Combine all the ingredients in a food processor or blender and blend. Chill.

Yield: 1 cup

Calories per tablespoon: 20

Protein per tablespoon: 1g

Fat per tablespoon: 2g

Saturated fat per tablespoon: trace

Cholesterol per tablespoon: trace

Carbohydrates per tablespoon: trace

Sodium per tablespoon: 11mg

Fiber per tablespoon: trace

BEYOND SIMPLE TOSSED . . .

No matter how innovative and imaginative your mix of greens, there are times when you yearn for something different. Perhaps a Fire and Ice Salad or the pleasant bite of Counter Slaw, or maybe the cool creaminess of Dilled Zucchini and Carrot Salad. Whatever your pleasure, scan these offerings for that which tempts you. These are side dishes, lunches, or light dinners; heavier offerings are found in the seafood and poultry chapters.

FIRE AND ICE SALAD

This salad gets its name from the flame of the brandy and the chill of the greens. Often when a recipe indicates flaming, it is purely for effect; here, igniting the liquor renders it mellow. A wonderful salad for chilly nights.

Yield: 4 servings

Calories per serving: 119

Protein per serving: 6g

Fat per serving: 2g

   Saturated fat per serving: trace

Cholesterol per serving: 1mg

Carbohydrates per serving: 19g

Sodium per serving: 321mg

Fiber per serving: 4g

The Salad

1 pound fresh spinach, stems and backbones removed, washed and
   spun dry

2 carrots, grated

1/2 small Bermuda onion, thinly sliced

chopped whites of 2 or 3 hard-boiled eggs

1 small Portabello mushroom, stem removed and cap sliced, or 6 ounces
   mushrooms, cleaned and sliced

The Dressing

6 ounces canned consomme or 6 ounces double-strength homemade
   chicken or beef stock

1 tablespoon cornstarch

3 tablespoons malt or balsamic vinegar

1 tablespoon lemon juice

2 teaspoons sugar

1/2–1 teaspoon Worcestershire sauce

1 teaspoon canola oil

1 teaspoon Dijon-style mustard

1/2 teaspoon seasoned salt

2 tablespoons brandy or bourbon

To Prepare the Salad

1. Tear the spinach into bite-size pieces in a salad bowl. Toss with the carrots, onion, and egg whites.

2. Spray an 8-inch nonstick skillet with nonstick cooking spray. Saute the mushrooms over medium-high heat until lightly browned, about 5 minutes. Toss with the greens. Set aside while preparing the dressing.

To Prepare the Dressing

1. *In a 2-cup glass measuring cup or other microwave-safe container, combine the consomme, cornstarch, vinegar, lemon juice, sugar, Worcestershire sauce, oil, mustard, and salt. Stir thoroughly to dissolve the cornstarch. Cover and microwave on high (100 percent power) for 2 minutes.* Alternately, bring to a boil in a small saucepan on the stove top and boil for 4 minutes.

2. Meanwhile, heat the liquor over medium-high heat in a small pot with a long handle and spout. When bubbles appear at the edge of the pot, ignite the liquor. Let it burn, tipping the pot to keep the flames going, about 1 to 2 minutes. Liquor will be reduced by half before the flames die out. Combine the reduced liquor with the hot dressing.

3. Microwave the dressing at high (100 *percent* power) another 30 seconds, or heat over high heat another minute. Toss with the chilled greens.

Black Bean and Corn Salad

This is an incredibly easy salad to put together, for most of the ingredients are pantry staples. It also keeps beautifully for several days, even improving in flavor as it mellows. Serve at room temperature.

1 1-pound can black beans, drained, or 2 cups cooked black beans (see
page 199)

1 17-ounce can whole kernel corn or 2 cups cooked fresh corn kernels

1 large tomato, diced, or 5 tablespoons "recipe-ready" tomatoes

3 scallions, minced

½ jalapeño pepper, seeded and diced, or 2 tablespoons minced canned
chilies

3 tablespoons minced fresh parsley

2 teaspoons olive or canola oil

1 tablespoon minced fresh coriander

1 tablespoon balsamic vinegar

1 tablespoon lime juice

1 clove garlic, minced

½ teaspoon Adobo seasoning (available in Spanish section of many
markets) or salt

Yield: 8 servings

Calories per serving: 97

Protein per serving: 4g

Fat per serving: 2g
   Saturated fat per serving: trace

Cholesterol per serving: 0

Carbohydrates per serving: 19g

Sodium per serving: 145mg

Fiber per serving: 3g

1. In a medium-size bowl combine the beans, corn, tomato, scallions, jalapeño, and parsley. Set aside while preparing the dressing.

2. Combine the remaining ingredients in a screw-top jar. Shake well to combine. Toss with the bean and corn salad.

Wilted Cucumber Salad

If soft-leafed lettuce dressed with vinaigrette is the national salad of France, a wilted cucumber salad is the fingerprint of Germany. Here's a reduced-calorie version that's as good the second day as the first.

1 cucumber

2 teaspoons salt

2 tablespoons canned consomme

1 tablespoon red wine vinegar

1 teaspoon honey or sugar

1 teaspoon oil

freshly ground pepper to taste

Yield: 2 servings

Calories per serving: 55

Protein per serving: 1g

Fat per serving: 2g

  Saturated fat per serving: trace

Cholesterol per serving: 0

Carbohydrates per serving: 8g

Sodium per serving: 2,213mg

Fiber per serving: 2g

1. Peel the cucumber and seed by slicing it in half the long way and removing the seed core with a teaspoon. Slice the cucumber very thinly by hand or in a food processor, and place it in a sieve or colander. Sprinkle salt over it and let it drain 20–30 minutes over a bowl or in sink. This removes excess water from the vegetable.

2. Rinse the cucumber repeatedly. Taste it to be sure the salt is removed. Press cucumber to help remove water. Drain it on an absorbent towel.

3. In a small saucepan, combine the consomme, vinegar, honey, and oil. Reduce the liquid over high heat until 2 tablespoons are left. Pour it over the drained cucumber, season with pepper, and chill until serving time.

Counter Slaw

Cynthia Young, a fine Nantucket cook, gave me this recipe some years ago when we honeymooned at her Polpis guest house. It's quick, easy, and delicious, just the thing to take on a picnic to Great Point—or your favorite summer afternoon getaway spot. Coleslaw prepared with mayonnaise-type dressings contains as many as 225 calories and 21 grams of fat in a ¾-cup serving; this counter slaw lets you save room for dessert. Add grated carrots, raisins, or a bit of onion for variety.

Yield: 6 servings

Calories per serving: 76

Protein per serving: 1g

Fat per serving: 5g

   Saturated fat per serving: trace

Cholesterol per serving: trace

Carbohydrates per serving: 9g

Sodium per serving: 186mg

Fiber per serving: 2g

1 small green pepper, grated

6 cups loosely packed, shredded cabbage (about ¹/₂ small head)

¹/₃ cup chicken broth

2 tablespoons light oil, such as safflower

2 tablespoons sugar

2 tablespoons red wine vinegar

1 teaspoon caraway seeds

¹/₂ teaspoon salt

freshly ground pepper to taste

1. In a medium-size bowl, combine the green pepper with the cabbage.

2. In a 1-quart nonaluminum saucepan, combine the broth, oil, sugar, vinegar, and caraway seeds. Cook over high heat until the sugar is dissolved, about 1 minute.

3. Toss hot dressing with the vegetables. Season to taste with salt and pepper. Cover the slaw with plastic wrap and leave it at room temperature for 4 hours. Chill until serving time.

Pear and Havarti Salad with Pine Nuts

A halved pear broiled until a cloak of Havarti cheese bubbles and browns, resting on a lightly dressed bed of curly salad bowl lettuce, makes a dish of pasta tossed with Basil Salsa (page 117) a wonderful dinner partner. You can have it on the table in less time than it will take to drive to McDonald's.

1 pear, any variety, slightly underripe is fine, peeled if desired
2 tablespoons (1 ounce) reduced-fat Havarti cheese, grated
1 tablespoon pine nuts
¼ head salad bowl or other leaf lettuce
4 tablespoons Herbed French Vinaigrette, page 100

Yield: 2 servings
Calories per serving: 158
Protein per serving: 6g
Fat per serving: 9g
  Saturated fat per serving: 3g
Cholesterol per serving: 10mg
Carbohydrates per serving: 18g
Sodium per serving: 147mg
Fiber per serving: 3g

1. Preheat the broiler. Cut the pear in half the long way, and remove its core and woody fiber leading to the stem. Sprinkle the halves with lemon juice if holding more than 20 minutes before broiling. Slice a sliver from the curved side of the pear halves so they will sit evenly. Place on a baking sheet.

2. Divide the grated cheese over the pear halves. Broil about 8 minutes, or until they are softened and cheese is bubbly and browned.

3. Meanwhile, toast the pine nuts by putting them in an 8-inch skillet over high heat. Shake the pan constantly for about 1 minute until nuts turn golden brown. Remove from skillet.

4. Wash, rinse, and dry the lettuce. Divide on two plates. Center each broiled pear half on lettuce. Drizzle 2 tablespoons dressing on each salad, and sprinkle pine nuts over.

Bibb, Tuna, and Green Bean Salad

One of my favorite lunchtime or light dinner salads.

½ pound green beans

1 small head Bibb lettuce

2 slices thin-sliced bread

1 6½-ounce can water-packed tuna, drained

4 tablespoons Balsamic-Walnut Oil Vinaigrette (page 102) or other
*   reduced-calorie vinaigrette dressing*

Yield: 2 servings

Calories per serving: 265

Protein per serving: 26g

Fat per serving: 7g

   Saturated fat per serving: 1g

Cholesterol per serving: 25mg

Carbohydrates per serving: 24g

Sodium per serving: 393mg

Fiber per serving: 4g

1. Prepare the beans for cooking by aligning several at a time and cutting off their tips. Turn the beans around, align again, and slice ends again. Continue until all are "tipped and tailed."

2. Bring a 2½-quart saucepan ¾ full of water to a boil. Add the beans and boil 4 minutes or until softened but still crisp. Drain and cool under running water. Pat dry.

3. Core and wash the lettuce. Spin dry the leaves or dry them on an absorbent towel. Chill until serving time.

4. With one slice bread atop the other, dice it into tiny cubes. Spray a baking sheet with cooking spray. Place the cubes in a single layer on the baking sheet and bake in a 325-degree oven for about 10 minutes or until they are toasted.

5. Remove chilled, washed lettuce from the refrigerator. Tear it into bite-size pieces and arrange it on individual plates or in a bowl. Arrange the beans, flake the tuna over, and sprinkle the salad with croutons. Dribble on the dressing.

APPLE-ARTICHOKE SALAD WITH HOLLANDAISE

The ingredients are reminiscent of a Waldorf salad, but the light Hollandaise adds a different dimension. You may expand the salad to a main-dish meal by grilling and dicing a swordfish steak, toss it with the celery and so on, and serve at room temperature or only slightly chilled. Make this salad early in the day so flavors may meld before serving time.

Yield: 4 servings

Calories per serving: 219

Protein per serving: 8g

Fat per serving: 11g

   Saturated fat per serving: 1g

Cholesterol per serving: trace

Carbohydrates per serving: 29g

Sodium per serving: 351mg

Fiber per serving: 9g

4 artichokes

2 tablespoons lemon juice

$1/4$ cup flour

1 quart water, plus a little more

2 celery ribs, diced

1 apple, Red Delicious recommended, diced

1 ounce walnuts, roughly chopped

$1/2$ cup Hollandaise, page 24

$1/4$ teaspoon salt

freshly ground pepper to taste

1. With a stainless-steel knife, cut off the stem and upper third of each artichoke. Using scissors, remove the sharp tips of the leaves. Cut around the artichoke with a sharp knife as if paring an apple, removing the tough outer leaves. When you get to the soft inner core, slice it off. Be sure all dark green skin is removed from the bottom of the artichoke. Drop each artichoke bottom into water with the lemon juice added.

2. Make a paste of about $1/4$ cup flour with enough water to moisten. Bring a quart of water to a boil, stir in the flour paste, and bring to a boil in a nonaluminum saucepan. Add the artichokes and simmer for 10 minutes or until easily pierced with a fork. Remove the artichokes from the cooking liquid with a slotted spoon and drain until cool.

3. With a grapefruit spoon, remove each artichoke's fuzzy center and discard. Set artichokes aside while preparing remaining salad.

4. In a bowl, toss together the celery, apple, walnuts, and Hollandaise (which may be cold). Season with salt and pepper. Add swordfish here if desired.

5. Line individual plates with a lettuce leaf. Place an artichoke bottom on lettuce. Fill to overflowing with celery-walnut mixture.

CONFETTI RICE SALAD

Carbohydrates, the bugaboo of the diet world for years, are no longer a dirty word. The diet conscious, particularly those who exercise regularly, need complex carbohydrates for energy; otherwise, the body will break down proteins for fuel, proteins better used to build and maintain tissues. Sadly, most carbohydrates taste better when lathered with fats: the butter on the bread, the sour cream on the potato, the dressing on the salad. Here's a cool salad, great for picnicking because it's ultimately portable, which makes the most of the carbohydrates and the least of the fat. A few smoked shrimp would make a wonderful addition.

Yield: 6 servings

Calories per serving: 190

Protein per serving: 3g

Fat per serving: 5g

  Saturated fat per serving: 1g

Cholesterol per serving: 0

Carbohydrates per serving: 33g

Sodium per serving: 180mg

Fiber per serving: 2g

2 medium tomatoes

2 medium green peppers

1 medium red pepper

3 cups cooked rice

2 tablespoons minced fresh parsley

10 fresh basil leaves, snipped, or 1 teaspoon dried basil

¹/₂ teaspoon salt

freshly ground pepper to taste

2 tablespoons oil, safflower or corn oil recommended

1 tablespoon plus 2 teaspoons rice wine vinegar, available at specialty
    food stores or oriental markets

1. Dice the tomatoes. Seed and dice the peppers.

2. Place the vegetables in a bowl with the rice, parsley, basil, salt, and pepper. Sprinkle all with oil and vinegar.

3. Spray a 1-quart mold or 6 1-cup ramekins with cooking spray. Fill each ramekin ¾ full with rice mixture, and press salad down with a glass or any utensil slightly smaller than the diameter of the ramekin. Cover with plastic wrap and chill at least 3 hours. (*Note:* For a decorative design, fashion a "flower" from a thin carrot slice and a "stem" from a parsley stem on the bottom of each ramekin.)

4. To unmold, run a flexible-bladed metal spatula between the salad and the mold. Invert a plate on mold, flip over, and lift mold off.

Pasta Salad with Basil Salsa

I could eat this salad, which is best at room temperature, nearly every day and not tire of it. The sauce is reminiscent of pesto, but it's much lighter. Delicious with garden-ripe tomatoes and a simple tossed salad, or flesh the meal out with a Chicken Breast Paillard.

> *12 ounces egg noodles, fresh if possible*
> *¾ cup Basil Salsa, page 31*
> *¼ teaspoon salt*
> *freshly ground pepper to taste*
> *freshly grated Parmesan cheese*

Yield: 4 servings

Calories per serving: 304

Protein per serving: 13g

Fat per serving: 5g

   Saturated fat per serving: 2g

Cholesterol per serving: 68mg

Carbohydrates per serving: 51g

Sodium per serving: 300mg

Fiber per serving: 3g

1. Cook the noodles according to package directions. Drain.

2. Toss the noodles with the salsa, salt, and pepper. Serve at room temperature or warm. Top with Parmesan cheese.

Pea Pod and Water Chestnut Salad with Sherry Ginger Dressing

Make the dressing, blanch the pea pods, and grate the water chestnuts early in the day, then assemble this salad at the last minute.

½ pound pea pods, strings removed

5 tablespoons double-strength homemade beef or chicken stock or canned consomme

1 tablespoon vegetable oil

2 tablespoons sherry wine vinegar, available at specialty food shops

1 tablespoon reduced-sodium soy sauce

1 teaspoon sesame oil, available at oriental or specialty food shops

1 teaspoon peeled and minced fresh ginger root

1 scant teaspoon sugar

4–6 radicchio lettuce leaves or soft-leafed lettuce such as Bibb

2 fresh mandarin oranges, peeled and sectioned, or 1 7-ounce can mandarin oranges packed in light syrup, drained

8 or 9 fresh water chestnuts, peeled and blanched, or 4 ounces canned chestnuts

Yield: 4 servings

Calories per serving: 97

Protein per serving: 2g

Fat per serving: 5g

Saturated fat per serving: 1g

Cholesterol per serving: trace

Carbohydrates per serving: 13g

Sodium per serving: 157mg

Fiber per serving: 2g

1. Bring a 2½-quart saucepan ¾ full of water to a boil. Immerse pea pods, remove from heat, and let peas sit 4 minutes. Drain and rinse the peas under cold running water until they're no longer warm. Drain peas on absorbent towels.

2. Combine the consomme, oil, vinegar, soy sauce, sesame oil, ginger, and sugar in a jar. Shake well to combine.

3. In a small bowl, combine half the dressing with the cooked pea pods. Let the mixture rest at least 15 minutes or up to several hours at room temperature or in the refrigerator.

4. Arrange the lettuce on individual plates or a serving platter. Arrange the pea pods and orange sections alternately in a circle on the lettuce.

5. Grate the water chestnuts in a Mouli grater or food processor. Arrange in the center of the pea pods and oranges. Dribble the salad with the remaining dressing.

GRILLED PEPPER SALAD

More than a cold side dish, this multicolored mélange of sweet bell peppers and leeks is also delicious served warmed over pasta, or as an accompaniment for grilled meats, such as chicken. It's even better the second day, so you might want to double the recipe. As a variation, stir in 2 tablespoons of the Basil Salsa (page 31). A tablespoon of yogurt cheese (page 54) is also a pleasing addition.

Yield: 2 cups; ½ cup serving
Calories per serving: 95
Protein per serving: 2g
Fat per serving: 3g
  Saturated fat per serving: 1g
Cholesterol per serving: 2mg
Carbohydrates per serving: 12g
Sodium per serving: 321mg
Fiber per serving: 2g

4 sweet bell peppers, 1 green, 1 red, 1 yellow (colors are only
  suggestions)
2 teaspoons olive oil
2 tablespoons minced shallots (1 large shallot)
2 cloves garlic, minced
1 cup thinly sliced leeks (2 leeks, white only)
½ cup white wine
1 tablespoon white wine vinegar
2 teaspoons dried oregano
½ teaspoon salt
freshly ground pepper to taste
1 teaspoon sugar
2 tablespoons freshly grated Parmesan cheese

1. Grill or broil the peppers, turning occasionally, until the skins are evenly blackened, about 10 minutes for broiling or as long as 20 minutes when grilled. Place peppers in a paper bag, roll tightly closed, and set aside to cool.

2. Meanwhile, heat the oil in an 8-inch skillet over high heat. Reduce heat to medium and saute shallots and garlic, stirring often until softened. Do not allow to brown.

3. Add the leeks, continue to cook, stirring often, until softened, about 5 minutes. Add the wine, vinegar, oregano, salt, pepper, and sugar. Cook over low heat until blended and leeks are thoroughly softened, about 5–7 minutes longer.

4. When peppers are cool, peel under running water. Discard skin, core, and seeds.

5. Stack the peppers and slice thinly lengthwise. Add the strips to the leek mixture. Cook over low heat for 2 minutes to warm peppers. Stir in the cheese. If using Basil Salsa and/or yogurt cheese, add now. The salad may be served at room temperature or warmed.

MEATS

THE RECIPES

MEATS

America produces more meat than any other country, and we eat almost all of it. Beef is still the national favorite; it's estimated every man, woman, and child will consume 120 pounds in a single year. While there are those who will view this as eating our way to the grave, others will claim it as evidence Americans are among the best-fed people in the world. Is eating meat a dietary liability or insurance of good nutrition? And what is its place in a reduced-calorie and -fat format?

Those on the pro side of the meat question will have us know that, ounce for ounce, meat is nutrient dense. Quite simply, it supplies outstanding nutritive value. It is an excellent source of high-quality protein and essential minerals such as iron, phosphorus, and copper while contributing vitamins, too. Those on the con side point to meats, particularly red meats, as major contributors of saturated fats, which have been linked to high cholesterol levels and heart disease. And because most meat is high in fat, as a rule it is a caloric pill of no little consequence.

Does that imply one should eschew meat for tofu? Give up taste for health? After all, *Gourmet Light* professes to be a "waist not—want not" style of eating, and for many, eating red meats is one of the pleasures of the table. Others enjoy a juicy pork chop or succulent veal cutlet, and with 4 billion pounds of hamburger typically consumed in a single year, it's not only children who hanker for America's signature food. Whether you're interested in reducing your intake of saturated fats, calories, or both, limiting—not eliminating—the amount of fatty meats in your diet may be the answer. Selection of the cut is key.

Disavowing Spartanism, which meat to choose when the carnivorous hunger strikes? Must one feel guilty savoring a fork-tender rib eye? No; moderation and trimming visible fat are the simple answer. And if meat is an important part of your diet, perhaps a look at sample calorie counts of each type will help when selecting a type of meat.

Veal, of course, is the leanest of the meats, because the 3-month or younger calf has developed little fat. A 4-ounce portion contains roughly 176 calories and 4 grams of fat. Lamb, marketed at about 6 months, has a hefty fat cover, but that can be removed before cooking. A 4-ounce serving contains about 275 calories and 9 grams of fat. Pork tenderloin weighs in at about 180 calories for a 4-ounce serving. And finally, all America's favorite, beef ranges from 342 calories with 25 grams of fat in a moderately fatty 4-ounce portion such as ground chuck to a surprisingly low 190 calories and 8 grams of fat in a similar-size portion of lean flank steak.

In moderation, any of these meats is perfectly permissible for the calorie conscious. But while 4 ounces of beef—about 340 calories—is within most people's limits, 6–7 ounces may not be. And you may be eating more than you think. Take careful note of package weights before cooking and determine just how much a 3½- or 4-ounce serving truly is. Or perhaps get in the habit of weighing portions for a while to train the eye to recognize how much (or little) the recommended portion size amounts to. "But it's good for me!" comes the lament. "What's wrong with a little extra meat?" For children, who need protein to grow, nothing; for the adult it may mean added pounds.

Just how much protein do we really need? And will it really make us strong? Here's a look at some protein myths and realities.

THE PROTEIN PEDESTAL

Of the three food classifications of protein, carbohydrates, and fats, protein has long been ballyhooed to all too often mythical proportions. It is, in fact, the one we should eat least of.

MYTH 1: To be healthy we need to eat lots of protein.

Nutritionists recommend that protein constitute the smallest percentage of the daily diet. It's been estimated that most Americans eat 2 to 3 times the amount of protein they need. And more is not necessarily better. Excess protein is burned for calories, stored as fat, or simply excreted.

The recommended daily allowance of protein is 42 grams for a 120-pound person and up to 73 grams for a 200-pound person. If in a typical day you eat something like this—a glass of 2 percent low-fat milk (4 grams protein), a ham sandwich on white bread (14 grams), and a 4½-ounce hamburger (30 grams)—you've received 48 grams of protein, to say nothing of protein also eaten in the course of the day in other forms, from vegetables to the flour in desserts.

MYTH 2: Protein isn't fattening.

In truth, protein supplies the same amount of calories per gram (4) as carbohydrates. And excess protein turns to the same kind of body fat as excess carbohydrates or fats.

MYTH 3: Protein increases athletic performance.

There are no magic potions for increasing athletic prowess. Protein alone will make no one a better athlete, or even increase one's stamina. The proverbial balanced diet (with protein on the low end) will allow us to perform at our individual best. Foods don't make for athletic performance; skill and training do. But without proper nutrition, we can't live up to our potential. Good nutrition is but one rung on the ladder.

For all these reasons—from a high concentration of saturated fats to bulging calorie counts—this chapter is necessarily lean. Those wishing to curb calories will do well to incorporate a larger percentage of fish and poultry in their diet. But when meat and only meat will do, by all means enjoy, for lean red meat is a nutritional powerhouse offering iron and zinc and vitamins thiamin, niacin, and B_{12}. Veal, selected cuts of beef and lamb, and even a lean pork tenderloin or cutlet are within the bounds of the calorie-conscious diner. Unfortunately, the leanest meats are often the toughest, and the tastiest cuts are the fattest. But even lean meats can be coaxed into tenderness if the cook understands a bit about the science of tender meat. The following factors apply mostly to beef. Tenderness for veal, pork, and lamb are discussed in the recipes for those meats.

The Science of Tender Meat

The tenderness of meat is the cumulative effect of these factors:

1. *Connective tissue*

There are two kinds of connective tissue in the muscles: collagen, which melts into gelatin quickly in the presence of heat, and elastin, which stubbornly refuses to melt unless subjected to long, slow cooking and even then may remain unchanged. If there is a great deal of either collagen or elastin in the meat, it is likely to be tough. Connective tissue is not to be confused with the streamlets of fat that run through the muscles; this marbling is an indication of tender meat.

2. *Where the cut is from*

As a general rule, the less exercised a muscle is, the more tender it will be. Choosing any cut that lies on either side of the backbone (the loin) will be the most tender, and, of course, the most fatty.

3. *Aging*

When beef is aged, enzymes in the meat naturally soften the connective tissue creating literally fork-tender meats. Aged meats are more costly because of the refrigeration and warehouse space involved. Home aging of meats is possible for good cuts of meat that are at least 4 pounds in weight, when they're covered with a protective flap of fat, which is later removed.

4. *Grade of the cut*

Meat is graded by government inspectors prior to sale. The carcass is inspected for conformation, quality, and finish—gibberish to you and me but the meat of the matter for the inspector before it is labeled prime, choice, or good. There are actually five lesser grades but not for retail sale. While prime meat is regarded as the best, the quality of choice meats is also excellent and, because of reduced marbling, may be slightly less fatty.

A naturally tender steak, then, has a lot of marbling, has little connective tissue, was cut from the loin, and was hopefully aged at least a week or more. It can be either of prime or choice quality. Meat that is not naturally tender can be made so by attention to the cooking technique used.

Moist vs. Dry Heat Cooking

Virtually all the recipes ever created for meat fall under one of but two categories: moist or dry heat cooking. Moist heat (stewing, braising, etc.) breaks down the collagen if the meat is allowed to cook at low temperatures for a long time. Naturally, a piece of meat may not be cooked rare if it is a tough cut; it will need to cook beyond the 120 internal degrees of pink meat. Not even meat tenderizers can transform a tough cut into fork-tender steak.

It is my experience that meat tenderizers promise more than they can deliver, much as a sparkling wine is not, after all, a fine champagne. Tenderizers for the most part are made from papain, an enzyme found in papayas. This enzyme, which incidentally is injected into humans to dissolve calcium deposits on the spine, does soften tissue. It has some drawbacks, however. It is only effective on the meat's surface, unless the meat is punctured, making little escape tunnels for the juices. Further, the tenderizing activity is slow unless the meat is quite warm—reaching its peak at 176 degrees—so it may actually do nothing at all on refrigerator-cold meat.

Marinating meat is another popular method for tenderizing tough cuts. Its effectiveness remains a moot point. While some cooks claim soaking meat in an acid (wine or vinegar) solution with oils and seasonings will tenderize it, there are scientific studies that both contradict and confirm the practice. It is an indisputable fact that marinating meats in an acid will result in some loss of minerals.

It seems wise then to choose the cooking method that best complements the meat. Dry heat cooking (sauteing, grilling, broiling, and roasting) is suitable for cuts that are naturally tender. These meats may be cooked rare. You can broil, pan-fry, or grill tender meat (not at too high a heat, which can destroy some of the protein) for a quick, delicious, and somewhat fattening meal. For beef lovers who wish to curb calories, fat, and cholesterol, a bit of finagling is called for, because the cut of choice for them is a leaner, thus a tougher cut. Top round, eye of the round, flank steak, and lean sirloin steaks are lower in fat. Of the tender cuts, filet mignon (tenderloin) is the better choice.

For those who relish a moist, juicy, rare beefsteak, the Roasted Tenderloin of Beef may be the answer. For the meat lovers, there are Beef Paupiettes with Parmesan-Zucchini Stuffing, Coriander and Lime Pork Kabobs with Hot Chili Chutney, and more. This section is thin, however, because of the generally high calorie count of most meats.

BEEF

Despite a slightly tarnished reputation because of a bit of bad press, I'll bet the hamburger is still one of America's favorite foods; it accounts for nearly 20 percent of all restaurant orders. From Monday's meat loaf to Saturday's prime rib, beef has been the backbone of the American diet. But unless you've been orbiting in space for the last decade or so, you also know that it is high in saturated fat, which has been fingered as a contributor to heart disease, and calories. Nutritionists have warned against indulging in too much fatty meat, which has sent the American Beef Council scrambling to remind the public that beef . . . indeed, "is good food." With $3\frac{1}{2}$ ounces of beef round supplying more than $\frac{1}{2}$ the daily requirement of protein, more than $\frac{1}{4}$ the phosphorus, $\frac{1}{6}$ the iron, and $\frac{1}{4}$ of the niacin for a 120-pound woman for only 261 calories, one wonders, what's the fuss? The *rest* of the story, of course, is the high concentration of saturated fats, which, if you're prone to high cholesterol levels, are health threatening. But one needn't give up fatty meats altogether. With proper cooking techniques and wise selection, moderate amounts of beef can be enjoyed.

From a calorie and a quality viewpoint, there is beef and there is beef. Unfortunately, the tastiest beef is the most fattening, the leaner the beef, the tougher and the more tasteless. Following the guidelines given above about tender meat, select and cook lean meats so as to maximize their tenderness and flavor.

BRAISED BEEF
WITH TOMATO AND BASIL

Call it boeuf en daube, boeuf à la mode, estouffade de boeuf, braised beef, or pot roast, the technique is all the same. A tough and often fatty cut of meat is browned, liquid and vegetables are added for flavoring, and the whole is simmered until tender. It's the sort of robust meal that justifies the existence of cold weather. But because it is often made with relatively fatty cuts that drip their fat into the sauce rather than into a broiler pan to be discarded, it should not be a common meal for the calorie concerned. This *Gourmet Light* version, made with a leaner cut than the more traditional chuck relies on the long, slow simmer of a Crockpot, the most energy-efficient means of cooking, rather than fatty meat, to produce a fork-tender, delicious dinner. Don't be put off by the 8 to 10 hours of cooking time, for preparation is only about 15 minutes' worth. This minimal time can be further reduced by substituting a large (28-ounce) jar of your favorite spaghetti sauce for the tomatoes, herbs, and broth. The cooking time can be shortened by microwaving, instructions for which are included here. Serve with some wide noodles and a simple green salad.

Yield: 10 servings

Calories per serving: 257

Protein per serving: 25g

Fat per serving: 12g

   Saturated fat per serving: 4g

Cholesterol per serving: 71mg

Carbohydrates per serving: 12g

Sodium per serving: 549mg

Fiber per serving: 2g

3 pounds top or bottom round beef roast, trimmed completely

3 medium onions, chopped

2 carrots, chopped

2 cloves garlic, minced

1 13³/₄-ounce can beef broth

¹/₂ cup red wine (optional)

1 28-ounce can ground peeled tomatoes

4 tablespoons tomato paste

1 tablespoon dried basil

2 teaspoons salt

freshly ground pepper to taste

1 teaspoon dried oregano

1 teaspoon sugar

1 bay leaf

1. Place all ingredients in a 4-quart or larger Crockpot. Cover and simmer at the low setting for 10 hours. Stir from time to time. The beef can cook as

long as 14 hours if you like fork-tender meat. If cooking for just 8 hours, cook for 2 hours at the high setting, then reduce heat to low. Remove bay leaf before serving.

2. To microwave, pierce the meat 10 to 12 times from both the top and bottom with a carving fork. Place in a 4-quart microwave-safe dish. Add the remaining ingredients. Microwave at high (100 percent power) for 10 minutes. Microwave at medium (50 percent power) for 2½ hours. Stir from time to time. Let rest 15 minutes before serving. Remove bay leaf before serving. *Note:* If you line the cooking container with a cooking bag, you'll have virtually no dishes to clean up!

FLANK STEAK IN GINGERED BEER SAUCE

Flank steak, a strip of muscle that lies on either side of the loin, is the leanest of all beef cuts, with about 163 calories in a 4-ounce serving. Because the muscle fibers are coarse and there is little fat, it is most often cooked with moist heat, though occasionally it is broiled or grilled as a steak. With its long, thin configuration, which is ideal for stuffing, flank steak makes an attractive presentation. Here it is rolled around a fruit stuffing and slow cooked in a fragrant sauce of gingered beer. The meat may be readied for cooking early in the day.

Yield: 6 servings

Calories per serving: 314

Protein per serving: 25g

Fat per serving: 12g

  Saturated fat per serving: 5g

Cholesterol per serving: 59mg

Carbohydrates per serving: 27g

Sodium per serving: 476mg

Fiber per serving: 4g

The Stuffing

5 dried apricots

2 tablespoons rum or hot water

1 small onion, minced

2 tablespoons beef broth

3 small apples, peeled, cored, and
*   chopped*

2 teaspoons minced ginger root

¼ teaspoon salt

freshly ground pepper to taste

dash ground cinnamon

The Meat

1³/₄ *pounds flank steak*

Dijon-style mustard

1 onion, chopped

2 celery ribs, chopped

1 carrot, chopped

¹/₂ teaspoon salt

freshly ground pepper to taste

a 12-ounce bottle dark beer

1¹/₂ *cups beef broth*

3 tablespoons tomato paste

3 or 4 allspice berries or ¹/₄ teaspoon ground allspice

1 bay leaf

1 tablespoon fresh thyme leaves or ¹/₂ teaspoon dried thyme

2 garlic cloves, minced

1 cinnamon stick

a quarter-size piece of fresh ginger root, peeled and minced

To Prepare the Stuffing

1. Plump the apricots in the rum or hot water in a microwave oven or on the stove top at high (100 percent power) for 5 minutes.

2. "Saute" the onion in the broth in a 10-inch skillet over medium heat until limp and the broth is evaporated.

3. Drain the apricot liquid into the onion skillet. Chop and add the apricots. Add the apples and ginger. Season with salt, pepper, and cinnamon. Cover and cook over medium-low heat for 4 minutes or until the fruits are soft. Remove from the heat and cool while preparing the pot vegetables and meat.

To Prepare the Meat

1. Place the meat between two sheets of wax paper and pound it with the side of a cleaver until somewhat thinner and enlarged. Dip a pastry brush into a pot of mustard and brush it over the inside of meat. Set aside.

2. Spoon the stuffing (from Step 3) onto the meat, completely covering the surface; reserve any extra. Starting at the small end, roll the meat up in jelly-roll fashion. Tie tightly with butcher's twine or secure with wooden skewers. Gather what stuffing falls out and reserve with other stuffing.

3. Spray the skillet used for stuffing (no need to wash) with cooking spray. Add the onion, celery, and carrot, cover, and cook at high heat until the vegetables are lightly browned. Scrape them into a 5-quart Dutch oven or electric Crockpot.

4. Add the meat and all remaining ingredients including any extra stuffing to the Crockpot.

5. Cook at high for 1 hour; reduce heat to low and simmer for another $2\frac{1}{2}$ hours. Alternately, place all ingredients in a Dutch oven or other ovenproof casserole and bake at 350 degrees for $\frac{1}{2}$ hour. Reduce heat to 300 degrees and cook an additional 2 hours. Broth should not boil. Check for evaporation, adding more broth if necessary.

To Serve

1. Remove the meat from the pot. Cut and discard strings or skewers. Let the meat rest, covered with a towel, while preparing the sauce.

2. Remove the cinnamon from the pot. If you prefer a smooth sauce, pour the sauce through a coarse strainer (or put through a food processor and then strain), pushing the vegetables with the back of a wooden spoon. Discard the

pulp in the strainer, taste the sauce, and adjust seasoning. If it's too thin, boil until somewhat reduced. If there's not enough sauce, add broth or red wine, heat, and stir until it reaches the desired thickness.

3. Slice the meat in ½-inch slices and arrange them in a circle on platter. Pour the sauce over and around the meat. Garnish the center of the platter with lightly buttered peas or glazed carrots or turnips.

Ginger

Ginger root has been the up-and-coming spice of recent years. It is used in sauces, blanched and julienned like orange rinds as a garnish for poultry dishes, and added to everything from salad dressings to ice creams. Oriental cooking has long known the wonders of this root of an orchidlike plant. In powdered form ginger has been used in baked goods literally for centuries. Our grandmothers used it in pickles and chutneys, and it is a component of curry powder. To use fresh ginger root, peel the outer skin and small knobs with a knife, exposing the pale yellow woody flesh. Cut off as much as you need and mince it finely. The remaining ginger root may be stored at room temperature in an airtight container (how long will depend on the age of the root when you buy it) or immersed in sherry and kept refrigerated for up to 6 months. The ginger-spiked sherry is delicious anywhere ginger is welcome: eggs, fish, poultry, carrots, squash, sweet potatoes, or your favorite way.

BEEF PAUPIETTES WITH PARMESAN-ZUCCHINI STUFFING

These beef rolls make a lot of a little beef. When purchasing the ground turkey, look for a brand that is 97 percent fat-free. The stuffing may be put together several hours before hand if desired. Grilled or sauteed, the paupiettes are delicious with a curried rice and perhaps Ratatouille (page 270) or Lemon-Glazed Carrots (page 244).

Yield: 6 servings

Calories per serving: 211

Protein per serving: 26g

Fat per serving: 10g

  Saturated fat per serving: 3g

Cholesterol per serving: 69mg

Carbohydrates per serving: 4g

Sodium per serving: 939mg

Fiber per serving: 1g

2 small zucchini

1 small onion

1 clove garlic

2 teaspoons salt

8 ounces ground turkey

$\frac{1}{2}$ teaspoon salt

freshly ground pepper to taste

$\frac{1}{2}$ teaspoon dried thyme

2 tablespoons grated Parmesan cheese

1 pound thinly sliced lean beef, such as sandwich steaks

prepared horseradish

To Prepare the Stuffing

1. In the bowl of a food processor or by hand, grate together the zucchini, onion, and garlic. Place the mixture in a sieve suspended over the sink.

2. Toss with the 2 teaspoons salt (to remove excess moisture from the squash) and let rest about 10 minutes.

3. Spray a nonstick skillet with cooking spray. Over medium-high heat, saute the turkey, breaking it up with a wooden spoon, until it is no longer pink, about 6 minutes.

4. Meanwhile, rinse the zucchini mixture in cold running water, squeezing it in your hand until the salt is rinsed away, about 30-45 seconds. Squeeze hard to remove water.

5. Stir the zucchini mixture into the turkey and continue to saute over medium-high heat another 4 minutes, stirring often to combine well and cook the vegetables.

6. Stir in the ½ teaspoon salt and pepper, thyme, and cheese. Remove from heat. The stuffing may be prepared several hours in advance and kept refrigerated, if desired.

To Finish the Paupiettes

1. Place the sandwich steaks between two long strips of waxed paper and pound them with a cleaver until thin.

2. Dip a pastry brush into the horseradish jar and spread a thin layer on one side of the meat.

3. Divide the turkey-zucchini mixture among the steaks, spreading it over the entire surface of the steaks with a broad-bladed knife or spatula. Tightly roll up the steaks, pressing the paupiettes in your palm to create rolls. They may be fastened with a piece of wooden skewer or toothpick, though this usually isn't necessary.

4. Spray a large nonstick skillet with cooking spray, place over high heat, and saute the rolls, reducing heat to medium once they are browned. Roll the paupiettes often; they will cook in about 10–12 minutes. They may also be grilled. Spray a fine-mesh grill rack, as well as the paupiettes themselves, with nonstick cooking spray. Place the paupiettes over the grill rungs to prevent them from falling into the coals.

Thinking Thin Tip

Cooking sprays are useful to keep on hand for coating both non-stick and regular skillets, grill rungs, baking sheets, and even food prior to grilling or high-heat roasting. Most manufacturers recommend a 2-second spray. An alternative is to dip a pastry brush or paper towel in oil and then over the pan and/or food, but this is a little more wasteful. Either method cuts down on added fats in cooking.

ROASTED TENDERLOIN OF BEEF

I've always felt that a tenderloin epitomized the best of beef. Fewer cuts are more tender, easier to carve, or serve. But tenderloin can lack flavor, for as meats go, it is fairly lean, particularly if well trimmed before cooking. Hence the tradition of wrapping a tenderloin steak in a slice of bacon before grilling, or serving the meat with a rich sauce such as Béarnaise.

To accentuate the tenderness, our *Gourmet Light* version calls for home aging (a process you may omit). For the ultimate in juicy perfection, the meat is then slow roasted in a salt crust, which, rather amazingly, doesn't penetrate the roast. This makes an excellent party meal served with *Gourmet Light* Béarnaise Sauce, which holds better than the traditional sauce, for everything may be done ahead. For an even more festive treatment, butterfly the meat and stuff it, after aging, with langoustine (available frozen), crab, or lobster. Retie the roast and proceed as directed.

Tenderloins freeze well so take advantage of an occasional sale. A typical tenderloin weighs 5½ pounds to about 8 pounds, before trimming. Allow about one-half pound per person of untrimmed weight for the generous servings you plan for when entertaining. A 7-pound tenderloin will weigh about 5 pounds after trimming, theoretically feeding 10 people, with a generous half pound. I've never found this to be true, however. In my experience a 7-pound tenderloin (before trimming) will feed 6–8 with seconds for some. Ask the butcher to trim and tie the roast, reserving the fat if you wish to age it at home.

Prime meat has already enjoyed a lengthy aging, but choice meat often has not. For truly fork-tender meat, follow this procedure 3 days before your dinner party.

Remove the store wrappings from the meat weighing at least 4 pounds, trim any fat that remains. Place the meat on a cake rack over a baking sheet. Lay the reserved fat on the meat, covering it as much as possible. Crease a piece of aluminum foil large enough to cover the meat down the center. Position the tent of foil over the meat loosely, do not wrap tightly. Air must circulate. Refrigerate for 3 days, turning the meat and repositioning the fat

Yield: 10 servings

Calories per serving: 333

Protein per serving: 46g

Fat per serving: 15g

  Saturated fat per serving: 6g

Cholesterol per serving: 135mg

Carbohydrates per serving: trace

Sodium per serving: 103mg

Fiber per serving: trace

once a day. During this time, the enzymes that are naturally present in the meat break down the fibers of the muscles, causing them to relax. In the process, the meat softens. You'll notice that any surface not covered by fat will darken and harden. To prepare the meat for cooking, untie the butcher's twine and discard the fat. Carefully pare away all the hardened flesh. Retie the roast; it is now ready for roasting.

a whole tenderloin, about 7 pounds before trimming, tied and trimmed
1 clove garlic, mashed or pressed
10 cups kosher salt
2 1/2 cups water
Béarnaise Sauce (page 25)

1. Preheat oven to 400 degrees. Pat the meat dry with paper towels. Trim away all visible fat. Rub the garlic over the meat.

2. In a large bowl, moisten the salt with the water bit by bit, stirring to form a paste. Because kosher salt has no additives to keep it free flowing, it is very susceptible to moisture and may or may not need the entire amount of water specified here. Add only as much (or more) as needed to form a thick paste.

3. Put half the salt paste in a roasting pan just large enough to hold the meat. Put the meat on top, add remaining salt paste, and pack tightly around the roast with your hands.

4. Place on the lowest shelf in a 400-degree oven and roast for 1 hour or until an instant-reading meat thermometer registers 120 degrees for rare or 135 degrees for medium rare. Begin temperature testing after 40 minutes to be on the safe side. The temperature of the meat at the time of roasting, the shape of the meat, and the density of the salt paste can all affect the actual roasting time; what worked last time may not work next time.

5. Remove the pan from the oven when the meat is the desired temperature. Let the meat sit for 10 minutes, and remove salt crust. Slice the meat before serving it, because the outside will be gray rather than brown since it was not seared. Serve with Béarnaise Sauce.

TWO-SESAME BEEF AND RED PEPPER STIR-FRY

A quick and satisfying stir-fry for busy schedules, it will need nothing other than rice to complete the meal. Keeping prechopped ginger on hand speeds preparation; you'll find it in specialty produce markets. Dried hot chili peppers are readily available in the spice section at the supermarket. Add the sesame oil at the last minute, as prolonged heat destroys its fragrance and flavor.

Yield: 4 servings

Calories per serving: 279

Protein per serving: 29g

Fat per serving: 11g

   Saturated fat per serving: 3g

Cholesterol per serving: 66mg

Carbohydrates per serving: 15g

Sodium per serving: 1,272mg

Fiber per serving: 3g

¾ pound lean beef, such as top round, partially frozen

½ cup reduced-sodium soy sauce

1 small dried hot chili pepper

1 clove garlic, minced

2 tablespoons Chinese cooking wine

1 tablespoon rice wine vinegar

1 tablespoon sugar

1 teaspoon minced ginger root

1 tablespoon sesame seeds

2 teaspoons canola or peanut oil

½ red onion, thinly sliced

1 red bell pepper, thinly sliced

1 stalk broccoli, cut into flowerets, and stalks peeled and thinly sliced

1 tablespoon cornstarch dissolved in 1 tablespoon water

1 teaspoon sesame oil

1. Slice the meat thinly on the bias. Place it in a 1-quart bowl.

2. Combine the soy sauce, chili pepper, garlic, cooking wine, vinegar, sugar, ginger root, and sesame seeds in a 2-cup measuring cup. Pour it over the meat. Marinate at least 20 minutes and as long as 24 hours.

3. Heat the oil in a wok or 12-inch skillet over high heat until very hot. Add the onion, red pepper, and broccoli and stir-fry until tender-crisp, about 4 minutes (time will vary with the shape of the cooking pot).

4. Push the vegetables to the rim of the wok, making a well in the center. Add the meat and marinade to the well and stir-fry until meat is no longer pink, about 3 to 4 minutes.

5. Add the cornstarch thickener and stir over high heat until sauce thickens, about 1 minute. Remove the dried chili pepper. Drizzle sesame oil over all. Serve with rice.

BLACK BEAN AND BEEF CHILI

This hearty dish is perfect fare after a few hours' activity in the frosty out-doors. Make it ahead and take it to the ski house or serve after sledding at home. A meal in itself, this chili calls for just some rice, maybe tossed with a little fresh coriander. It will keep frozen, without flavor loss, for up to two months.

Yield: 10 servings

Calories per serving: 289

Protein per serving: 26g

Fat per serving: 5g

   Saturated fat per serving: 2g

Cholesterol per serving: 40mg

Carbohydrates per serving: 35g

Sodium per serving: 581mg

Fiber per serving: 6g

9 plum tomatoes

1 jalapeño pepper

3 medium onions, chopped

4 cloves garlic, chopped

1/2 cup red wine or beef broth

1 1/2 pounds lean red beef, such as top or bottom round, partially frozen

3 tablespoons minced fresh coriander

1 tablespoon ground cumin

2 teaspoons dried oregano

2 tablespoons chili powder

1 teaspoon salt

*6 cups black beans, cooked (see page 199), or 4 1-pound cans black
    beans, drained and rinsed*

4 beef bouillon cubes

3 tablespoons cornmeal

1. Blacken the tomatoes and jalapeño pepper in a 10-inch skillet over high heat for 15 minutes, shaking the pan from time to time to blacken evenly. Reduce heat to medium-high as tomatoes become blackened. Remove toma-toes and pepper from pan to cool.

2. Meanwhile, combine the onions and garlic with the red wine or beef broth in a 4-cup glass measuring cup or other microwave-safe container.

Cover with plastic wrap and microwave at high (100 percent power) for 6 minutes or until the onions are softened. Place onions and cooking broth in a 1.3-gallon microwave-safe container.

3. Thinly slice the partially frozen meat either by hand or using a food processor. Add meat to onions.

4. When tomatoes are cool enough to handle, core and chop them roughly. Add to the onion-meat mixture.

5. Wearing rubber gloves, peel, stem, and seed the jalapeño. Mince. Using the whole pepper will produce a medium-hot chili; using a level tablespoon of minced jalapeño produces a mildly spicy dish. Add as much as you like to the tomato-onion-meat mixture.

6. Stir in the coriander, cumin, oregano, chili powder, salt, and beans. Dissolve the bouillon cubes in 2 cups boiling water. Add to the tomato-onion-meat mixture.

7. Cover and microwave at high (100 percent power) for 15 minutes. Stir. Cover and microwave again at medium-high heat (75 percent power) for an additional 40 minutes. Stir in cornmeal if needed for thickening. Microwave at high (100 percent power) for an additional 5 minutes to thicken. (If the chili is being reheated, it will thicken during chilling and may not need the cornmeal.)

SOFT BEEF TACOS SEDONA

At a charming Mexican restaurant in Sedona, I discovered how good a taco filling made from a fresh brisket of beef can be. A relatively lean cut when trimmed of all fat, the brisket makes a delicious and authentic filling for tacos, salads, burritos, and other south-of-the-border dishes. The filling freezes beautifully and is even better the second or third day, making this dish a good candidate for weekend cooking. Adding carrots to the more traditional taco fixin's adds fiber and a rich source of beta carotene while helping to reduce the amount of yellow cheese you might otherwise help yourself to. Serve low-fat refried beans to complete the meal.

Yield: 6–8 servings (filling for 14–16 tacos)

Calories per serving: 500

Protein per serving: 41g

Fat per serving: 16g

   Saturated fat per serving: 3g

Cholesterol per serving: 90mg

Carbohydrates per serving: 46g

Sodium per serving: 784mg

Fiber per serving: 4g

For the Filling

2 pounds fresh beef brisket, trimmed of all fat, thinly sliced on the bias

1 13¾-ounce can beef broth

8 ounces water

2 tablespoons chopped onion

3 cloves garlic, minced

2 tablespoons chili powder

1 tablespoon minced fresh or canned jalapeño (less if you prefer a mild mixture)

1 tablespoon coriander seed, crushed (measure whole seed)

1 teaspoon dried oregano

1 teaspoon ground cumin

3 tablespoons cornmeal

For the Tacos

14–16 whole wheat, flour, or corn tortillas
shredded lettuce
minced scallions
chopped chilies
shredded carrots
shredded reduced-fat cheddar cheese
salsa

1. Combine the beef with all the other filling ingredients. Cover and bring to a simmer over high heat. Reduce heat to low, partially cover, and simmer 1½ to 2 hours. Cool.

2. Shred the meat in your fingers. Bring to a simmer over high heat. Reduce heat to medium, sprinkle in the cornmeal, and cook, stirring often, until thickened, about 4 minutes.

3. To serve the tacos, heat the tortillas according to package instructions or wrap in a damp towel and microwave at high (100 percent power) for 4-5 minutes or until heated through.

4. Arrange condiments attractively on a platter. Line a serving bowl with lettuce or red cabbage leaves and mound beef filling in center. Each diner serves him or herself.

CORIANDER AND LIME PORK KABOBS WITH HOT CHILI CHUTNEY

This easily prepared dish, festive enough for guests, pairs the cool tang of yogurt-coriander marinated pork with a chili-tinged apple-based chutney, a modern variation on the traditional combination of pork and apples. While tenderloin is called for, another pork cut, well trimmed, would be fine. Make the chutney a day ahead if you like when you marinate the meat. Serve with rice flecked with a bit of tomato and chilies to further the southwestern theme and Zucchini Saute (page 267). Left over chutney is excellent with grilled poultry and will last, chilled, up to one month.

1 pound pork tenderloin, trimmed of all fat and cut into 2-inch chunks

1 cup plain nonfat yogurt

¹/₄ cup lime juice

3 tablespoons minced fresh coriander

¹/₂ teaspoon salt

1 Spanish or other sweet onion, cut into 2-inch chunks

1. Combine the pork and yogurt, lime juice, coriander, and salt in a plastic bag. Tie the bag and knead with your hands to mix seasonings. Marinate in the refrigerator for 4–24 hours.

2. Thread 4 skewers with the meat and onion. Grill the kabobs over a medium-hot fire for approximately 20 minutes, basting often with the remaining marinade. Serve with hot chutney.

Yield of meat with chutney:
    4 servings

Calories per serving: 211

Protein per serving: 30g

Fat per serving: 5g
    Saturated fat per serving: 2g

Cholesterol per serving: 85mg

Carbohydrates per serving: 11g

Sodium per serving: 372mg

Fiber per serving: 1g

Hot Chili Chutney

2 Granny Smith apples, peeled, cored, and diced
1/2 cup diced dried mixed fruits, such as prunes, apricots, and peaches
1 tablespoon chopped canned chilies
1 tablespoon minced fresh coriander
2 teaspoons balsamic vinegar
1 teaspoon sugar
1 teaspoon ground cinnamon
1/2 teaspoon salt
1/4 teaspoon ground cloves

Yield of chutney: 4 servings:
   (4 tablespoons each)
Calorie per serving: 41
Protein per serving: trace
Fat per serving: trace
   Saturated fat per serving: trace
Cholesterol per serving: 0
Carbohydrates per serving: 11g
Sodium per serving: 153mg
Fiber per serving: 1g

1. Combine the ingredients in a 1-quart heavy-bottomed saucepan. Cover. Bring to a boil over high heat, reduce to medium-low, and simmer, stirring occasionally, for 1/2 hour. Chutney may be prepared several days in advance.

2. If the chutney has been refrigerated for more than 2 hours, mix with 3 tablespoons liquid such as water, cider, or white wine. Microwave at high power (100 percent) for 4 minutes, or simmer on the stove top, covered, about 5 minutes, stirring occasionally. Serve chutney hot with the kabobs.

Yogurt

Yogurt is a fermented milk product that has long been used in the Middle East but has only been used here since the 1940s. Widely regarded as a health food, it should be noted that it supplies no more nutrients than a glass of partially skimmed milk, although it does aid in digestion. Yogurt, like its roly-poly cousin, sour cream, must be cooked at low temperatures or it will curdle. Fruit-flavored yogurts are comparatively high in calories, one cup supplying about 260–300 calories.

Pork Cutlet
in Cider Cream Sauce

Here's a quick and delicious meal for midweek dining when time is of the essence. Pork cutlets are lean, boneless cuts taken from the loin, and they cook with little waste. After an initial searing, the pork must be slowly cooked to avoid toughening.

1 to 1 1/4 pounds boneless pork cutlets, trimmed of all fat

3/4 cup cider (hard or nonalcoholic sparkling cider recommended)

4 small apples, peeled, cored, and thinly sliced

1/4 teaspoon salt

freshly ground pepper to taste

2 teaspoons (or to taste) stone-ground mustard (the kind made with
*   horseradish is excellent)*

1/2 cup crème blanc (page 34), made without milk, or nonfat plain
*   yogurt or nonfat sour cream.*

Yield: 4 servings

Calories per serving: 302

Protein per serving: 26g

Fat per serving: 12g

    Saturated fat per serving: 4g

Cholesterol per serving: 81mg

Carbohydrates per serving: 23g

Sodium per serving: 269mg

Fiber per serving: 2g

1. Spray a 10-inch heavy-bottomed nonstick skillet with cooking spray. Pat the cutlets dry. Sear the cutlets for about 1 minute on each side or until well browned.

2. Reduce the heat, add the cider and apples, season with salt and pepper, and half cover the pan. Stirring the apples occasionally, simmer for 8 minutes, or until the pork is cooked through and the apples are tender but not mushy.

3. Remove the cutlets from the pan to a serving plate, cover with a towel to keep them warm. Boil pan juices, if necessary, to reduce to 1/4 cup. Cool about 1 minute; cider that's too hot will curdle the crème blanc.

4. Stir the mustard into the crème blanc or yogurt or sour cream. Whisk this mixture into the cider. Pour the sauce and apples over the pork cutlets.

ROASTED PORK TENDERLOIN WITH CURRIED FALL FRUIT COMPOTE

Pork has always been considered a fatty meat, but with better breeding today's animal is less fatty than in previous years. The tenderloin, a long thin strip of meat taken from the unexercised backbone area, is among the leanest of the cuts. Pork tenderloins range from 2 inches to 3 inches thick, tapering down to a mere flap of meat. If you're only able to buy the thinner tenderloin, purchase two and tie them together with one thin tail abutting the thick body of the other. This way you'll have a "log" of meat of uniform thickness. This recipe may be prepared early in the day and roasted just before serving. Serve it with the Curried Fall Fruit Compote for a delicious dinner worthy of a festive occasion.

Yield of meat: 5 servings
Calories per serving: 240
Protein per serving: 38g
Fat per serving: 7g
  Saturated fat per serving: 2g
Cholesterol per serving: 119mg
Carbohydrates per serving: 4g
Sodium per serving: 452mg
Fiber per serving: trace

Dijon-style mustard
1³/₄ pounds pork tenderloin
¹/₂ teaspoon salt
freshly ground pepper to taste
1 clove garlic, minced
¹/₄ cup unseasoned dried bread crumbs
4 to 5 fresh sage leaves, snipped, or ³/₄ teaspoon dried sage

1. Preheat oven to 450 degrees. Brush the mustard over the meat with a pastry brush. Sprinkle half the salt over the meat.

2. Spray an 8-inch skillet with cooking spray, add the garlic, and cook over medium heat about 30 seconds. Add the bread crumbs and sage. Cook, stirring, until the crumbs begin to brown. Season with remaining salt and pepper.

3. Put half the crumbs in a roasting dish just large enough to hold the meat. Put the roast on top and pat remaining crumbs around and on top of roast.

4. Place roast in the bottom third of the preheated 450-degree oven for 10 minutes. Then reduce heat to 325 degrees and roast for an additional 50 minutes. Check meat's internal temperature after it has roasted 45 minutes. It is done when internal temperature registers 160 to 165 degrees. Let the tenderloin rest 5–10 minutes before slicing. Serve with Curried Fall Fruit Compote.

Curried Fall Fruit Compote

¹/₂ small onion, chopped

4 tablespoons beef or chicken broth

1 teaspoon curry powder

¹/₂ teaspoon ground cumin

1 pear, peeled, cored, and chopped

1 Granny Smith apple, peeled, cored, and chopped

1 Red Delicious apple, peeled, cored, and chopped

*2 dried apricots, soaked 20 minutes in 2 tablespoons apricot or other
    fruit-flavored brandy*

4 tablespoons golden raisins

Yield of compote: 4 servings

Calories per serving: 128

Protein per serving: 1g

Fat per serving: 1g

  Saturated fat per serving: trace

Cholesterol per serving: trace

Carbohydrates per serving: 30g

Sodium per serving: 4mg

Fiber per serving: 4g

1. "Saute" the onion in 2 tablespoons of the broth until limp. Sprinkle on the curry powder and cumin. Cook over medium-high heat, stirring, about 15 seconds.

2. Add the remaining ingredients, including the brandy, cover, and cook over low heat 20 minutes or until flavors are blended. Serve with pork dishes. Leftovers are easily reheated in a bit of broth or cider.

VEAL CHOPS WITH RED PEPPER BUTTER

Really watching calories for a few days? How about a veal chop for lunch? Too much, too fattening? Would you believe these succulent chops slathered with red pepper butter actually have fewer calories than a tuna on white bread? More costly perhaps, but would you rather pay with your pocketbook or your waistline? Besides the calorie count, an added payoff is the feeling of satisfaction after such a pampered lunch that will last till dinnertime. Because the red pepper butter keeps in the freezer indefinitely, make it in quantity—even frozen, it is sliceable. It flames a simple green vegetable, chicken, or fish fillet with flavor and color.

Yield: 4 servings

Calories per serving: 277

Protein per serving: 40g

Fat per serving: 11g

Saturated fat per serving: 3g

Cholesterol per serving: 149mg

Carbohydrates per serving: 1g

Sodium per serving: 287mg

Fiber per serving: trace

For the Red Pepper Butter

5 medium red bell peppers

4 tablespoons minced fresh parsley

1 clove garlic, minced

1/2 teaspoon salt

freshly ground pepper to taste

1 teaspoon fresh lemon juice

2 tablespoons reduced-calorie margarine

For the Meat

4 loin or shoulder (sometimes called arm) veal chops

1/4 teaspoon salt

freshly ground pepper to taste

To Prepare the Red Pepper Butter

1. Halve the peppers, discard the seeds, and flatten the peppers with your hand. Place on a baking sheet and broil until blackened and charred, about 8

minutes. Turn the sheet around once or twice to ensure even cooking. See the illustration on page 259.

2. Scrape the peppers into a plastic or paper bag, roll it closed, and chill until cool enough to handle, about 10 minutes. (The freezer makes quick work if you're in a hurry.)

3. Peel and discard the skins and chop the flesh roughly.

4. Puree the roasted peppers in a food processor with the remaining ingredients, adding the margarine after the other ingredients have been pureed. Lacking a food processor, puree the peppers in a blender or a food mill, adding the remaining ingredients, and puree again.

5. Scoop the pepper butter onto a double thickness of wax paper. Form it into a log shape, roll and twist ends to compact. Wrap in aluminum foil. Chill. The butter may be used as is or frozen and sliced as needed. You will only need about half the red pepper butter for the chops.

To Prepare the Chops

1. Preheat oven to 400 degrees. Sear the chops in a Teflon-coated skillet over high heat, for a little less than a minute on each side. Season with salt and pepper.

2. Tear off 4 pieces of parchment paper (17 inches by 15 inches). The paper may be used as is, with the chops wrapped as you would a sandwich. Or for a more decorative presentation, stack the four sheets and fold in half the long way. Trim the corners so you're left with four heart shapes. Place a chop on a half of each heart. Place a tablespoon of red pepper butter on each. Fold top of heart over. Starting at the rounded top, fold and pleat the paper, making a tight seal. Tuck the pointed end under the packet. Place each packet on a baking sheet. Place in the lower third of the preheated 400-degree oven for 15 minutes or until the paper puffs. Remove the baking sheet from the oven, and let each diner open the paper at the table and enjoy the heady aroma.

VEAL SCALLOPS WITH SUN-DRIED TOMATOES AND SHIITAKE MUSHROOMS

Don't let time-pinched schedules rob you of a fine meal now and again. This dish with its classy, yet conveniently prepared ingredients makes for quick, though still special occasion fare. It is wonderful with Risotto (page 281) and a steamed green vegetable.

1 ounce sun-dried tomatoes, broken up or sliced

½ cup chicken or beef broth

2 tablespoons skim milk

1 egg white

4 tablespoons flour, instant-blending recommended

4 tablespoons bread crumbs

1 pound veal scallops, pounded thin

salt and pepper to taste

3 tablespoons dry sherry

½ cup canned consomme or beef broth

4 ounces shiitake mushrooms, stems discarded and caps sliced

1 clove garlic, minced

1 tablespoon minced fresh parsley (optional)

4 very thin lemon slices (optional)

1. *Heat the tomatoes with the ½ cup broth in a microwave oven for 3 minutes on high (100 percent power). Set aside.* Alternately, bring the broth to a boil on the stove, add the tomatoes, remove from heat, and set aside while preparing the meat.

2. Beat together the milk and egg white. Pour onto a plate.

Yield: 4 servings

Calories per serving: 446

Protein per serving: 58g

Fat per serving: 15g

   Saturated fat per serving: 6g

Cholesterol per serving: 179mg

Carbohydrates per serving: 17g

Sodium per serving: 471mg

Fiber per serving: 1g

3. On a large sheet of waxed paper, make a circle of the flour and another of the bread crumbs. Dip the meat in the milk mixture, then in the flour, and finally in the bread crumbs, lightly coating both sides. Set the meat aside on another sheet of waxed paper. Season with salt and pepper.

4. Spray a 10- or 12-inch nonstick skillet with nonstick cooking spray and place over high heat. When the pan is very hot, add the meat. All the meat may not fit at one time; as it shrinks you will be able to add the remaining veal scallops. Cook over high heat about 3 minutes; turn and cook over medium-high heat about 2 to 3 minutes more. Transfer the meat to a plate or sheet of waxed paper.

5. Deglaze the pan with the sherry. Boil over high heat until only about a teaspoon of liquid remains. Add the consomme or beef broth, mushrooms, garlic, and reserved tomato-broth mixture. Cook over medium-high heat about 3 to 4 minutes, stirring frequently.

6. Return the meat to the pan, reduce heat to low, and spoon the sauce over, cooking about another 3 minutes or until the sauce is somewhat thickened and syrupy. Arrange veal on a serving plate and garnish with parsley and lemon slices if desired.

Thinking Thin Tip

Veal has more cholesterol than some cuts of beef because cholesterol, a fatlike substance, is concentrated not in the fat but in the muscle, the meaty portion, of the animal. Calves, with a higher muscle-fat ratio because of the tender age, thus have higher concentrations of cholesterol.

MOCK TENDERLOIN

This is one of my favorite ways to enjoy lamb, pink and succulent with a texture and taste much like that of a fine beef tenderloin. A lamb leg is completely stripped of fat, the muscles separated, marinated, cut into noisettes, and then grilled. Serve this with a mustardy hollandaise made by stirring a tablespoon of stone-ground mustard into *Gourmet Light* Hollandaise (page 24). Alternately, the muscles may be left whole and roasted in a 450-degree oven for 15 minutes for rare meat.

> *¹/₂ leg of lamb, the shank half (about 3¹/₂ pounds total)*
>
> *4 tablespoons red wine vinegar*
>
> *4 tablespoons red wine*
>
> *2 tablespoons minced fresh parsley*
>
> *1 clove garlic, minced*
>
> *a few drops hot pepper sauce*
>
> *Dijon-style mustard*
>
> *¹/₈ teaspoon salt*
>
> *freshly ground pepper to taste*

Yield: 4 servings

Calories per serving: 397

Protein per serving: 45g

Fat per serving: 22g

   Saturated fat per serving: 9g

Cholesterol per serving: 154mg

Carbohydrates per serving: 1g

Sodium per serving: 308mg

Fiber per serving: trace

1. Have the lamb boned or do it yourself. Lay the meat flat on the counter top with what was the skin side facing up. Trim and discard all the fat and gristle from the meat.

2. Cut off and freeze for another use the thin flap of meat that you'll find on one side. Pull the meat with your hands; you'll notice natural "breaks" in the muscles. Separate the muscles by pulling the white veil of connective tissues. You'll need a knife in only a few places. You'll have three separate muscles. Fold the thin ends of each muscle toward the middle and tuck underneath. Cut each muscle into rounds (noisettes), about 1¹/₂-inches thick. Each noisette will be about 3 inches across and look like a slice of beef tenderloin. Reserve and freeze any untidy chunks of meat with the flap and use for a curry or kebabs.

3. Combine the vinegar, wine, oil, parsley, garlic, and hot pepper sauce in a jar and shake to combine. Put the meat and marinade in a leak-proof plastic bag and refrigerate, turning occasionally, for about 12 hours.

4. Pat the meat dry, brush with the mustard, season with salt and pepper, and grill until done to your liking. Or "saute" in a nonstick skillet, or broil. Serve with a mustard hollandaise.

Note: The noisettes will be even juicer if you sear the meat on both sides, then remove it from the fire and let it rest 20 minutes before finishing the cooking.

How to Cut Lamb Noisettes

1. Lay the boned lamb on the counter. Trim and discard the fat and gristle from the meat.

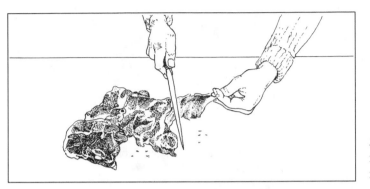

2. Turn the lamb over so what was the fat side is now facing down. Remove the thin triangular flap of meat. It may be saved for another use.

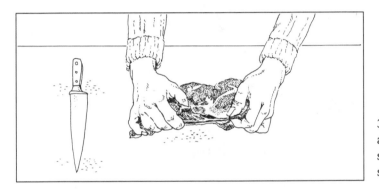

3. The meat will pull apart into three segments that are held together by a white, gossamer tissue and some gristle. Use your fingers and a small knife to separate the meat into three muscles.

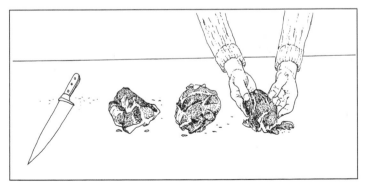

4. Fold the thin ends of each muscle toward the middle and tuck underneath.

5. Slice each muscle into noisettes about 1½ inches thick.

6. The finished noisettes will be about 3 inches across and look like a slice of beef tenderloin.

POULTRY

THE RECIPES

POULTRY

Back when Grandma simmered a pot of baked beans on the wood stove all day long and whipped up a mess of biscuits, mile high and puffy as you please, chicken was Sunday fare, a to-do worthy of company. Today, thanks to scientific advancements in the breeding and feeding of the barnyard birds, chicken has become a standard rather than a luxury. Because the birds now come to market in a matter of weeks, rather than months, the reduced production costs translate into reduced consumer prices, making chicken not only one of our more economical but also nutritionally bountiful buys, as well. Just 4 ounces of white meat, without skin, supplies about half an adult's protein needs for less than 150 calories. But half a cup of skinned, boned chicken is hardly something to feast on, and certainly no culinary inspiration. This chapter offers more tempting treatments.

Chicken, like red meat, must be inspected for wholesomeness, but there's no law stating it must be graded—a letter classification (A or B) based on the bird's physical appearance. Chickens wearing a Grade A shield do so because the processor has paid USDA inspectors to grade the product, a cost that the producer, and ultimately the consumer, must pay for. And it's not likely you'll spot a Grade B shield boldly displayed on a chicken breast—who wants the world to know your product is second best? This is not to say that nongraded birds are necessarily of poor quality, only that they've not been graded. You can be assured they'll be less expensive, and in some cases, just as good.

Here are some tips when purchasing chicken:

1. The bird should be fresh, not previously frozen.

Each time a chicken is thawed it loses some of its juices. If you suspect your market is selling previously frozen birds, or ones that have unintentionally frozen when shipped on ice, snap a leg bone after roasting. It will appear reddish-black if the bird was once frozen.

2. Match the cooking technique to the bird's size.

Roasters, over 3 pounds—roast or fricassee
Fryer, 2–3 pounds—saute, roast, or fricassee
Broiler, 1½ to 2½ pounds—grill or roast

Chickens range from broiler/fryers (smallest) to roasters (largest), which is not to say a fryer couldn't be broiled or a broiler roasted. However, the long, slow cooking such as that required for a Coq au Vin might render a small bird mushy, and grilling a cut-up roaster might take far too long, burning the skin before it was ever done at the bone. Adapt the recipe to the bird, remembering (logically) that large birds do best with long, slow cooking, while small birds are better suited to shorter cooking methods. Old, tough birds—fowl—need long, slow cooking in a liquid to make them tender.

3. Look for a plump bird, with a good covering of fat.

The plumper the bird, the more tender the meat. While buying only Grade A chickens pretty much ensures the best, buying plump ungraded chickens will get you to the same place for a few pennies less per pound.

4. Skin color is not an indication of flavor.

Some chicken producers routinely monitor the birds' skin pigment by taking blood samples from a few chickens. Those to be marketed in the Northeast, where yellow-skinned chickens are preferred, may have their feed bolstered by marigold petals, a completely natural substance that yellows the skin color but does not affect the flavor.

The very methods responsible for the relative inexpensiveness of chicken are held responsible by some cooks for production of a bland, flavorless bird. Free-range chickens, available at some specialty markets, are brought up "the old-fashioned way," pecking away in the barnyard. These same cooks feel the increased exercise and natural feed supplements make for a better-flavored bird. If you can find a supplier of free-range chickens, you can test the theory yourself . . . but because the old-fashioned method is more dear, be prepared to pay more.

Like fish, chicken is very perishable. It is best to freeze it if not using it within 24 hours of purchase. If you choose to rinse the chicken before cooking and it is to be browned, pat it thoroughly dry or it will more likely stew than saute.

A frozen chicken, or any other poultry, is best thawed under refrigeration, well wrapped, to inhibit water loss. This can take anywhere from 1–3 days, depending on the size of the bird.

BONING CHICKEN BREASTS

Chicken breasts are a favorite in *Gourmet Light* cooking for they make a tidy serving and neatly solve the "just one more bite" temptation. A typical chicken breast weighs 3 ounces and supplies a mere 125 calories, 3 grams of fat, and 20 grams of protein—about half the daily requirement for most women. It's wonderfully versatile, nutrient dense, skinny, and economical, too—don't be caught without a supply in the freezer.

Although chicken breasts are readily available boned and skinned, you may wish to do the work yourself. Not only is it more economical, but the bones are almost indispensable for enriching store-bought chicken broth or making your own. As you bone the breasts, toss the bones into a plastic bag in the freezer. You may add to and use from your stash as needed.

Use any sharp knife for boning chicken breasts; you don't need a special boning knife. Place the breast on the work surface, skin side up. If whole, flatten with the heel of your hand and split by cutting through or just to one side of the breastbone. With the breastbone to the right and the rib cage section to the left, slice against the breastbone and scrape down the bones, pulling back the meat with your fingers. Always angle the knife toward the bones. Don't worry about making gorgeous, clean cuts. The meat is very gelatinous and will "glue" together as it cooks, and the bit of meat left on the bones will only serve to enrich your stock. When the meat is scraped free of the bones, cut loose at the shoulder end. This is called a supreme. Turn the supreme so the skin side is down. Notice the small strip of meat, called the filet mignon, with the white tendon running its length. By the way, if the filet became detached in cutting, don't despair, just stick it back on! Grasp the end of the tendon in your finger tips and pull it free by scraping the meat away with the tip of a small, sharp knife. Although this is a pesky task and may be omitted, the tendon, if left, tends to pull the breast out of shape as it doesn't shrink with the cooking meat. To skin, simply lift the skin in your fingertips, cutting loose where needed. With your fingertips check to be sure the supreme is free of any remaining cartilage. Trim away yellow fat. Freeze the breasts or use within 24 hours.

Eating Fat

On average each adult American eats 138 pounds of fat a year. That's about 6 ounces or ¾ cup of fat a day.

CHICKEN PAILLARDS

A paillard is the culinary term for a piece of beef, chicken, or veal that is cooked without fat. Although this can be accomplished in a good heavy non-stick skillet, it is best suited for grills, either the indoor models with their wonderfully effective fans or a more typical outdoor version. What follows are basic instructions for preparing chicken paillards and some suggestions for varying the routine. You'll soon devise some wonderful alternatives that reflect your own tastes for this simplest and skinniest of meals. Technically, a chicken paillard is the breast boned and skinned.

4 boneless chicken breasts
juice of half a lemon
$1/8$ teaspoon salt
freshly ground pepper to taste

1. Skin the chicken breast. Place the chicken between sheets of wax paper and pound just to an even thickness, not to make thin. Spray the chicken on both sides with nonstick cooking spray or dip a pastry brush in oil and sparingly brush both sides.

2. Heat a grill or skillet with grill ridges. Place the chicken perpendicular to the grill rungs. After the chicken has seared, turn $1/4$ turn (90 degrees) to make customary grill marks. Season with a few drops lemon juice. Turn over after 3 minutes. Repeat above procedure to make grilling pattern. Season with salt, pepper, and lemon juice. Continue to cook until chicken is firm when poked with your finger in several places, about 6–7 minutes. Because the grill's heat and the thickness of chicken will vary, watch it closely. Chicken may be cooked in anywhere from 4–8 minutes.

Yield: 4 servings

Calories per serving: 144

Protein per serving: 27g

Fat per serving: 3g

   Saturated fat per serving: 1g

Cholesterol per serving: 73mg

Carbohydrates per serving: 1g

Sodium per serving: 129mg

Fiber per serving: trace

Mustard Paillards

Dip a pastry brush in stone-ground mustard and lavish over uncooked chicken. Spread on additional mustard if desired during cooking. This is also delicious with some of the sweet mustards on the market, such as Russian or champagne mustard. (The nutritional content is not available.)

Basil Salsa Paillards

When fresh basil is in season, make several batches of the wonderfully delicious Basil Salsa on page 31. It is an all-purpose flavor booster with a tiny caloric price tag. Brush 2 tablespoons on each chicken paillard before and as it cooks and serve with sauteed cherry tomatoes.

Yield: 4 servings

Calories per serving: 165

Protein per serving: 28g

Fat per serving: 4g

  Saturated fat per serving: 1g

Cholesterol per serving: 74mg

Carbohydrates per serving: 2g

Sodium per serving: 96mg

Fiber per serving: trace

Red Pepper Butter Paillards

When red peppers are plentiful in early spring and fall, make the Red Pepper Butter on page 149 in quantity and freeze it. Sliced right from the freezer, it cloaks a simple chicken paillard with a scarlet robe at once subtle yet piquant. Add a slice after the chicken has cooked on one side, and another when the chicken is done, just before serving, covering briefly while still on the grill to melt the butter.

Yield: 4 servings

Calories per serving: 160

Protein per serving: 27g

Fat per serving: 4g

  Saturated fat per serving: 1g

Cholesterol per serving: 73mg

Carbohydrates per serving: 2g

Sodium per serving: 184mg

Fiber per serving: trace

GRILLED CHICKEN BREAST WITH BLACKENED TOMATO SALSA

The simple process of blackening the plum tomatoes and the fresh chili lends a rich, smoky flavor to the salsa, which will keep up to two weeks chilled. Use it to enhance green beans, as a dip for raw vegetables and no-oil taco chips, or to flavor an egg white omelet. The recipe-ready tomatoes called for are available at most major markets in the canned tomato section. Be sure to select those that are not processed with oil.

4 skinless, boneless chicken breasts

4 plum tomatoes

1 fresh jalapeño pepper

1 14¹/₂-ounce can recipe-ready tomatoes

1 cup diced red onion

2 cloves garlic

2 tablespoons minced fresh parsley

¹/₃ cup minced fresh coriander, stemmed

1 teaspoon dried oregano

1 teaspoon salt

minced parsley or coriander for garnish (optional)

Yield of chicken: 4 servings

Calories per serving: 160

Protein per serving: 27g

Fat per serving: 3g

   Saturated fat per serving: 1g

Cholesterol per serving: 73mg

Carbohydrates per serving: 4g

Sodium per serving: 220mg

Fiber per serving: 1g

Yield of salsa: 3¹/₂ cups

Calories per tablespoon: 5

Protein per tablespoon: trace

Fat per tablespoon: trace

   Saturated fat per tablespoon: trace

Cholesterol per tablespoon: 0

Carbohydrates per tablespoon: 1g

Sodium per tablespoon: 43mg

Fiber per tablespoon: trace

To Prepare the Salsa

1. Place the plum tomatoes and jalapeño in a small skillet over high heat. Add no oil or liquid. Shake the skillet from time to time until tomato and jalapeño skins are blistered and blackened, about 12 to 15 minutes. Remove from skillet and cool.

2. When cool enough to handle, quarter the tomatoes (no need to discard the skin) and place in the bowl of a food processor. Wearing rubber gloves,

hold the jalapeños under running cool water and peel and discard the blackened skin. Split in half and discard seeds and stem. Add flesh to food processor.

3. Process a few seconds to chop up tomatoes. Add all remaining ingredients. Salsa will keep in the refrigerator up to two weeks.

To Prepare the Chicken

1. Spray the chicken breasts with nonstick cooking spray or dip a pastry brush in oil and lightly brush over the chicken. Heat a grill or broiler. Grill the chicken breasts, spreading salsa on the chicken as it cooks to keep it from drying out. Flip the chicken after about 5 minutes and grill on the other side about 3 minutes more, again topping with salsa.

2. Serve with additional salsa at the table. Garnish with chopped parsley or coriander if desired.

Thinking Thin Tip

Portion control is vital to weight control. Invest in a small food scale and use it until you can pretty well judge what a 4-ounce portion looks like.

SESAME CHICKEN SALAD

This chicken salad is Chinese in spirit with its soy marinade, Japanese in soul with its yolk-enhanced grilling technique (see Nutrition Note on the next page), and very much "today" with its lightness, attention to color, and emphasis on vegetables. It is served warm, not chilled.

6 tablespoons reduced-sodium soy sauce

2 tablespoons rice wine vinegar, available at oriental or specialty food shops

1 scallion, minced

a quarter-size piece of fresh ginger root, peeled and diced

1 teaspoon sesame oil, available at oriental or specialty food shops

4 boneless, skinless chicken breasts

1 egg yolk

3 tablespoons chicken broth

1 scant teaspoon sugar

1 carrot, cut into narrow strips about 3 inches long

1 small zucchini, cut like the carrot

1 small summer squash, cut like the carrot

red leaf lettuce

2 tablespoons sesame seeds, toasted

Yield: 4 servings

Calories per serving: 239

Protein per serving: 31g

Fat per serving: 8g

  Saturated fat per serving: 2g

Cholesterol per serving: 126mg

Carbohydrates per serving: 11g

Sodium per serving: 983mg

Fiber per serving: 2g

1. Combine the soy sauce, vinegar, scallion, ginger, and sesame oil in a bowl. Pour the mixture into a leakproof plastic bag or shallow baking dish, add the chicken, and marinate overnight or at least 4 hours in the refrigerator.

2. Drain the chicken, reserving marinade. Mix 4 tablespoons marinade with the egg yolk and set aside.

3. Mix the remaining soy marinade with the chicken broth and sugar. Set aside.

4. Bring a 2½-quart saucepan three quarters full of water to a boil. Add the carrots, 30 seconds later add the zucchini, and 30 seconds later add the squash. Time 1 minute more, drain and cool under running water. Toss the vegetables with half the soy-broth-sugar mixture from Step 3. Set aside while preparing chicken.

5. Grill chicken 3 minutes on each side, basting frequently with the yolk-enriched marinade. When the chicken is cooked (firm when poked with a finger), remove and slice in thin strips on the diagonal.

6. Line a serving platter with the lettuce. Drizzle with the remaining dressing from Step 3. Place dressing-tossed vegetables on lettuce and chicken strips arranged in a V-shaped column down the center. Sprinkle with toasted sesame seeds.

Note: To toast sesame seeds, place them in a skillet over high heat until they pop, shaking constantly. Sodium-reduced soy sauce is available in many markets for those wishing to restrict the amount of sodium.

Nutrition Note

While it is true that egg yolks are high in cholesterol, containing about 213 milligrams each, the American Heart Association does not suggest they must be eliminated from the diet altogether. The current advice is to eat no more than 4 whole eggs per week.

Apricot-Orange Glazed Chicken

This inexpensive, quick family meal goes well with curried rice flecked with a little red pepper. To speed preparation, look for prechopped ginger, sold in some specialty produce markets. While the recipe specifies thighs, skinned whole cut-up chicken or chicken legs would be just as successful.

12 chicken thighs, skinned

5 tablespoons instant-blending flour

1 teaspoon salt

freshly ground pepper to taste

1/4 teaspoon crushed red pepper

1 cup orange juice

2 tablespoons dry sherry

2 tablespoons apricot preserves or orange marmalade, fruit only

1 teaspoon minced fresh ginger root

1 teaspoon stone-ground mustard

1/2 teaspoon minced garlic

3 tablespoons golden raisins

1/2 orange, very thinly sliced (optional)

Yield: 6 servings

Calories per serving: 294

Protein per serving: 28g

Fat per serving: 12g

  Saturated fat per serving: 3g

Cholesterol per serving: 98mg

Carbohydrates per serving: 17g

Sodium per serving: 463mg

Fiber per serving: trace

1. Combine the chicken, flour, salt, pepper, and crushed red pepper in a plastic bag. Seal bag and shake to coat chicken evenly. Place chicken in a microwave-safe 1-gallon container.

2. Combine the orange juice, sherry, preserves, ginger root, mustard, and garlic in a glass measuring cup. Microwave at high (100 percent power) for 2 minutes or until preserves are melted. Mix well. Pour over chicken.

3. *Add raisins to chicken. Cover and microwave at high (100 percent power) for 10 minutes. Turn chicken over. Microwave at medium-high (75 percent power) for 20 minutes, turning once. Let chicken rest 5 minutes before serving.* Alternately, bake chicken in a 350-degree oven for 1 hour. Garnish with orange slices if desired.

CHICKEN SAUTE WITH CEPES

This recipe is ideal for today's overscheduled cook who's bored with routine meals. In just 15 minutes you can turn out a moist chicken breast with a sauce perked by raspberry vinegar and cepes. Serve it with Pea and Leek Puree (page 253) and a simple rice studded with a handful of golden raisins.

Yield: 4 servings

Calories per serving: 175

Protein per serving: 28g

Fat per serving: 5g

   Saturated fat per serving: 1g

Cholesterol per serving: 74mg

Carbohydrates per serving: 4g

Sodium per serving: 111mg

Fiber per serving: 1g

³/₄ cup chicken broth

1 ounce dried cepes (or porcini), available at specialty food shops

4 boneless and skinless chicken breasts

3 tablespoons raspberry or red wine vinegar

1 clove garlic, minced

12 mushrooms, sliced

1 tablespoon reduced-calorie margarine

1 tablespoon minced fresh parsley (optional)

1. *Combine the broth and cepes in a glass measuring cup or other microwave-safe container. Cover with plastic wrap and heat at high power (100 percent) for 17 minutes.* Set aside. Alternately, bring the broth to a boil. Break the cepes up in your fingers, add them to the hot broth, cover, and steep 20 minutes. Set aside.

2. Spray a 10-inch nonstick skillet with nonstick cooking spray. Place on high heat. When hot, add the chicken. Cover and saute 3 minutes, reducing heat if needed to avoid burning. Turn the chicken, cover, and continue to saute 3 minutes more, again reducing heat if needed. When chicken is firm to the touch, place it on a serving platter in a 150-degree oven while completing the sauce.

3. Remove the skillet from heat. Deglaze it with vinegar. Return the skillet to heat when sizzling stops and boil until the vinegar is reduced to a film on the bottom of skillet.

4. Wet a coffee filter (or a piece of cheesecloth or heavy paper towel), and suspend it in a wide-mouthed jar or measuring cup. Pour the mushroom-broth liquid through, removing cepes with a slotted spoon.

5. Pour the strained mushroom liquid into the vinegar skillet. Add garlic, mushrooms, and cepes. Boil until the liquid is reduced to about ⅓ cup.

6. Reduce heat to medium-low. Whisk in the margarine, pour sauce over chicken, and sprinkle with parsley if desired.

CHICKEN FRICASSEE WITH LEEKS AND CARROTS

This economical meal makes the most of some rather simple ingredients. Chicken thighs (you may use the whole leg for larger servings) are braised with leeks and carrots, then served up in a rich sauce that promises everything but high calories. True to its word, this dish pleases children and parents alike. The chicken thighs may be made ahead and kept chilled for up to 6 hours before cooking. You also may freeze them. This dish is also good reheated.

Yield: 4 servings

Calories per serving: 364

Protein per serving: 38g

Fat per serving: 15g

   Saturated fat per serving: 4g

Cholesterol per serving: 132mg

Carbohydrates per serving: 13g

Sodium per serving: 307mg

Fiber per serving: 2g

8 or 9 chicken thighs (about 2½ pounds), skinned

¼ teaspoon salt

freshly ground pepper to taste

1 cup chicken broth

1 cup dry red wine

1 sprig fresh tarragon or 1 teaspoon dried tarragon

1 bay leaf

1 clove garlic, minced

a few grindings fresh pepper

4 leeks, white part only, thinly sliced

2 carrots, scrubbed and julienned

1 teaspoon cornstarch

1 tablespoon chicken broth or wine

8–10 washed and dried fresh spinach leaves, stems and spines removed

1. Season chicken with salt and pepper.

2. Spray a 12-inch nonstick skillet with cooking spray. Add the chicken, cover, and brown for 5 minutes over high heat. When browned, add broth, wine, tarragon, bay leaf, garlic, pepper, leeks, and carrots. Cover and simmer.

3. Transfer the chicken and vegetables to a heated platter. Dissolve the cornstarch in the remaining broth. Remove and discard the bay leaf from cooking broth. Whisk in the dissolved cornstarch and stir until thickened over medium heat.

4. Make a stack of the spinach leaves. Roll them tightly. Slice them crosswise into thin strips (known as chiffonade). Add the spinach to the sauce over high heat. Stir for 30 seconds or just until wilted. Pour the sauce around chicken.

How to Chiffonade

1. Stack the lettuce, or other item, to be cut, then roll it up tightly, jellyroll fashion.

2. Slice it crosswise into thin strips.

PARCHMENT CHICKEN WITH TOMATO VINAIGRETTE

Oven poaching a chicken breast in oodles of sweet butter is neat, simple, and fattening. Neat and simple is nice, but fattening is as welcome as the taxman. Here the French technique of oven poaching is adapted, omitting the butter and encasing the poultry in parchment paper, which seals in the natural juices of the bird and anything else you might add, such as the tangy Tomato Vinaigrette used here. Or the chicken may be oven poached in its packet and lathered with a sauce after the fact. This Tomato Vinaigrette is one with panache. The feather in its cap is a dash of vinegar—just the right touch for a moist and juicy chicken breast. Because the sauce is actually better the second day, make some ahead; it will keep under refrigeration for about a week. The Hollandaise, the Béarnaise, the Basil Salsa, all in Chapter 2, or the Lemon Caper Sauce (page 218) also would be appropriate.

For the Chicken

1 boneless, skinless chicken breast

1/8 teaspoon salt

freshly ground pepper to taste

2 tablespoons Tomato Vinaigrette, recipe follows

2 or 3 mushrooms, sliced

parchment paper, available in specialty food shops

To Prepare the Chicken

1. Preheat oven to 425 degrees. Trim the breast of fat and gristle. Place on a square of parchment paper (see page 216 for instructions on wrapping food in parchment paper hearts if preferred). Sprinkle the chicken with salt and pepper, spoon on the Tomato Vinaigrette, and place mushrooms on top. Fold the paper around the chicken as you would for a sandwich. Place on a baking sheet in the preheated 425-degree oven. Cook for 12–15 minutes.
2. To serve, open and discard the paper and spoon juices over chicken.

Yield of Chicken: 1 serving

Calories per serving: 164

Protein per serving: 28g

Fat per serving: 3g

  Saturated fat per serving: 1g

Cholesterol per serving: 73mg

Carbohydrates per serving: 5g

Sodium per serving: 420mg

Fiber per serving: 1g

Yield of Vinaigrette: 1¾ cups (serving size 2 tablespoons)

Calories per serving: 13

Protein per serving: trace

Fat per serving: trace

  Saturated fat per serving: trace

Cholesterol per serving: 0

Carbohydrates per serving: 3g

Sodium per serving: 85mg

Fiber per serving: 1g

Tomato Vinaigrette

A wonderfully versatile sauce, Tomato Vinaigrette may be a thick but thinning hot or cold soup, tossed with marinated chilled zucchini as a salad and used as a braising sauce for veal chops or grilled chicken. It is best, though, made with tomatoes plump with the sun, rather than those ripened by ethylene gas.

> *1¹/₂ pounds tomatoes (2–3 large), quartered*
>
> *1 tomato, blanched, peeled, seeded, and chopped*
>
> *1 tablespoon raspberry or red wine vinegar*
>
> *4–6 fresh basil leaves or 1 teaspoon dried basil*
>
> *1 tablespoon minced fresh parsley*
>
> *1 teaspoon sugar*
>
> *¹/₂ teaspoon salt*
>
> *3–4 drops hot pepper sauce*

1. Quarter the tomatoes, place in a heavy-bottomed saucepan, cover, and bring to a boil over medium heat. Simmer, uncovered, 45–50 minutes or until somewhat reduced.

2. Puree the tomatoes in a food processor, blender, or food mill. Strain the tomatoes into a bowl to remove the seeds and skin.

3. Add the remaining tomato to the bowl along with the oil, vinegar, basil, parsley, sugar, salt, and pepper sauce. Stir to combine.

Thinking Thin Tip

A gram of carbohydrate and protein each supply 4 calories; a gram of fat supplies 9 calories.

CHICKEN BOUILLABAISSE

Bouillabaisse—a mélange of tomatoes and leeks flavored with saffron—is a natural in low-fat cookery. Use this recipe as a starting point and let your imagination run. Without the chicken, this could be a sauce for white fish and/or shellfish, or you could simmer vegetables such as zucchini, summer squash, and fresh corn kernels in the bouillabaisse until cooked, then spoon it over thick slabs of grilled bread and pass freshly grated Parmesan at the table. Low-fat, low-calorie, fabulously flavorful and satisfying. Serve this bouillabaisse with Risotto (page 281) or with plain rice. This is excellent the second day.

Yield: 6 servings

Calories per serving: 126

Protein per serving: 15g

Fat per serving: 2g

  Saturated fat per serving: 1g

Cholesterol per serving: 46mg

Carbohydrates per serving: 11g

Sodium per serving: 413mg

Fiber per serving: 2g

3 leeks, white part only, chopped

2 cloves garlic, minced

1 shallot, minced

³/₄ cup chicken broth or white or rosé wine

*5–6 tomatoes (about 1¹/₂ to 1³/₄ pounds), peeled and seeded, juice
    reserved*

¹/₄ cup orange juice or the juice of 1 orange

zest of 1 orange (optional)

1 bay leaf

1 teaspoon dried thyme

1 teaspoon sugar

1 teaspoon salt and freshly ground pepper to taste

¹/₂ teaspoon fennel seed

¹/₄ teaspoon ground saffron or a pinch of saffron threads

1 cut-up broiler chicken, skinned (about 2 pounds), wings discarded

To Microwave

1. Combine the leeks, garlic, shallot, and chicken broth in a 4-cup glass measuring cup or other microwave-safe dish. Cover and microwave at high power (100 percent) for 6 minutes.

2. Add all the remaining ingredients except the chicken. Stir, cover, and cook at high (100 percent power) for 6 minutes.

3. Place the chicken in a single layer in a 1-gallon microwave-safe container. Add leek and tomato mixture. Cover. Microwave at high power (100 percent) for 15 minutes; stir and microwave at medium power (50 percent) for 30 minutes more. Let rest 5 minutes before serving.

To Cook in a Crockpot

1. Combine the leeks, garlic, shallot, and chicken broth in an 8-inch skillet and saute over medium high heat, stirring often until the leeks are softened, about 10 minutes. Scrape into a crockpot.

2. Add all remaining ingredients. Cover and cook at high heat 1 hour, then reduce heat to low and simmer an additional 4 to 5 hours. Stir occasionally. Remove cover the last hour of cooking.

Thinking Thin Tip

Don't baste that turkey or roast chicken with oils or butter. Use broth heated with a little reduced-calorie margarine for equally good and skinnier results.

Stir-Fried Chicken and Vegetables

The signature of the world's oldest cuisine, the stir-fry, may be tailored to fit the modern principles of good nutrition perfectly. This recipe is rich in carbohydrates, while frugal with both proteins and fats. Just 10–12 ounces of meat or poultry with the bountiful use of vegetables and rice easily feeds 4. Stir-fries are also quick to cook once the chopping and slicing are accomplished, a task that can often be done as much as 5 hours in advance. This stir-fry is made spicy with hot red pepper and chili paste—both may be omitted if a milder dish is preferred. All this dish needs is a side of rice or Chinese noodles to complete the meal. The oriental ingredients are available at specialty or Chinese food shops.

Yield: 4 servings

Calories per serving: 225

Protein per serving: 25g

Fat per serving: 7g

    Saturated fat per serving: 2g

Cholesterol per serving: 59mg

Carbohydrates per serving: 14g

Sodium per serving: 380mg

Fiber per serving: 2g

2 tablespoons reduced-sodium soy sauce

1 tablespoon rice wine or semisweet sherry

1 tablespoon rice wine vinegar (white wine vinegar may be substituted)

1 teaspoon sesame oil

2 tablespoons chicken broth

2 teaspoons sugar

1 clove garlic, minced

1 stalk green onion, minced

a 1-inch piece ginger root, peeled and minced

³/₄ pound skinless, boneless breast of chicken

1 tablespoon vegetable or peanut oil

¹/₂ red bell pepper, sliced

¹/₂ green bell pepper, sliced

8 ounces fresh mushrooms, sliced

1 cup Chinese cabbage, sliced

1 carrot, blanched 5 minutes and julienned

4 ounces snow peas, strings removed

¹/₂–1 teaspoon minced hot chili pepper (optional)

¹/₂–1 teaspoon chili paste with garlic (optional)

2 teaspoons cornstarch

¹/₃ cup chicken broth

1. Combine the soy sauce, wine, vinegar, sesame oil, broth, sugar, garlic, onion, and ginger in a measuring cup. Mix well. Pour it into a plastic bag.

2. Cut the chicken into thin strips and marinate in the above soy mixture for 2 hours in the refrigerator or 20 minutes at room temperature.

3. Heat the oil in a wok or heavy 10-inch skillet until very hot. Lift the chicken from the soy marinade a few pieces at a time (reserving the marinade for Step 7). Stir-fry in hot oil until flesh firms and becomes opaque, about 4 minutes.

4. Remove the chicken with a slotted spoon or chopsticks and drain on paper towels. Continue stir-frying until all the chicken is cooked.

5. Add the peppers and mushrooms to wok. Add a bit of chicken broth or oil if necessary. Stir-fry for 1 minute. Add the Chinese cabbage and stir-fry another minute. Add the carrots and snow peas, and stir-fry about 1 minute more or until pea pods are done.

6. Stir in the chili pepper and paste if desired.

7. Moisten the cornstarch in the chicken broth; combine it with the reserved marinade from Step 3. Add to the vegetables along with the cooked chicken. Stir until thickened over high heat. Serve with boiled rice or noodles.

POACHED CHICKEN BREAST WITH MUSTARD HOLLANDAISE

Reheating a traditional Hollandaise is a bit like space-walking: There's little room for error. You won't find yourself in orbit, though, with the *Gourmet Light* version; it may be made early in the day and reheated over low heat. Or you may choose to keep it warm in a bowl set atop an electric warming tray. Serve this dish with the Pea and Leek Puree (page 253) and some broccoli or a rice pilaf.

1 scallion or half a small onion, minced

1 sprig fresh tarragon or ½ teaspoon dried tarragon

1 cup water

4 chicken breasts, with skin and bones

juice of half a lemon

1 recipe Hollandaise, page 24

1 tablespoon stone-ground mustard, or to taste

minced fresh parsley or watercress (optional)

Yield: 4 servings

Calories per serving: 192

Protein per serving: 27g

Fat per serving: 7g

Saturated fat per serving: 2g

Cholesterol per serving: 66mg

Carbohydrates per serving: 3g

Sodium per serving: 253mg

Fiber per serving: trace

1. In a food processor or blender, combine the scallion, tarragon, and water. Blend.

2. Pour into a skillet just large enough to hold the chicken. Add chicken, skin side down. Add the lemon juice. Add water to cover. Bring to a boil, then immediately reduce to a simmer. Cover and cook 15–20 minutes or until the chicken flesh feels firm when poked with a finger.

3. Remove the chicken with a slotted spoon (cooking liquid may be reserved for making stock).

4. Meanwhile, make the *Gourmet Light* Hollandaise. Stir in the mustard and set aside.

5. Discard the skin. Lift the chicken from bones in one piece, place on warmed plates. Spoon Hollandaise over and garnish with the parsley or watercress if desired.

Scotch Chicken

Chicken, cream, and mushrooms make for a tempting trilogy often found in French cooking. What a pity the cream brings out the calorie-conscious cringes. Fortunately, there's crème blanc, the *Gourmet Light* replacement for overfatted dairy products. The sauce base must be cooled a full minute as directed to avoid a curdled mess. Vary this simple supper with the addition of some dried mushrooms such as cepes or chanterelles.

2 boneless, skinless chicken breasts

¹/₈ teaspoon salt

freshly ground pepper to taste

2 tablespoons Scotch

¹/₂ cup chicken broth

4 ounces mushrooms, sliced

1 tablespoon crème blanc, page 34, or nonfat sour cream

a few gratings fresh nutmeg

Yield: 2 servings

Calories per serving: 183

Protein per serving: 29g

Fat per serving: 4g

Saturated fat per serving: 1g

Cholesterol per serving: 75mg

Carbohydrates per serving: 4g

Sodium per serving: 219mg

Fiber per serving: 1g

1. Place the chicken in a 10-inch nonstick skillet that has been sprayed with nonstick cooking spray. Season chicken with salt and pepper. Sear it, covered, over high heat 3 minutes. Turn the chicken over, reduce heat to medium, cover, and continue cooking another 3–4 minutes.

2. Transfer the chicken from skillet to plate. Off the heat, deglaze the skillet with the Scotch. When the liquor quiets down, return to high heat, stirring constantly with a wooden spoon to loosen the particles stuck to the pan bottom. Reduce the liquid until it's just a film.

3. Add the broth and mushrooms to the skillet, cover, and boil, stirring occasionally until it's reduced to about 3 tablespoons liquid.

4. Remove the skillet from heat, stir, and cool about 1 minute. Stir in crème blanc, season with nutmeg, and pour it over the chicken.

Herbed Chicken Breasts

This recipe calls for stuffing the breast with an herbed rice mixture. Bag the proverbial two birds with one stone by doubling the stuffing portion and serving it as a side dish. All you need then to complete the meal is a salad or possibly some broccoli with *Gourmet Light* Hollandaise, which will also complement the chicken. Although this dish needs no sauce, you might like to nap it with the Tomato Vinaigrette, page 174, the Lemon Caper Sauce, page 218, or the Reduced-Calorie Béarnaise, page 25.

Yield: 4 servings

Calories per serving: 192

Protein per serving: 28g

Fat per serving: 3g

  Saturated fat per serving: 1g

Cholesterol per serving: 73mg

Carbohydrates per serving: 11g

Sodium per serving: 334mg

Fiber per serving: 1g

1/2 small green pepper, diced

1/2 small onion, diced

4 tablespoons chicken broth

1/2 cup cooked white or brown rice

5–6 mushrooms, sliced

5 leaves fresh or oil-cured basil, snipped, or 1 teaspoon dried basil

1/2 teaspoon salt

freshly ground pepper to taste

4 boneless, skinless chicken breasts

1. "Saute" the green pepper and onion in 3 tablespoons broth (reserving 1 tablespoon for Step 3), covered, in an 8-inch skillet until limp.

2. Combine the pepper and onion with the rice.

3. "Saute" the mushrooms in the same skillet with the remaining tablespoon broth until limp. Add it to the rice-pepper mixture.

4. Stir basil, 1/4 teaspoon salt, and pepper into the rice mixture.

5. Cut a pocket in the chicken breast by pressing down on the skin side with one hand while slicing parallel with the counter top almost, but not all the way, to the back of the breast. Open the breast (like a book) and stuff it with a tablespoon of the rice-pepper mixture. Lay the meat back over stuffing; it will "glue" together while cooking. Lift a chicken breast onto a baking dish.

Repeat with the remaining chicken breasts. Sprinkle with the remaining salt. Refrigerate, if desired, up to 6 hours, until ready to cook.

6. Roast the chicken breasts, covered with foil, in a preheated 350-degree oven for 20 minutes.

CHICKEN BAKED IN A SALT CRUST

Meats and poultry roasted in a crust of salt are amazingly succulent, flavorful, and juicy. The moistened salt forms a shell, locking in moisture that would otherwise evaporate. Happily, the salt doesn't penetrate the food either. For this family meal, a broiler is stuffed with rice seasoned with a garlic puree (made mild by a long simmer), trussed to keep the legs from breaking through the salt crust, then roasted. Carve the bird and serve on a platter with the natural juices retrieved from the carving board. The rice stuffing may be prepared a day ahead or early in the day, the chicken stuffed and packed in salt just before roasting. Although the bird does take 2 hours to cook, it is not lengthy to prepare for roasting, and all you need to complete the meal is a green vegetable or salad.

Yield: 4 servings

Calories per serving: 424

Protein per serving: 41g

Fat per serving: 10g
   Saturated fat per serving: 3g

Cholesterol per serving: 112mg

Carbohydrates per serving: 40g

Sodium per serving: 384mg

Fiber per serving: 1g

1 2- or 3-pound broiler chicken

1 whole head garlic, cloves separated

2½ cups cooked rice

1 small tomato, diced

*4–5 fresh basil leaves or 1 teaspoon
   dried basil*

½ teaspoon salt

freshly ground pepper to taste

10 cups kosher salt

1¾ cups water

1. Prepare the bird for roasting by cutting off the excess fat at the cavity opening. Cut off the wing tips at the joint, add them to your bone collection for making stock, or discard. Set aside the bird while preparing the stuffing.

2. Separate but don't peel the garlic cloves. Bring a 1-quart saucepan ¾ full of water to a boil. Boil the garlic cloves 1 minute, lift with a slotted spoon to a sieve, and cool under running water. Slip skins off. Return peeled cloves to boiling water and simmer 30 minutes. Drain, reserving 2–3 tablespoons cooking water. Puree the garlic in a food processor, adding reserved cooking water as needed, or force through a fine mesh sieve with a wooden spoon.

3. Combine the cooked rice, garlic puree, tomato, basil, salt, and pepper. Adjust seasoning if necessary.

4. Stuff the cavity of the chicken with the rice mixture, but don't pack too tightly; any remaining rice may be heated in a small casserole the last 20 minutes of roasting. To truss the bird, which will keep the legs from breaking through the salt crust during baking, follow the illustrations on the next page, or use another trussing technique. Pack any stuffing that might have come loose back into cavity.

5. Preheat oven to 475 degrees.

6. Line a roasting pan big enough for the chicken with a sheet of aluminum foil that extends 10 inches over short sides.

7. Moisten the salt with some of the water, but don't use all the water at once. Paste should be just wet enough to hold together when packed with your hands. Place about a third of the paste on the foil-lined roasting pan. Place the chicken on top. Pack the remaining salt all around the bird, covering any exposed spots. Pull the foil up snug to the bird; use it to help pack down the salt. Roast in the lower third of a preheated 475-degree oven for 2 hours.

8. To serve, peel back the foil. Break and discard the top salt crust. Lift the chicken from roasting pan by the trussing string to a cutting board or plate, one that will trap the juices. Snip and discard string. Brush away any clinging salt. Pull and discard skin from bird. To carve, cut off legs first, cut in half at the joint. Cut off breast meat. Flip bird, remove skin, cut back in half. Scoop stuffing on to serving platter. Dribble juices from cutting board on to chicken.

Thinking Thin Tip

Check serving sizes when reading labels. Some manufacturers paint a misleading, yet pretty, nutritional picture by analyzing smaller-than-average serving sizes.

How to Truss a Chicken

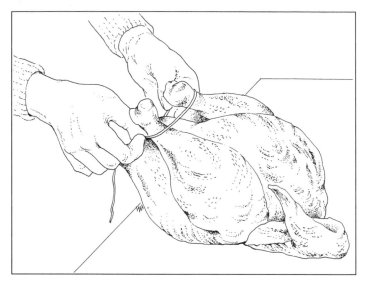

1. Fold a three- or four-foot length of butcher's twine in half, then lay the midsection over the knee joints of the whole chicken.

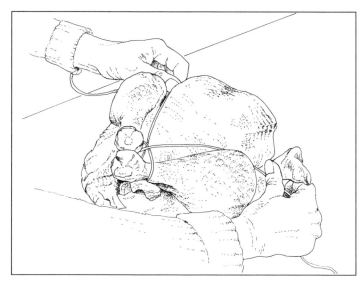

2. "Lasso" the leg ends by pulling the twine up, then lay the twine in the hollow between the leg and the breast.

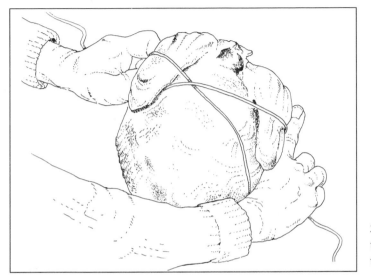

3. Flip the chicken over and cross the twine. Pull the wings snug to the body by laying the twine over them.

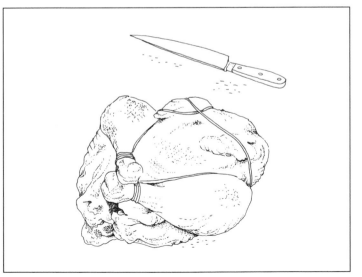

4. Flip the chicken back over so the breast side is up. Knot the twine and cut off the excess.

POACHED CHICKEN BREASTS WITH HONEY-MUSTARD SAUCE

Quick, delicious, and very low in fat. There are two ingredients in this recipe to note. The chicken base called for is available at most markets in the spice section. A concentrated chicken bouillon, it is very useful to have on hand for flavoring sauces. The other ingredient, which might raise an eyebrow, is the skimmed evaporated milk. Another staple in the fat-conscious pantry, it lends the thickness of cream without the fat. Seasonings such as sherry, honey, and mustard—all nonfat—contribute the flavor.

4 boneless, skinless chicken breasts

For Honey-Mustard Sauce

1 tablespoon reduced-calorie margarine
2 scallions, white part only, minced
4 ounces mushrooms, sliced thinly
1/4 cup dry sherry
1 teaspoon cornstarch
2/3 cup evaporated skimmed milk
1 teaspoon stone-ground mustard
1 teaspoon honey
1/2 teaspoon paprika
1/2 teaspoon salt
freshly ground pepper to taste
1/8 teaspoon chicken-flavored base

Yield of Chicken: 4 servings
Calories per serving: 217
Protein per serving: 31g
Fat per serving: 5g
  Saturated fat per serving: 1g
Cholesterol per serving: 75mg
Carbohydrates per serving: 9g
Sodium per serving: 453mg
Fiber per serving: 1g

Yield of Sauce: 2/3 cup
Calories per tablespoon: 27
Protein per tablespoon: 1g
Fat per tablespoon: 1g
  Saturated fat per tablespoon: trace
Cholesterol per tablespoon: 1mg
Carbohydrates per tablespoon: 3g
Sodium per tablespoon: 133mg
Fiber per tablespoon: trace

1. Melt the margarine in a heavy-bottom 1-quart saucepan until bubbling. Add the scallions and mushrooms and saute over medium-high heat 3 minutes or until vegetables are limp.

2. Add the sherry and boil until liquid is reduced to about 2 tablespoons.

3. While the sherry reduces, poach (or microwave) the chicken. To poach, fill a skillet just large enough to hold the chicken ¾ full of water (add a bouillon cube if you wish to intensify the flavor). Bring to a boil. Add chicken, cover, reduce heat to medium, and poach for 15 to 20 minutes. Water should just barely bubble; a fast boil will toughen the meat. Drain and cool. To microwave, place the chicken in a microwave-safe dish, cover with plastic wrap and cook at high (100 percent power) for 4 minutes (longer if doing more than a single breast) or until flesh is firm. Let rest 5 minutes.

4. When the sherry has reduced, dissolve the cornstarch in the milk. Add the remaining ingredients. Stir this mixture into the sherry-mushrooms. Stir over medium heat until thickened, about 1 minute.

5. Arrange chicken breasts on a platter and nap with the sauce. Garnish with a dash of paprika, if desired.

CHICKEN AND PASTA SALAD WITH GOLDEN RAISINS AND CAPERS

Here is a delicious pasta salad with absolutely no added fat, thanks to a dressing based on egg whites instead of the more traditional yolk and/or oil dressing. Use a food processor to make quick work of julienning the vegetables. To roast peppers, refer to the illustrated directions on page 259, or purchase a jar of roasted peppers from the Italian section of your market. Serve the salad at room temperature.

1 1/2 cups water

1 chicken bouillon cube

4 split chicken breasts, with bones and skin

1 leek, white only, julienned

1 summer squash, julienned

1 zucchini, julienned

1 carrot, julienned

8 ounces vermicelli or other thin pasta, cooked according to package instructions

1/2 cup roasted red peppers, sliced thinly

1/4 cup golden raisins

2 tablespoons or to taste capers

2 egg whites

1 tablespoon lemon juice

2 tablespoons fat-free mayonnaise

1 tablespoon honey

2 teaspoons curry powder

1/2 teaspoon cumin powder

Yield: 4 servings

Calories per serving: 463

Protein per serving: 37g

Fat per serving: 6g

　Saturated fat per serving: 1g

Cholesterol per serving: 73mg

Carbohydrates per serving: 66g

Sodium per serving: 905mg

Fiber per serving: 5g

1 teaspoon Dijon-style mustard
1 teaspoon prepared horseradish
1 teaspoon salt
freshly ground pepper to taste
1 tablespoon minced fresh parsley (optional)

1. In a skillet just large enough to hold the chicken, bring the water and bouillon cube to a boil. Add the chicken, skin side down, cover, bring back to a boil, and then reduce heat to a simmer. Cook 15 minutes or until chicken flesh feels firm.

2. Remove chicken with a slotted spoon, and set it aside to cool. Reserve the broth.

3. While the chicken is cooking, *combine leek, summer squash, zucchini, and carrot in a 4-cup glass measuring cup or other microwave-safe container. Add 3 tablespoons water, cover with plastic wrap, and microwave on high (100 percent power) for 4 minutes.* Alternately, steam the vegetables until tender-crisp.

4. Drain vegetables and combine them in a bowl with the pasta, red pepper, raisins, and capers. Set aside.

5. To make the dressing, beat the egg whites and lemon juice in the bowl of a food processor for 30 seconds or until frothy. Bring the chicken cooking broth to a boil. Dribble 4 tablespoons of the hot broth into the whites with the processor on full power. Add remaining ingredients. Taste to correct seasoning.

6. Discard the skin and bones from the chicken. Shred the meat into the pasta-vegetable mixture. Toss with the dressing. Garnish with parsley if desired.

TURKEY CUTLET WITH CRANBERRIED APPLE SAUCE

Turkey cutlets—thin slices from the breast—make a quick and satisfying meal not unlike veal. If cutlets aren't available in your market, they may be cut from a whole turkey breast and the remainder of the breast may be roasted or smoked (page 191). Purchase cranberries in the fall and freeze them whole in the plastic bag for up to a year, scooping out just what you need for this sauce, which may be made ahead and reheated.

Yield: 4 servings

Calories per serving: 238

Protein per serving: 35g

Fat per serving: 4g

  Saturated fat per serving: 1g

Cholesterol per serving: 78mg

Carbohydrates per serving: 13g

Sodium per serving: 340mg

Fiber per serving: 1g

¹/₂ cup chicken broth

¹/₂ cup uncooked cranberries

2 medium apples, McIntosh recommended, peeled, cored, and chopped

¹/₃ cup flour

¹/₂ teaspoon salt

freshly ground pepper to taste

1¹/₄ pounds turkey cutlets

4 tablespoons dry sherry

6 tablespoons chicken broth

¹/₂ cup of the cranberry-apple sauce

thin orange slices for garnish (optional)

1. In a 1-quart saucepan, combine the broth, cranberries, and apples. Bring to a boil, reduce heat, and simmer 10 minutes. Puree in a food processor, food mill, or blender. Set this cranberry-apple sauce aside.

2. Season the flour with the salt and pepper. Dredge the cutlets in the flour.

3. Spray a 12-inch nonstick skillet with cooking spray. Add the floured cutlets and sear them over high heat 1 minute. Reduce heat, cook 1 minute more, turn, and repeat the procedure. Meat is done when it feels firm to the touch. Transfer to a heated platter while completing the sauce.

4. Deglaze the skillet with sherry, stirring over high heat with a wooden spoon to loosen the coagulated proteins. When reduced to a syrupy glaze, add the broth, and reduce it until ¼ cup remains. Stir in ½ cup or to taste of the cranberry-apple sauce. Remaining cranberry-apple sauce may be kept in the refrigerator for a little more than a week. Serve the sauce over turkey cutlets. Garnish the platter with orange slices if desired.

CHINESE TEA–SMOKED TURKEY

Tea smoking is a lovely way to impart smoked flavor to fish or poultry without a major investment of time or expensive equipment. You need a wok or any pan with a tight cover, such as an electric skillet, and Chinese black tea. While the instructions are written for a boned turkey, you may use a turkey breast or even a chicken. Start the recipe a day before serving, and if using a frozen turkey or breast, 2 days before. The smoked turkey may be served sliced warm or at room temperature or used in other recipes such as a turkey salad. It is wonderful sliced for the buffet table accompanied with small pumpkin biscuits and pots of herbed jellies.

Yield: 12 servings

Calories per serving: 153

Protein per serving: 29g

Fat per serving: 3g

   Saturated fat per serving: 1g

Cholesterol per serving: 68mg

Carbohydrates per serving: 0

Sodium per serving: 328mg

Fiber per serving: 0

1 4-pound boned turkey or turkey breast

1 tablespoon whole black peppercorns

3 tablespoons kosher salt

2 tablespoons Chinese black tea or contents of 4 Chinese tea bags
    (available at specialty food shops)

2 tablespoons uncooked regular rice

2 tablespoons brown sugar

1. Thaw the turkey if frozen and wipe it dry.

2. Combine the peppercorns and salt in a small skillet and saute over medium-high heat until the mixture is fragrant, about 2–3 minutes. Let the mixture cool and rub it into the turkey breast. Wrap the turkey in aluminum foil and refrigerate overnight.

3. Rinse the turkey breast free of peppercorn-salt mixture. Steam the breast in a steamer over 3 inches of water for 40–50 minutes. Remove the breast from steamer, let it stand at room temperature (or refrigerate overnight) until cool (about 2 to 3 hours); pat thoroughly dry. This step is important, for if the meat is not cool and continues to "sweat," the moisture will prevent it from browning in the smoking step.

4. Line a wok or other deep pot that has a tight-fitting lid with a double thickness of aluminum foil. Combine the tea, rice, and sugar. Spread over the foil. Set a rack in the pot. Place the breast on rack, skin side up. Cover and place over medium heat until the tea leaves crackle or wisps of smoke escape. Smoke the turkey for 10 minutes. Remove the lid. If the meat is not browned, cover and smoke another 5 minutes. Discard skin before serving. Turkey is ready to serve or use in any turkey recipe.

Smoked Foods

Smoking foods, used as a preservation technique in a time without refrigeration, has enjoyed a revival of late. Many restaurants feature smoked foods or garnish dishes with smoked tidbits. Smoked turkey breasts, hams, fishes, and shellfish are available by mail from many a modern smokehouse. Those on sodium-restricted diets should know that most smoked foods are treated heavily with salt. Some companies will supply salt-free smoked foods.

FISH AND SHELLFISH

THE RECIPES

FISH AND SHELLFISH

"Food is meant to tempt as well as nourish and everything that lives in the sea is seductive." —JEAN-PAUL ARON

Fish is to the calorie-conscious gourmet what polish is to wood—a gleam on the palate. Few foods are as calorie economic or as nutritionally rich. Yet fish varies in calorie count from variety to variety. So-called fat fish (tuna, salmon, trout, and pompano), with a higher percentage of natural oils, are higher in calories than lean fish (cod, flounder, and red snapper). But a fat fish may need less oils added to it during cooking to avoid drying out.

All fish is high in protein and relatively low in fat. A 3½-ounce serving of flounder supplies 30 grams of protein (¾ of the daily requirement for a 120-pound woman) and 8 grams of fat for a very reasonable 202 calories. A similar-size serving of beef rump supplies somewhat less protein (24 grams) and three times the amount of fat (27 grams) for 347 calories. All other things being equal, substituting fish for beef two nights a week for twelve weeks would save 3,500 calories—which if not converted into energy transforms into a pound of fat.

Care must be taken in the purchase and storage of fish, perhaps more so than with any other food, or the delicate flavor suffers. Today, most of us purchase fish that is already dressed, eviscerated, and scaled, with the head, fins, and tail cut off. Unfortunately, this convenience erases some of the freshness indicators, making it impossible to know if the eyes were bright, clear, and bulging; if the scales were firmly affixed; and if the internal body walls were bright in color with no bones protruding. It really isn't practical to poke fillets, either, but if you were so minded you could judge the fish's freshness by its resiliency, for your fingerprint would not make a lasting impression on a truly fresh fillet. Given the lack of physical evidence, what is a buyer to do?

Your most important clue in shopping for fresh fish is the odor of the fish. A strong smell indicates age, which in turn means poor taste. Unfortunately, fish begins to deteriorate almost as soon as it leaves the water, unlike beef which actually improves with age. This deterioration may be slowed if the fish is kept at about 30 degrees, which does not freeze the flesh but seems to stabilize it. So look for fish sold on ice. There's no way of knowing, of course, if the fish was iced aboard ship or during any processing. But again, the odor of fish cannot be masked, so if the fish you're buying smells fishy, it's time to find a new supplier. Buying from a reputable store should erase fears of purchasing something second rate. A reputable store is one supplied daily, not twice a week—don't hesitate to ask when the product came in.

With the freshest possible fish at hand, the rest is up to the consumer. Just as at market, the fish should be put in a bowl of ice (protected in a plastic bag) in the refrigerator if held more than 4 hours before cooking. Very fresh fish, just 1 or 2 days out of water, will keep this way with very little flavor loss for 3–4 days. Remember to replenish the ice and pour off the water.

Not all parts of the country can get fresh fish; some must use frozen. Properly prepared it can be quite good. Again, there should be no odor, the package should be intact, and the edges of the fish should not be freezer burned.

In most cases, fish cooks quickly. And if it's impeccably fresh, fish needs little adornment. It is one of the few foods that truly needs only "a little lemon juice" to be enjoyable. Following are recipes for more elaborate treatments, because even the most ardent fish fan must yearn for something a little different now and again. You will need to substitute your local varieties of fish in these recipes. Unlike beef or poultry, products that are largely uniform from Anaheim, California, to Bangor, Maine, fish types vary from coast to coast, and in between.

Shellfish, other than shrimp, may be even more regional than fish fillets. Bivalves, such as mussels and clams, should be alive when purchased and cooked. Frozen langoustine is a somewhat credible substitution for lobster. Having been spoiled by Nantucket's November scallops, I am admittedly biased, but many feed happily on the frozen Florida bay variety.

If you've never much cared for fish but are somewhat tempted by its high-nutrition/low-calorie ratio, I urge you to give it a try with the freshest catch money will buy. Good food with little fat, what better lure is there?

SEDONA SHRIMP WITH COCONUT AND CORIANDER

On a trip to Arizona, we enjoyed an outstanding Malaysian-inspired meal in a log cabin nestled beneath dense trees amid the gurgles of a rushing stream. With nary a chili pepper or cactus in sight, the meal was a most delicious anomaly. Here are my efforts to recreate the entree; to my mind, it is perhaps one of the best of this chapter. Double the recipe to serve 4.

Yield: 2 servings

Calories per serving: 342

Protein per serving: 24g

Fat per serving: 5g

    Saturated fat per serving: 2g

Cholesterol per serving: 179mg

Carbohydrates per serving: 42g

Sodium per serving: 344mg

Fiber per serving: 6g

½ red bell pepper, minced

½ carrot, minced

1 leek, white part only, minced

½ zucchini, diced

4 mushrooms, sliced

2 teaspoons reduced-calorie margarine

½ pound jumbo shrimp, shelled

2 tablespoons shredded coconut

¾ cup white wine

1 teaspoon minced fresh coriander

1 cup cooked white rice

1. Saute the pepper, carrot, leek, zucchini, and mushrooms in the margarine in an 8-inch nonstick skillet over medium-high heat about 8 minutes or until softened. Stir often, avoid browning. *Alternately, combine these ingredients in a microwave-safe container. Cover with plastic wrap and microwave at high (100 percent power) for 6 minutes, or until vegetables are softened.*

2. Add the shrimp, shredded coconut, wine, and coriander to vegetables; stir to combine. *To microwave, cook at high (100 percent power) about 8 minutes or until shrimp are pink throughout.* To cook on the stove top, combine the same ingredients in the skillet, cover, and cook over medium-high heat, stirring often until shrimp are pink throughout. Serve over rice.

GRILLED SHRIMP ON WHITE BEANS

Different, but decidedly do-able even when time is tight, this dish makes a first-rate starter or main course when served with a loaf of crusty Italian bread and a crisp tossed salad. Canned white beans curtail cooking chores, but you can prepare your own in the microwave, as indicated below. This recipe serves four as a main course.

1½ pounds jumbo shrimp, shelled and deveined

juice of 1 lemon

⅓ cup rice wine vinegar

2 scallions, minced

2 tablespoons minced fresh tarragon or 1 teaspoon dried tarragon

1 clove garlic, minced

¾ teaspoon salt

1 teaspoon olive oil

2 16-ounce cans white beans, drained

¾ cup diced red onion

¾ cup minced fresh parsley

½ cup minced red pepper

1 large carrot, shredded

4 tablespoons red wine vinegar

1 tablespoon plus 1 teaspoon olive oil

1 tablespoon water

1 teaspoon sugar

1 clove garlic, minced

½ teaspoon salt

freshly ground pepper to taste

Yield: 2–2½ cups cooked beans
Calories per ½ cup: 196
Protein per ½ cup: 9g
Fat per ½ cup: 4g
  Saturated fat per ½ cup: 1g
Cholesterol per ½ cup: 0
Carbohydrates per ½ cup: 32g
Sodium per ½ cup: 216mg
Fiber per ½ cup: 5g

Yield of shrimp: 4 servings
Calories per serving: 127
Protein per serving: 23g
Fat per serving: 2g
  Saturated fat per serving: trace
Cholesterol per serving: 216mg
Carbohydrates per serving: 3g
Sodium per serving: 289mg
Fiber per serving: trace

1. Marinate the shrimp in the lemon juice, rice wine vinegar, scallions, tarragon, garlic, ¾ teaspoon salt, and teaspoon of olive oil for at least 20 minutes or as long as 8 hours.

2. Thread the shrimp on wooden skewers. Spray a mesh grill screen with nonstick cooking spray. Spray the shrimp skewers lightly as well. Grill the shrimp over medium coals about 5 to 6 minutes, turning once or twice and basting frequently with the remaining marinade. Alternately, broil the shrimp until pink and cooked through, about the same length of time.

3. While the shrimp cook, combine the beans in a microwave-safe bowl with the onion, parsley, red pepper, carrot, red wine vinegar, oil, water, sugar, garlic, salt, and pepper. Stir to combine. Cover and microwave at high (100 percent power) for 5 minutes or until hot. Beans may also be served without heating, at room temperature.

4. To serve, spoon beans onto a luncheon plate and top with skewered shrimp.

To Microwave Beans

1. Rinse a heaping cup of white or black beans in a sieve. Remove any stones. Place beans in a microwave-safe 4-quart container, such as a vegetable steamer with a removable basket.

2. Add 2 quarts water, cover, and microwave at high (100 percent power) for 45 minutes. Lift basket from steamer, discard cooking water, and rinse beans under running water one full minute.

3. Refill container with 2 quarts fresh water, replace basket with beans, cover, and cook at high (100 percent power) another 45 minutes or until tender. A quartered unpeeled onion may be added to the cooking water at this time. Rinse beans well. Beans may be refrigerated up to 4 days or frozen up to 3 months.

The New American Grill

Grilling is hot. The day when barbecue meant hamburgers, steaks, and the occasional sausage is past. America's imaginative chefs are grilling everything from shrimp to squab and accompanying dishes with sauces that would leave Grandma gasping. From barbecue Hollandaise to Spicy Plum, from Burgundy Cherry to Mustard Mousse, today's concoctions make ketchup sound about as appealing as a plastic tomato. The innovations don't stop with the food and sauces, either. Where once charcoal would do, mesquite, applewood, hickory, cabernet grapevine cuttings, and cords of other woods now smoke. And all this on equipment that makes the backyard grill look about as current as a Model T. Gas and electric grills, covered models, water smokers, and 55-gallon tin drums are among the grill chef's options, making what was once the finest and simplest of cooking techniques one where only the most sophisticated take charge.

SAUTEED SCALLOPS

This is an example of the "less is more" culinary school of thought, which believes food is best enhanced by simple rather than complicated cooking techniques. Its most basic tenet, "nothing but the best and the freshest," keeps the simply prepared fare from being nothing more than a bare bones offering. For this dish it is imperative the scallops be sweet and never frozen. Serve with Orange-Carrot Puree (page 245) and Fire and Ice Salad (page 108). Ingredients may be doubled or tripled to accommodate more diners.

1 pound scallops

2 tablespoons flour

freshly ground pepper to taste

1 tablespoon reduced-calorie margarine

2 tablespoons dry white wine or, for a sweeter touch, sherry

1. Dredge the scallops in the flour, season with pepper.

2. Melt the margarine in a 10-inch skillet. When foamy, add the scallops and saute over high heat, turning often, until opaque, about 5–7 minutes.

3. Add the wine to pan and stir until reduced to a syrupy glaze. Divide scallops and sauce between 3 to 4 baking shells and serve.

Yield: 3–4 servings

Calories per serving: 108

Protein per serving: 16g

Fat per serving: 2g

Saturated fat per serving: trace

Cholesterol per serving: 30mg

Carbohydrates per serving: 5g

Sodium per serving: 181mg

Fiber per serving: trace

SCALLOPS IN CHAMPAGNE

The delicate, sea-fresh flavor of scallops is enhanced with champagne and Pernod, a French liquor; for a more budget-conscious preparation use a chablis and Anisette.

1 pound scallops

1 tablespoon flour, instant-blending recommended

¹/₂ teaspoon salt

freshly ground pepper to taste

1 teaspoon canola or other vegetable oil

1 tablespoon bread crumbs

1 cup champagne or other white wine

¹/₄ cup egg substitute

2 tablespoons crème blanc (page 34) or nonfat sour cream

1 teaspoon Pernod

2 tablespoons bread crumbs

Yield: 3–4 servings

Calories per serving: 172

Protein per serving: 19g

Fat per serving: 2g
  Saturated fat per serving: trace

Cholesterol per serving: 31mg

Carbohydrates per serving: 9g

Sodium per serving: 482mg

Fiber per serving: trace

1. Dust the scallops with the flour, salt, and pepper.

2. Spray a 10-inch nonstick skillet with nonstick cooking spray. Add the oil, turn heat to high, and saute the scallops over medium-high heat for 2 minutes, shaking the pan from time to time.

3. Add the tablespoon of bread crumbs and continue to saute for 3 minutes more or until scallops are opaque and lightly browned.

4. Add the champagne and simmer 4 minutes over medium-high heat.

5. With a slotted spoon, transfer scallops to a broiler-safe serving dish such as a quiche dish. Cover with a towel while completing the sauce.

6. Turn heat to high under pan juices and boil 2 minutes or until reduced to about ¾ cup.

7. Combine the sauce with the egg substitute, crème blanc, and Pernod in the bowl of a food processor. Mix at full power about 30 seconds.

8. Return sauce to the skillet and whisk over medium heat until it thickens, about 1 to 2 minutes.

9. Pour sauce over scallops, sprinkle remaining bread crumbs on top, and broil 2 minutes or until top is lightly browned.

MUSSELS IN WHITE WINE AND SAFFRON

Mussels, long enjoyed on the continent, are coming into such favor here that we can now buy a cultivated breed. These bivalves are much cleaner than naturally occurring mussels, making light work of a once time-consuming chore. Be wary when purchasing any mussels, though. The shellfish should be kept on ice, be as fresh as possible (ask the vendor when they came in and pass over any more than two days old), and the shells should be closed. This is not a do-ahead meal, but it is very quickly cooked. The mussels may be enjoyed as a first course, light dinner, or served on a bed of pasta for a heartier fare.

Yield: 4 servings

Calories per serving: 268

Protein per serving: 29g

Fat per serving: 7g

  Saturated fat per serving: 1g

Cholesterol per serving: 67mg

Carbohydrates per serving: 13g

Sodium per serving: 485mg

Fiber per serving: trace

3–4 pounds mussels

1 shallot, minced

2 cloves garlic, minced

a few threads saffron

a few parsley stems

1 sprig thyme

1 bay leaf

1 cup white wine

1 tablespoon reduced-calorie margarine, softened

1 tablespoon flour, instant-blending recommended

¹/₂ teaspoon turmeric (optional, for color)

2 tablespoons skimmed evaporated milk

1 tablespoon minced fresh parsley

1. To clean the mussels: Scrub each mussel with a brush and remove the "beard" with a sharp knife. Drop them into cold water and soak 1 to 2 hours. Some cooks add a handful of cornmeal or flour on the theory that it is ingested, thus plumping and cleansing the mussels. Lift the mussels from the soaking water and rinse again.

2. In a saucepan large enough to hold the mussels, put the shallot, garlic, saffron, parsley stems, thyme, bay leaf, and wine. Add the mussels, cover, and bring to a boil, shaking the pan frequently. When the shells open, about 5 minutes, remove from heat.

3. Pour the mussels and cooking liquid into a strainer set over a bowl. Discard the bay leaf, parsley stems, and thyme sprig. Pour cooking liquid back into saucepan (but not the grit at the bottom) and boil over high heat until reduced by a third.

4. Mash the margarine and flour together. Whisk it into the simmering stock in two parts over medium-low heat. Stir in turmeric and milk. Whisk over medium-low heat until sauce thickens slightly.

5. To prepare the mussels for serving, discard one half of each shell. Neatly arrange the mussels on a platter. Pour the sauce over mussels and garnish with the parsley.

Saffron

The world's most expensive spice is the dried stigma of a crocus. There are only three such threads in each flower, and they must be picked by hand. Since it takes 225,000 stigmas to make a pound of saffron, small wonder it is so costly. Saffron is the signature spice of paella, a Spanish rice dish. It is also used in breads, pilafs, and with some shellfish. It comes in powdered and dried form.

CLAMS, MUSSELS, AND LOBSTER IN BLACK BEAN SAUCE

Any combination of shellfish would be delicious in this oriental-inspired sauce. The basic premise, however, could be applied to whatever is available—a firm-fleshed white fish or a thick fish steak, such as monkfish or shark. Fermented black beans, oddly enough a soybean product, can be found in the Chinese section of your market and will last indefinitely. This dish is excellent as a first course, as part of a Chinese–style meal served with other entrees, or—my favorite—as a sauce for pasta. Easily reheated in the microwave (about 5 minutes on high, 100 percent power), it is a convenient dish for entertaining as well as a special family treat.

Yield: 6 servings

Calories per serving: 164

Protein per serving: 20g

Fat per serving: 3g

  Saturated fat per serving: trace

Cholesterol per serving: 50mg

Carbohydrates per serving: 12g

Sodium per serving: 945mg

Fiber per serving: trace

For the Fish

1¹/₂ dozen littleneck or other hard-shell clams, scrubbed

8 ounces clam broth, bottled or reconstituted

1¹/₂ dozen mussels, bearded and scrubbed

1 1¹/₂ -pound lobster, cooked and cooled

For the Black Bean Sauce

1¹/₂ tablespoons oriental fermented black beans

4 tablespoons dry sherry

2 tablespoons rice wine vinegar

2 cloves garlic, chopped

¹/₃ cup chopped fresh ginger root

*1 tablespoon plus 2 teaspoons cornstarch dissolved in 3 tablespoons
    cold water*

4 tablespoons oyster sauce

2 tablespoons reduced-sodium soy sauce

1 tablespoon minced fresh coriander

1 tablespoon minced fresh parsley

2 scallions, green only, chopped

¹/₄ teaspoon sesame oil

To Prepare the Fish

1. Steam the clams for 3 to 4 minutes in the clam broth. Add the mussels and continue to steam until all the shellfish have opened, about 4–5 minutes more. Transfer shellfish with a slotted spoon to a bowl. Strain the broth through a moistened coffee filter into a 2-cup glass measuring cup or other microwave-safe container. Set aside both shellfish and broth while preparing the lobster.

2. Remove the legs from the lobster; discard the body. Cut the tail and claws into roughly 3-inch pieces, leaving the meat in the shell. Add lobster legs and meat to the bowl with clams and mussels. Set aside while preparing the sauce.

To Prepare the Sauce

1. Soak the black beans in water to cover for 10 minutes if they have been preserved in salt. Drain and rinse under running water. Place them in the bowl of a food processor with the sherry, rice wine vinegar, garlic, and ginger root. Process at high until mashed. Leave in the food processor bowl and set aside.

2. *Stir the cornstarch mixture into the strained shellfish broth. Microwave at high (100 percent power) for 2 minutes or until thickened.* Alternately, combine the broth with the dissolved cornstarch in a 1-quart saucepan. Bring to a boil over high heat, stirring constantly until thickened, about 2–4 minutes.

3. Add the thickened broth to the bean mixture in the bowl of the food processor with the oyster sauce, soy sauce, coriander, parsley, and scallions. Process at high just until combined. Add sesame oil and blend.

To Assemble

1. Combine sauce with the seafood; stir to combine. Sauce may be chilled up to 8 hours before serving. Reheat in microwave for 5 minutes at high (100 percent power) or on the stove over medium heat. Sauce should not boil.

MONKFISH À L'AMERICAINE

Monkfish, also known as monkey fish or lotte, is called poor man's lobster in France for its firm-fleshed texture. Here, much like mussels, it's been regarded as a junk fish and used as bait or sometimes exported to France, where it is in demand. More recently it's become available in our fish markets, and the price has risen as has interest in it. Ask your fish merchant for it if he does not now carry this mild-flavored fish. The origin of the culinary term "L'Americaine" is obscure. Whether it was a term attached to a seafood dish prepared with tomatoes and olive oil in commemoration of an American customer by a French restaurateur or a dish brought to America by a French chef then re-exported to France isn't known—but it is decidedly *provençale* in its origin, rich in onion, garlic, parsley, and oil. You know what's been left out here.

Yield: 4 servings

Calories per serving: 222

Protein per serving: 23g

Fat per serving: 3g

   Saturated fat per serving: trace

Cholesterol per serving: 35mg

Carbohydrates per serving: 17g

Sodium per serving: 363mg

Fiber per serving: 3g

4 tomatoes or a 14-ounce can of tomatoes

2 leeks, white part only, thinly sliced

3 tablespoons chicken broth

1/2 teaspoon salt

freshly ground pepper to taste

2–3 tablespoons flour

1 1/2 pounds monkfish, skinned and boned, or other firm-fleshed
   whitefish, at least 2 inches thick

3 tablespoons Pernod

2/3 cup dry white wine

1 clove garlic, minced

3–4 tablespoons tomato paste

1 teaspoon fresh tarragon leaves or 1/2 teaspoon dried tarragon

1 tablespoon minced fresh parsley

1. Core the tomatoes and cut a cross in each one's bottom. Bring a 2½-quart saucepan ¾ full of water to a boil. Blanch the tomatoes 30 seconds to 1 minute, depending on ripeness. Drain and cool under running water. Spear on a fork and peel off the skins. Halve the tomatoes and extract seeds with your thumb or a spoon into a strainer held over a bowl. Dice the pulp. Press the seeds with the back of a wooden spoon to extract the juices. Discard the seeds. Add the juices to pulp. Set aside. Canned tomatoes may be used as is or seeded if desired.

2. "Saute" the leeks in the broth over medium-high heat, covered, until limp, about 5 minutes.

3. Mix the salt and pepper with the flour. Dredge the fish. Spray a 12-inch skillet with cooking spray. Place the skillet over high heat. Sear the fish for about 1 minute on each side to brown. Adjust heat as needed.

4. Add the Pernod and ignite it. When flames die out add the wine, leeks, broth, garlic, tomatoes, tomato paste, and tarragon.

5. Cover and simmer 10 minutes until the fish is cooked through; plan on about 5 minutes per inch thickness. *Note:* If monkfish fillets are over 4 inches thick, you may cut them into rounds 2-inches thick to hasten the cooking.

6. Remove the fish to a platter; cover and keep warm. If sauce is too thin, reduce it by boiling until it reaches desired consistency. Spoon over fish and garnish with the parsley.

FILLETS OF SOLE WITH SALMON MOUSSE

Gussy up a plain fish fillet with a quick-as-a-snap salmon mousse, then drizzle it with *Gourmet Light* Hollandaise or Béarnaise—it's a meal sure to please company or a justly deserved midweek treat for the family.

1 pound white fish fillets, such as sole

juice of 1 lemon (about 2 tablespoons)

salt and pepper to taste

¹/₂–³/₄ pound salmon steaks, skinned and boned

1 egg white

¹/₂ teaspoon minced fresh tarragon or 1 teaspoon dried tarragon

a few gratings fresh nutmeg or ¹/₁₆ teaspoon ground nutmeg

¹/₂ teaspoon salt

freshly ground pepper to taste

1 tablespoon white wine or additional lemon juice or vermouth

1 recipe Hollandaise (page 24) or Béarnaise sauce (page 25)

Yield: 3–4 servings

Calories per serving: 222

Protein per serving: 35g

Fat per serving: 8g

   Saturated fat per serving: 2g

Cholesterol per serving: 102mg

Carbohydrates per serving: 1g

Sodium per serving: 4,534mg

Fiber per serving: trace

1. Place the sole fillets, with what was the skin side facing up, between two pieces of waxed paper and pound lightly to flatten. Season with juice of half the lemon and salt and pepper to taste. Set aside.

2. Place the salmon in a 6-inch-round microwave-safe dish, such as a pie plate. Season with remaining lemon juice. Cover with plastic wrap and microwave on high (100 percent power) for 3 minutes.

3. Process the salmon and cooking juices, egg white, tarragon, nutmeg, salt, and pepper in a food processor until well blended, about 30 seconds.

4. Spread salmon mousse mixture over the fillets. Roll up fillets and place them in the same dish that was used to cook the salmon. Sprinkle with the wine. Cover with plastic wrap and microwave at high (100 percent power) for 6 minutes or until the white fish flakes easily with a fork and the salmon mousse is heated through. Serve with Hollandaise or Béarnaise.

FISH IN A FLASH

Simple, delicious, and very quick. Purchase presliced vegetables for stir-fry to speed preparation even further. You may substitute either the *Gourmet Light* Hollandaise or Béarnaise for the similar sauce used here.

1¼ pounds thick white fish fillets, such as scrod

juice of half a lemon (about 1 tablespoon)

salt and pepper to taste

1 pound, about 3 cups, mixed sliced vegetables, such as bok choy,
    carrots, green and red peppers, broccoli

¾ cup white wine (reduced-calorie recommended)

1 tablespoon minced fresh herb such as tarragon, basil, or thyme or
    1 teaspoon dried herb (same suggestions)

1 shallot, minced

½ cup reduced-calorie white wine

2 teaspoons reduced-calorie margarine

½ cup egg substitute

½ teaspoon salt

freshly ground pepper to taste

Yield: 3–4 servings

Calories per serving: 342

Protein per serving: 33g

Fat per serving: 8g
  Saturated fat per serving: 1g

Cholesterol per serving: 68mg

Carbohydrates per serving: 31g

Sodium per serving: 681mg

Fiber per serving: 7g

1. Place fish, tail folded under to make thickness uniform, in the center of a microwave-safe 10- or 12-inch pie plate. Season with lemon, salt, and pepper. Surround with vegetables, without covering the fish. Pour the ¾ cup wine over all and sprinkle with herbs. Cover with plastic wrap. Microwave at high (100 percent power) for 8 minutes.

2. While the fish cooks, prepare the sauce. Combine the shallot and ½ cup wine in a 3-cup heavy-bottomed saucepan. Boil over high heat until reduced to about ¼ cup. Add the margarine and stir over medium-high heat, until it has melted.

3. While the wine reduces, combine the egg substitute, salt, and pepper in the bowl of a food processor. Process 45 seconds on full power.

4. With food processor running, dribble in the hot wine and margarine. Process 30 seconds on full power.

5. Return egg/wine mixture to 3-cup saucepan. Whisk constantly over high heat about 4 minutes, adjusting to medium-high if necessary to prevent curdling. When fish is cooked, dribble in fish cooking juices and continue to whisk over medium-high heat until thickened, an additional 3 minutes. Drizzle a little sauce over fish and vegetables and pass remaining sauce at the table.

FILLETS OF SOLE WITH BASIL AND TOMATO

You may prepare the sauce for this dish early in the day, or even 24 hours ahead, and finish the cooking in about 10 minutes on top of the stove. A few steamed mussels or clams in their shells would be a welcome addition to the sauce; add them the last 5 minutes of cooking. Complete the meal with a simple tossed salad and parsleyed rice.

Yield: 6 servings

Calories per serving: 177

Protein per serving: 29g

Fat per serving: 2g

   Saturated fat per serving: trace

Cholesterol per serving: 70mg

Carbohydrates per serving: 9g

Sodium per serving: 481mg

Fiber per serving: 2g

6 tomatoes or 3 tomatoes plus a 10 1/2-ounce can tomatoes or 1 16-ounce
   can recipe-ready tomatoes

1 shallot, minced

1 clove garlic, minced

1/2 teaspoon fresh thyme or 1/4 teaspoon dried thyme

1 teaspoon fresh tarragon or 1/2 teaspoon dried tarragon

1/4 teaspoon fennel seed

6–8 leaves basil or 1 teaspoon dried basil

1 bay leaf

1 teaspoon sugar

1 teaspoon salt (1/2 teaspoon if using canned tomatoes)

freshly ground pepper to taste

grated zest of 1 orange

2 tablespoons orange juice (half an orange, squeezed)
2 pounds sole or other firm-fleshed white fish fillets
half a lemon
6 ounces mushrooms, sliced
1 tablespoon minced fresh parsley

1. Blanch the tomatoes by bringing a 2 1/2-quart saucepan 3/4 full of water to a boil. Immerse tomatoes, 30 seconds for very ripe ones, up to 1 minute for others. Drain and cool under running water. Spear the tomatoes on a fork, peel, and discard skins. Pull tomatoes in half. Put a strainer over a bowl. Squeeze the tomatoes over the strainer to remove seeds. Press the seeds with the back of a wooden spoon so juice drips into bowl. Discard the seeds, add squeezed tomatoes to juice. (Canned tomatoes are generally peeled; seed them as described here if desired. Recipe-ready tomatoes do not need this preparation.)

2. In a 12-inch skillet, combine the tomatoes with their juice, shallot, garlic, thyme, tarragon, fennel, basil, bay leaf, sugar, salt, pepper, zest, and orange juice. Bring to a boil. Reduce to a simmer, cover, and cook for 40–50 minutes. (You may need to add 1/4 cup red wine or chicken stock if the tomatoes boil dry.) *Alternately, combine the ingredients in a 4-cup glass measuring cup or other microwave-safe container. Cover with plastic wrap and microwave at medium-high (75 percent power) for 15 minutes.*

3. Meanwhile, prepare the fish. Place the fillets on a sheet of waxed paper or aluminum foil with what was the skin side facing up. Cover with another sheet of waxed paper and pound lightly with a cleaver or flat-bottomed heavy pan. Remove the paper, sprinkle fish with a few drops lemon juice. Roll the fillets loosely with what was the skin side facing inward. Set aside or refrigerate until ready to cook. (May be held, chilled, up to 6 hours.)

4. Remove and discard the bay leaf from the simmering sauce. Puree the tomato sauce in a food processor if desired. Strain back into the skillet. Discard dry pulp that remains in strainer. (Straining may be omitted if you prefer the sauce chunky.)

5. Add the mushrooms to the simmering sauce. Simmer 5 minutes. Refrigerate, if desired, until you're ready to complete the dish.

6. Bring the sauce back to a simmer. Lay the rolled fish fillets on top. Spoon a bit of sauce over. Cover pan. Cook 5 minutes per inch thickness of fish, about 12–15 minutes in total, at medium heat. The sauce should just simmer, not boil. Spoon the hot sauce over fish once or twice. When done, remove fish with a slotted spoon to a platter. Cover with a towel. *Alternately, place the fish fillets on the tomato sauce, then spoon some of the sauce on top. Cover with plastic wrap and microwave at high (100 percent power) for 8 minutes.* Remove fish with a slotted spoon and cover to keep warm. Return sauce to the microwave and cook, uncovered, at high (100 percent power) for 4 minutes or until sauce boils and reduces somewhat. Spoon sauce over fish to serve.

7. Raise heat under tomato sauce to reduce the juices the fish gave off during cooking. When reduced to about 2 cups, pour the sauce over fish and garnish with the parsley.

FILLETS OF FISH MARTINI

Steaming fish helps to retain its fresh, clean flavor better than any other cooking technique. This quickly done dinner is easily accomplished with a Chinese steamer and wok, but you may fashion a steaming arrangement with a cake rack set on custard cups inside a deep electric frying pan.

1 1/4 pounds fillets of fish—haddock, cod, or other thick white-fleshed fish

freshly ground pepper to taste

2 cups broccoli flowerets and stems

2 carrots, peeled and julienned

4–5 strips lemon peel

2 cups fish stock or 2 8-ounce bottles clam juice

1/4 cup dry white vermouth

3 juniper berries, crushed (optional)

1 tablespoon minced fresh parsley

2 tablespoons gin

1/4 cup egg substitute

1 teaspoon cornstarch or potato starch

1 tablespoon reduced-calorie margarine

Yield: 4 servings

Calories per serving: 211

Protein per serving: 31g

Fat per serving: 3g

   Saturated fat per serving: trace

Cholesterol per serving: 64mg

Carbohydrates per serving: 11g

Sodium per serving: 199mg

Fiber per serving: 3g

1. Place the fish on the rack of a Chinese bamboo steamer. Season with pepper (add salt only if using homemade fish stock, the commercial clam juice is salty).

2. Place broccoli flowerets on one side of fish. To prepare the stems, peel the tough outer skin with a knife or vegetable peeler. Slice the peeled stem thinly on the diagonal; add to the flowerets. Arrange the carrots on the other side of the fish. Arrange the lemon strips decoratively on top of fish.

3. In the bottom of a wok or deep electric skillet, combine the fish stock (reserving 2 tablespoons for Step 7), vermouth, juniper berries, and half the parsley. Place the bamboo steamer or rack over the wok, cover, and bring to a boil over high heat. Begin timing when the liquid boils; steam 5–6 minutes.

4. Lift the steamer or rack from wok. Boil the fish stock, uncovered, until reduced to 1 cup.

5. Meanwhile, heat the gin in a long-handled, small saucepan, preferably one with a lip, until bubbles just appear at the edge. Ignite the gin and pour it over fish (still in steamer, placed over a plate). After the flames die out, cover with a towel while completing the sauce or keep warm in a turned-off oven.

6. Beat the egg substitute in a small bowl or measuring cup with a fork. Dribble ¼ cup of the reduced fish stock into the eggs, while stirring with a fork. Whisk the egg-fish stock mixture into the remaining fish stock in wok over very low heat. Adjusting the heat as necessary, whisk until the sauce becomes opaque and foamy.

7. Dissolve the cornstarch in the 2 tablespoons reserved fish stock. Whisk this into the egg-fish stock mixture over medium-low heat until thickened. Whisk in margarine. Garnish fish with the remaining parsley. Serve fish right from the bamboo steamer with the sauce passed at the table.

Parsley

Fresh parsley is to dried parsley flakes as Wimbledon's grass courts are to Astroturf. Fresh parsley is readily available, inexpensive, and easy to use, if you have a good knife for mincing it. Store parsley, stem ends down, in a large glass of water in the refrigerator. This will help keep it fresh for a few days longer.

Lemon-Lime Fillets
in Parchment Paper Hearts

Cooking in parchment paper locks in natural juices and flavors and makes serving a snap. The paper hearts may be readied up to 3 hours ahead, but no longer or the paper will become soggy. If desired, top each of the fillets with a few scallops or shrimp. Serve with Bourbon Squash Soufflé (page 278) and a salad.

1 lime and 1 lemon

2 cups water

2 tablespoons reduced-calorie margarine

2 tablespoons lemon juice

1 tablespoon lime juice

1 teaspoon minced ginger root

1¼ pounds white-fleshed fish fillets, such as sole, cod, or haddock,
*   cut into 4 serving-size pieces*

¼ teaspoon salt

freshly ground pepper to taste

1 tablespoon minced fresh parsley

Yield: 4 servings

Calories per serving: 159

Protein per serving: 27g

Fat per serving: 5g

   Saturated fat per serving: 1g

Cholesterol per serving: 68mg

Carbohydrates per serving: 2g

Sodium per serving: 317mg

Fiber per serving: trace

1. With a vegetable peeler, remove the rind of both the lemon and the lime, taking care to remove only the colored skin and none of the white, which tends to be bitter. Julienne the peels into strips nearly as fine as pine needles.

2. Bring the water to a boil, immerse the julienned peels, and boil 2 minutes. *Alternately, combine the peels and water in a microwave-safe container, cover, and cook at high (100 percent power) for 4 minutes.* Drain.

3. Mash the julienned peel with the margarine, half the lemon juice, all the lime juice, and the ginger root.

4. Preheat oven to 425 degrees. Cut four parchment paper hearts and place a fish fillet on each. (You may use a double thickness of waxed paper if parchment paper is unavailable.) Season the fish with salt, pepper, and

remaining lemon juice. Divide the lemon-lime mixture over it. Garnish with parsley. Fold as shown in the illustration above, pleating the edge and turning the tip under. Place on a baking sheet and bake 8 minutes in a preheated 425-degree oven. Let each diner open his/her own package and enjoy the aroma.

Cooking in Parchment Paper Hearts

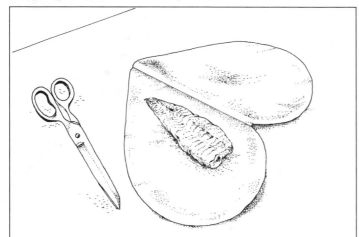

1. Lay the fish fillet, or other food, on half the paper heart, then fold the paper over it.

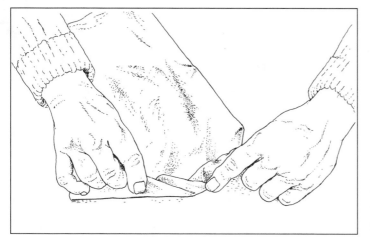

2. Pleat the paper tightly, securing the pleat with your fingertips as you move along the perimeter of the heart. Each pleat is made by making 1/4-inch folds at 1 1/2-inch intervals.

3. Continue making the pleats along the perimeter of the heart.

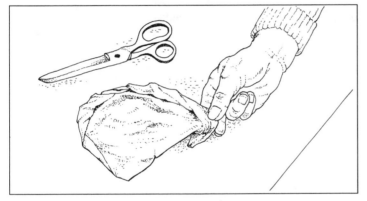

4. Secure the end by tucking the tip of paper under the package.

GRILLED HALIBUT WITH LEMON-CAPER SAUCE

This lemon-caper sauce reheats beautifully, so I've purposefully given instructions for a double batch that would amply serve 8. Offer it tonight with the halibut and the day after tomorrow with a poached or grilled chicken breast. It will keep up to 5 days in the refrigerator. You may substitute 3 tablespoons drained "recipe-ready" tomatoes for the fresh tomato if the season and/or time are conspiring against you. I'm partial to the big capers packed in salt (look for them in the Greek section of your market); just be sure to rinse them thoroughly.

Yield: 4 servings

Calories per serving: 202

Protein per serving: 34g

Fat per serving: 5g

Saturated fat per serving: 1g

Cholesterol per serving: 51mg

Carbohydrates per serving: 3g

Sodium per serving: 374mg

Fiber per serving: trace

1 ¹/₂ pounds halibut steaks or other firm-fleshed thick white fish steaks

1 tablespoon lemon juice

salt and pepper to taste

Lemon-Caper Sauce

2 tablespoons reduced-calorie margarine

¹/₂ teaspoon minced garlic

1 tablespoon cornstarch

1 cup bottled or reconstituted clam broth

1 tablespoon lemon juice

2 tablespoons nonfat sour cream

2 tablespoons capers

1 tablespoon minced fresh parsley

¹/₂ teaspoon paprika

1 peeled, seeded, chopped tomato

1. Season the fish with the lemon juice, salt, and pepper. Spray both sides of the fish and the grill rack with nonstick cooking spray. Grill the fish until flesh is opaque, turning once, about 4 minutes on each side. Alternately,

poach the fish in 2 cups clam broth over medium heat for about 10 minutes. (Freeze cooking broth for another use.)

2. While the fish cooks, prepare the sauce. Melt the margarine in a 3-cup heavy-bottomed saucepan over high heat until it bubbles. Add the garlic and cook over medium heat, stirring once or twice, for about 1 minute. Dissolve the cornstarch in the clam broth. Stir the broth into the margarine. Cook over medium heat 3 to 4 minutes, stirring often, until the mixture thickens. Reduce heat to low if the sauce starts to boil.

3. Over low heat, stir in the lemon juice, sour cream, capers, parsley, paprika, and tomato. Taste and adjust seasoning as needed. You might like a smidgen of pepper and/or nutmeg. Sauce may be made up to 5 days ahead. Reheat at high (100 percent power) in microwave or over medium-low heat on the stove. Sauce should not boil.

Unopened Flower Buds

Two spices in your kitchen are actually unopened flower buds: cloves, from a kind of evergreen tree, and capers, from a Mediterranean shrub. Capers are priced by their size, the smaller the more costly. They are most frequently preserved in vinegar, occasionally in salt. Used in salads, sauces, and as a garnish for egg dishes, they lend a distinction totally their own. They will keep in the refrigerator for up to one year. Cloves are dried flower buds; they come powdered or whole. Add a few to a bouquet garni destined for a tomato dish for a pleasant, peppery sweet taste.

BROILED FISH STEAKS WITH BASIL SALSA

A perfect Monday night dinner to atone for a calorie-taxing weekend, these broiled fish steaks may be readied in less time than it takes to empty the dishwasher if you have the Basil Salsa tucked away in the refrigerator or freezer. If you have none or if basil is out of season or unavailable, the Lemon Parsley Sauce, page 30, is also good on these fish steaks. Note that the fish does not have to be turned during broiling, since no one sees the underside anyway. This would be very nice with Fettuccine with Cepes, page 249, and a tossed salad.

Yield: 4 servings

Calories per serving: 146

Protein per serving: 25g

Fat per serving: 3g

   Saturated fat per serving: 1g

Cholesterol per serving: 60mg

Carbohydrates per serving: 2g

Sodium per serving: 402mg

Fiber per serving: trace

1 1/4 to 1 1/2 pounds fish steaks or fillets such as cod, haddock, or halibut, about 1-inch thick

1/2 teaspoon salt

freshly ground pepper to taste

1 tablespoon reduced-calorie margarine, at room temperature

juice of half a lemon

1/4 cup dry white wine

1/4 cup Basil Salsa (page 31)

1. Lay the fish in a broiling pan or roasting pan. Measure it at its thickest part. Season fish with salt and pepper and smear with margarine. Squeeze a few drops lemon juice over fish. Pour the wine into pan (it should just cover the bottom; add more or less as needed). Broil 4 minutes, cover the top of fish with Basil Salsa, and broil an additional 1–2 minutes, allowing about 5 minutes per inch thickness.

Note: For juicy fish, err on the side of undercooking.

GRILLED SWORDFISH WITH THREE-MELON SALSA

Make the melon salsa early in the day or preferably the day before, as its flavors intensify with time. Any remaining salsa is delicious as a condiment with other grilled meats or fishes. Just bring it to room temperature before serving. The Black Bean Cakes (page 238) are an excellent accompaniment.

1 1/2 cups diced mixed melon, such as cantaloupe, watermelon,
    and honeydew
1/4 cup minced red onion
2 tablespoons lime juice
1 tablespoon minced fresh coriander
2 teaspoons or to taste diced green chili pepper
2 teaspoons sugar
1/4 teaspoon salt or to taste
1 1/4 pounds swordfish

1. Combine the melons, onion, lime juice, coriander, chili pepper, sugar, and salt in a small bowl. Cover with plastic wrap and chill at least 4 hours or, preferably, overnight. Bring to room temperature before serving.

2. Grill the fish over medium-hot coals, about 4 minutes on each side. After turning the fish, slather the melon salsa on the cooked side to prevent it from drying out. Pass additional salsa at the table.

Yield of fish: 4 servings
Calories per serving: 155
Protein per serving: 25g
Fat per serving: 5g
  Saturated fat per serving: 1g
Cholesterol per serving: 50mg
Carbohydrates per serving: 0
Sodium per serving: 115mg
Fiber per serving: 0

Yield of salsa: 1 3/4 cups
Calories per tablespoon: 5
Protein per tablespoon: trace
Fat per serving: trace
  Saturated fat per serving: 0
Cholesterol per serving: 0
Carbohydrates per serving: 1g
Sodium per serving: 14mg
Fiber per serving: trace

Seared Ginger Tuna with Wasabi Butter

This simple preparation is a compromise between my love for raw tuna and the more common preference for it cooked. Here the tuna is just seared in a very hot pan, leaving the center a hearty hue of red. Be watchful, for tuna cooks to a gray, well-done stage quite quickly. It is excellent served with rice sticks or oriental noodles and steamed pea pods with a garnish of grated carrot.

Yield: 3–4 servings

Calories per serving: 202

Protein per serving: 26g

Fat per serving: 9g

  Saturated fat per serving: 2g

Cholesterol per serving: 41mg

Carbohydrates per serving: 4g

Sodium per serving: 678mg

Fiber per serving: trace

For the Tuna

1 pound tuna steaks

4 tablespoons reduced-sodium soy sauce

1 tablespoon minced fresh coriander

2 teaspoons sesame oil

1 tablespoon lemon juice

1 tablespoon minced ginger root

1 scallion, minced

1 clove garlic, minced

For the Wasabi Butter

1 tablespoon reduced-calorie margarine

1 teaspoon lemon juice

$^1/_8$ teaspoon powdered wasabi (available in Japanese or specialty
*   food stores)*

1. Place the tuna in a bowl just large enough to hold it. Marinate the fish in the soy sauce, coriander, sesame oil, lemon juice, ginger root, scallion, and garlic for at least 20 minutes or as long as 4 hours.

2. Combine the margarine, lemon juice, and wasabi until smooth. Set aside.

3. Spray a nonstick skillet with cooking spray. Heat the skillet over high heat about 30 seconds. Sear the fish about 3 minutes, basting with a bit of the

marinade. Reduce heat to medium, flip fish, and cook until desired degree of doneness—about 2 minutes more will produce a rare steak. Baste with a bit more marinade.

4. Transfer fish to plate and smear each steak with a bit of wasabi "butter." Extra marinade may be spooned over steaks or mixed with the noodles; be sure to boil it for 30 seconds beforehand.

SANTA FE SEAFOOD SALAD WITH CILANTRO CREAM

Yield: 6 servings

Calories per serving: 313

Protein per serving: 26g

Fat per serving: 2g
    Saturated fat per serving: trace

Cholesterol per serving: 111mg

Carbohydrates per serving: 46g

Sodium per serving: 735mg

Fiber per serving: 6g

Like millions of other tourists, I fell in love with the colors and flavors of Santa Fe. This salad is my attempt to replicate those indigenous tastes—the corn, beans, chiles, and coriander of New Mexican cooking—without the fat, of course. I've used a pasta, orzo, rather than rice, which would be more traditional, but either rice or another pasta shape would be fine. While somewhat time consuming to prepare, this salad is none the less an excellent choice for summer entertaining, for it can be prepared as much as 24 hours in advance, needs no last minute fussing, and is served at room temperature. I like to serve it with blue-cornmeal muffins and steamed green beans that have been tossed with Basil Salsa (page 31) and chopped, blackened tomatoes.

For the Salad

2 bay leaves

2 tablespoons white wine vinegar

$^1/_2$ teaspoon salt

1 tablespoon peppercorns

1 pound shell-on medium shrimp

$^1/_4$ cup white wine, clam broth, or water

$^1/_2$ pound scallops

3 plum tomatoes, cored

2 cups orzo, cooked according to package instructions and rinsed

1 16-ounce can black beans, drained, or 1 1/2 cups cooked black beans
  (see page 199)

1 cup cooked corn kernels, cut from 2–3 cobs, or canned and drained

4 tablespoons minced fresh parsley

For the Cilantro Cream

2 egg whites

6 tablespoons boiling scallop cooking broth

5 tablespoons lime juice (about 1 1/2 limes)

1 tablespoon minced red onion

1 tablespoon minced canned jalapeño pepper or 1/2 fresh jalapeño,
  blackened, peeled, seeded, and minced

1 teaspoon salt

lettuce leaves to line the serving platter (optional)

additional cilantro sprigs for garnish (optional)

To Prepare the Salad

1. Bring 2 quarts water to a boil with the bay leaves, vinegar, salt, and peppercorns. Add the shrimp, cover, and return water to a boil. Reduce heat to medium and simmer the shrimp 4 minutes. Drain, cool, and peel.

2. While shrimp cool, bring the wine to a boil in a 6-inch skillet. Add the scallops, cover, and cook at high heat for 5 minutes or until they are opaque and milky white. Remove scallops with a slotted spoon and reserve cooking broth for cilantro cream.

3. Blacken the tomatoes in a heavy-bottom skillet over high heat, for about 15 minutes. Add no oil, but reduce heat to medium if excessive smoking occurs. Shake the pan from time to time to blacken the tomatoes evenly. Remove tomatoes from pan. When they are cool enough to handle, seed and chop.

4. Combine the peeled shrimp, scallops, chopped tomatoes, orzo, beans, corn, and parsley in a large bowl. Set aside while preparing the cilantro cream.

To Prepare the Cilantro Cream

1. Place the egg whites in the bowl of a food processor and process on high power for 30 seconds. Bring the scallop cooking broth to a boil, either on the stove or in the microwave.

2. With the food processor on high, slowly drizzle 6 tablespoons of the broth into the egg whites. Add the remaining ingredients and continue to process. The cream will be thick and frothy like a very light mayonnaise. Combine with the orzo-seafood mixture. Taste to correct seasoning.

To Finish the Salad

1. Line a serving platter with lettuce leaves and mound salad on top. Garnish with cilantro sprigs if desired.

Warm Seafood Salad with Chinese Noodles

This fragrant toss of seafood and noodles is a meal all by itself. Although presented here as a warm dish, it is very good served at room temperature as well. (Do not serve it chilled, because chilling shrouds some of the flavor.) To serve at room temperature, prepare the salad in advance, tossing the seafood, vegetable, and noodles with the dressing to prevent the noodles from becoming gummy. Or prepare the seafood and vegetable, marinating them in the dressing for several hours but cooking the noodles at the last minute. All the oriental ingredients listed here can be found at specialty food stores. The noodles are increasingly available in produce sections of larger supermarkets.

Yield of salad: 4 servings

Calories per serving: 396

Protein per serving: 49g

Fat per serving: 4g

   Saturated fat per serving: 1g

Cholesterol per serving: 173mg

Carbohydrates per serving: 41g

Sodium per serving: 245mg

Fiber per serving: 6g

For the Court Bouillon

2 quarts water

1/2 cup rice wine vinegar or white wine vinegar

1 onion, sliced

3–4 sprigs parsley

1/2 teaspoon salt

1 teaspoon whole peppercorns

1 bay leaf

For the Seafood Salad

1/2 pound firm-fleshed whitefish, such as cod, haddock, or halibut

1/2 pound medium raw shrimp, shelled and deveined

1/4 pound scallops

2 stalks broccoli

For the Dressing

6 tablespoons reduced-sodium soy sauce

1 tablespoon sesame oil

1 tablespoon vegetable oil

2 tablespoons rice wine, Chinese cooking wine, or sherry

2 teaspoons minced scallion

2 teaspoons finely minced ginger root

6 tablespoons reduced court bouillon

1/2 pound fresh Chinese noodles

10–12 cherry tomatoes, halved

Yield of dressing: 4 servings (1 1/2 cups)

Calories per serving: 85

Protein per serving: 2g

Fat per serving: 7g

   Saturated fat per serving: 1g

Cholesterol per serving: 0

Carbohydrates per serving: 4g

Sodium per serving: 1,000mg

Fiber per serving: trace

1. Make the court bouillon by combining the water, vinegar, onion, parsley, salt, peppercorns, and bay leaf in a 4-quart saucepan. Bring to a rolling boil.

2. Wrap the fish and shellfish, individually, in double thicknesses of cheesecloth. Lower the fish into the court bouillon first, remove from heat, cover, and let it rest 30 seconds. Then add the scallops and shrimp, cover, and let them rest 5–6 minutes. Lift the fish and shellfish from the liquid and set aside to cool. Boil the court bouillon at high heat, uncovered, until reduced to about 1 cup, about 30 minutes.

3. Meanwhile, cut the stems from the broccoli flowerets. Slice the flowerets. Peel the stems and slice thinly on the diagonal. Bring a 2-quart saucepan 3/4 full of water to a boil, blanch the broccoli 4 minutes, drain, and rinse under cool water.

4. Combine all the dressing ingredients in a screw-top jar and shake heartily to combine. Set aside.

5. Cook the Chinese noodles by immersing them in 2 quarts of boiling water for 2–4 minutes. Drain and rinse under cool water.

6. Heat the dressing in a wok or large skillet over high heat. *Alternately, microwave at high (100 percent power) for 1 minute.* Remove and discard the cheesecloth from the fish, scallops, and shrimp. Toss the seafood with the broccoli and cherry tomatoes in the warm dressing to heat through.

7. Place drained noodles in shallow, wide soup bowls (reheat if needed by dousing with a kettle of boiling water), and add the seafood salad.

Note: Noodles may be cooked as much as 30 minutes in advance, but rinse well under running water after cooking. Reheat noodles by dousing with at least 2 quarts of boiling water.

Sole, Scallop, and Pea Pod Salad

This salad may be prepared early in the day and served several hours later. Be sure to remove it from the refrigerator at least 30 minutes before dining, as it is better closer to room temperature than chilled. Serve with crusty bread and offer a refreshing fruit sherbet for dessert.

For the Court Bouillon

1 quart water

2 cups dry white wine

1/4 cup tarragon vinegar

3–4 stems parsley

1 bay leaf

8 peppercorns

1/2 teaspoon salt

Yield: 6 servings

Calories per serving: 179

Protein per serving: 22g

Fat per serving: 7g

   Saturated fat per serving: 1g

Cholesterol per serving: 48mg

Carbohydrates per serving: 6g

Sodium per serving: 313mg

Fiber per serving: 2g

For the Salad

1¹/₂ pounds sole

³/₄ pound scallops

pieces of cheesecloth

³/₄ pound pea pods, strings removed

10 walnut halves, roughly chopped

For the Dressing

6 tablespoons reduced court bouillon

2 tablespoons vegetable oil

1 tablespoon fresh lemon juice

3 tablespoons tarragon vinegar

1 tablespoon freshly chopped basil or ¹/₂ teaspoon dried basil

1 garlic clove, speared on a toothpick

¹/₂ teaspoon salt

a few grindings fresh pepper

1. Combine all the ingredients for the court bouillon in a 3-quart nonaluminum saucepan and bring to a boil. Reduce heat and simmer for 45 minutes.

2. Wrap the fish and scallops in a double thickness of cheesecloth. Bring court bouillon back to a boil. Lower the fish and scallops into bouillon, cover, and remove from the heat. Let stand for 5 minutes. Lift the fish and scallops from liquid and rinse under cold running water to stop the cooking. Chill.

3. Put 1 cup court bouillon in a saucepan over high heat. Boil until reduced to 6 tablespoons. Set aside.

4. Bring a 2¹/₂-quart saucepan ³/₄ full of water to a boil. Immerse the pea pods, remove from heat, and let them sit for 4 minutes. Drain and rinse under cold running water until peas are at room temperature.

5. Combine all the dressing ingredients in a jar, shake well, and set aside for 1 hour. Remove the garlic just before serving.

6. The salad may be assembled as much as 4 hours before serving, but it is best done no more than an hour before. Flake the fish into a serving bowl and add the scallops, pea pods, and walnut halves. Toss with enough dressing to coat lightly. Serve on lettuce cups or in hollowed navel oranges, lined with lettuce.

Thinking Thin Tip

Scallops, mussels, clams, shrimp, and lobster, once considered to be high in cholesterol, have recently received a cleaner bill of health. Researchers now believe that a substance once thought to be cholesterol is actually another sterol—in fact, a beneficial one that may actually inhibit cholesterol absorption. Enjoy!

CHAPTER 9

VEGETABLES, BEANS, AND MEATLESS ENTREES

The Recipes

Note: Asterisked dishes may be served as meatless entrees.

VEGETABLES

Vegetables in this health-aware era have come into their own. Who wants the good old days when the 1941 edition of the *Fannie Farmer Cookbook* instructed Grandma to boil the green beans for 20 minutes! The vegetable is no longer an obligatory token item on the plate. Today we herald crisp but tender garden-fresh vegetables, not only for their flavor, but for their health-enhancing qualities as well.

Predominantly carbohydrates, supplying us with fuel for energy, vegetables are the best source of antioxidants, which include beta-carotene and vitamins C and E. These nutrients, researchers believe, may help keep certain cancers, heart disease, cataracts, and rheumatoid arthritis at bay.

Antioxidants fight and may deactivate toxins, known as free radicals, released by normal cell functioning. These free radicals may injure body cells and result in disease if not kept in check.

Dark yellow and orange vegetables as well as dark leafy greens are excellent sources of beta-carotene. Broccoli is an excellent source of vitamin C, and all vegetables provide vitamin E. Other vegetables supply several important minerals such as calcium and iron, and still others are good sources of fiber. Vegetables therefore not only provide energy-food with little fat but heaps of disease-preventative nutrition as well.

Aim for 3 to 5 servings of veggies a day—a serving is one cup of raw leafy greens or a ½ cup of any other vegetable. Have 2 to 4 servings of fruit, too.

In this chapter you will find dishes suitable for both the weekday's restraint and also for the weekend's indulgences. As with all the recipes in this book, some can be accomplished with microwave speed, others require the old-fashioned investment of time. Some are truly sidekicks, others demand—and receive—the spotlight. All trade on their upbringing, nothing but the freshest and the best.

ASPARAGUS

Royalty has its privilege—Louis XIV had a gardener who provided the palace kitchen with asparagus year-round. It's still a class act, though we commoners must content ourselves with a five-month season, stretching from February to June, peaking in April and May.

When purchasing asparagus, look for tightly closed heads and smooth, unwrinkled stalks. A pound of medium-size stalks holds between 16 and 20 spears, feeding 2–4 people depending on the menu. Asparagus's strong suit is vitamin A as well as appreciable amounts of vitamin C, potassium, and phosphorus. To protect those nutrients, store asparagus in the refrigerator crisper in a closed plastic bag or standing in an inch or so of water.

To prepare asparagus for cooking, cut or snap the stalks where the white turns to green. If the spears are more than a half inch in diameter, or if you're using white asparagus, peel to remove the stringy fibers, rendering the whole stalk edible. To peel, lay an asparagus flat on the work surface, tip facing you. Starting an inch or two beneath the tip, pull a vegetable peeler down the stalk, turning the spear after each stroke until you've peeled the circumference.

Asparagus may be boiled or steamed. Because green vegetables tend to turn drab olive green when cooked with covers in place (see page 240 for more explanation), boiling will better retain the emerald green hue. To boil, fill a 12-inch or larger skillet $3/4$ full of water. Add $1/2$ teaspoon salt. Bring to a boil. Immerse asparagus and boil for 6–8 minutes; the spears should be softened but still have some bite. Remove asparagus spears by lifting them with a slotted spoon or spatula. If you pour the water and all into a colander, they may break at the tip.

If you prefer to steam the asparagus, tie the stalks into a bundle with kitchen twine. Place an inch of water in the bottom of an asparagus steamer, stand asparagus upright, cover, and cook at high heat about 8 minutes or until somewhat softened but still crunchy. You may also fashion a steamer from any deep saucepan. Cover it with an inverted bowl or a double-boiler insert.

Asparagus looks wonderful laid upon a white linen napkin, with no more garnish than a lemon twist at the base. Pass *Gourmet Light* Hollandaise at the table, or try the simple recipe that follows. Asparagus is so elegant a vegetable, it may be served as a first course, but it also makes a first-rate casual supper alongside several other vegetables.

ASPARAGUS MIMOSA

The crumb topping may be prepared far in advance and gently reheated just before serving.

1 pound asparagus, peeled

1 teaspoon reduced-calorie margarine

2 tablespoons dried bread crumbs

1 hard-cooked egg white

1 tablespoon reduced-calorie margarine

a few drops lemon juice

$1/8$ teaspoon salt

freshly ground pepper to taste

Yield: 4 servings

Calories per serving: 46

Protein per serving: 3g

Fat per serving: 2g

   Saturated fat per serving: trace

Cholesterol per serving: trace

Carbohydrates per serving: 5g

Sodium per serving: 153mg

Fiber per serving: 1g

1. Prepare the asparagus for cooking by following instructions as outlined in the introduction. While bringing the water to a boil, prepare the topping.

2. Spray an 8-inch nonstick skillet with cooking spray. Place it over medium-low heat, add the margarine, and when it's foamy, add the bread crumbs, stirring occasionally until lightly browned. Remove the skillet from the heat, and sieve the hard-cooked egg white into the bread crumbs. Stir to combine. Scrape onto a piece of waxed paper.

3. Boil or steam the asparagus, and drain it when tender but still crunchy. Lay the asparagus on a serving platter.

4. Melt the margarine with the lemon juice in the now-empty skillet. Pour it over the asparagus, season with salt and pepper, and sprinkle the bread crumb mixture over the top.

BEANS

Dried beans—they're inexpensive, nutritionally correct, versatile, readily available, and good. So why do you rarely cook them? Time, probably. Overnight soaking? Forget it! If you're put off from dealing with beans because of the presoaking and lengthy cooking involved, look no farther than your microwave. An hour or two's stint in this kitchen timesaver is all it takes for most dried bean varieties to be ready to be turned into your favorite soup, ragout, or vegetable dish.

Just how good are beans for you? As a protein substitute, you're getting the good without the bad, the sound nutrition without the fat. Throw in a healthy dose of fiber and tip the scales with heaps of complex carbohydrates and you have a food perhaps rivaled only by that nutritional super hero, broccoli. Most dried beans can be soaked and cooked by the following methods.

Microwave: Pick over 1 pound of beans, removing any stones or foreign bodies. Rinse them and place in the steamer basket of a microwave-safe 4-quart container. Cover with water to within 2 inches of the top. Microwave covered on high power (100 percent) for 45 minutes to 1 hour. Discard water and rinse. Add fresh water as before, cover, and microwave on high power (100 percent) another 30 minutes to 1 hour. Test the beans from time to time; some will require less cooking time, others more. If you wish to combat the gas-producing substance in beans somewhat, discard the cooking water half way through, adding fresh water for the remaining time. Some of the nondigestible oligosaccharides will be drained away.

Traditional Overnight Soak: Pick over 1 pound of beans, removing any foreign matter. Rinse them and cover with 2 quarts cold water; soak overnight. Rinse beans and place in a Dutch oven or other heavy-bottomed pot. Cover with 2 quarts of water and simmer for 45 minutes to as long as 2 hours for very hard beans like white, black, and pinto beans.

Quick Soak: Pick over and rinse beans as above. Bring the beans to a boil and simmer for 5 minutes. Remove from heat and soak 2 hours. Rinse. Place beans in a Dutch oven or other heavy-bottomed pot. Cover with 2 quarts of cold water and simmer 45 minutes to as long as 2 hours.

Regardless of your cooking method, do not add salt to the beans until about the last 30 minutes of cooking time; salt tends to toughen them. Flavoring ingredients such as onions may be added after the initial soaking process or, if microwaving, after the first cooking cycle.

BLACK BEAN CAKES

Black bean cakes are a delightful change of pace from rice. They can be made as much as 2 to 3 days ahead of time and sauteed when needed. Indeed, the patties will be easier to form if the mixture can chill about 30 minutes after mixing. Serve them with fish or chicken dishes such as the Grilled Chicken Breast with Blackened Tomato Salsa (page 165).

Yield: 6 cakes

Calories per cake: 78

Protein per cake: 5g

Fat per cake: trace

   Saturated fat per cake: trace

Cholesterol per cake: 0

Carbohydrates per cake: 15g

Sodium per cake: 365mg

Fiber per cake: 2g

1 1-pound can black beans, drained and rinsed or 1¹/₂ cups cooked
   black beans (see page 199)

2 cloves garlic, roughly chopped

¹/₂ Spanish onion, roughly chopped

1 tablespoon minced fresh coriander

2 teaspoons canned minced chilies

2 teaspoons red wine vinegar

1 teaspoon chili powder

1 teaspoon salt

¹/₂ teaspoon ground cumin

instant-blending or regular flour

2 tablespoons nonfat sour cream

1 peeled, seeded, chopped tomato or 3 tablespoons drained "recipe-
   ready" tomatoes

coriander sprigs for garnish (optional)

1. Combine ⅔ cup of the black beans in the bowl of a food processor with the garlic, onion, coriander, chilies, vinegar, chili powder, salt, and cumin. Process into a thick paste. Add the remaining beans and process briefly, just to combine. The second addition of beans should not be processed too smoothly but remain chunky.

2. Chill the mixture, if time allows, for at least 30 minutes or as long as 3 days.

3. Line a dinner plate with waxed paper. Dust the paper and your hands with instant-blending flour. Shape the black bean mixture into 6 patties. Roll patties in flour on both sides. Patties may be cooked now or covered and chilled, on the same waxed paper, for as long as 24 hours.

4. Spray a nonstick 12-inch skillet with nonstick cooking spray. Place it over high heat. Add the patties, reducing heat to medium if they start to stick. Saute on both sides about 5 minutes or until warmed through and nicely browned.

5. To serve, top each patty with a dollop of nonfat sour cream and a bit of tomato. Garnish with the coriander sprigs, if desired.

GREEN BEANS

Thanks to modern horticulture, the string in string beans has been permanently pulled. No longer do we have those pesky strings to contend with! And thanks to modern transportation methods, fresh green beans are available almost year-round. They are an excellent source of vitamin A and supply a fair amount of calcium, too, for their very little 31 calories a cup.

When selecting green beans, look for those that are pliant and smooth, not coarse and tough. Frequently, when harvested by mechanical means, the bean is snapped from the stem exposing the meat, leaving a spot prone to rapid decay. Avoid these beans if given a choice. One pound of beans serves 4. Store the beans in the refrigerator crisper in a plastic bag; use within three days of purchase or they will be tough.

Prepare beans a handful at a time. Align the ends and cut across. Turn beans around, realign, and cut again.

Beans may be boiled or steamed. To boil, bring 6 cups of water to a rapid boil, with or without salt. Immerse beans and boil, uncovered, about 8 minutes, sometimes more, sometimes less. Time is a variable that is dependent on your heat source, the size and maturity of beans, and so on. Count on inconsistency because what works this time may not work next. During cooking, remove a bean and bite into it or pierce it with a fork. It should be crunchy but not raw. If holding the beans for later use, as much as 5 hours, undercook them a bit, then cool under running water.

To steam beans, prepare as above, then place in a steamer over 2 inches of boiling water, cover, and cook until tender, about 8 minutes. Again, check during cooking for tenderness.

To steam or to boil? Is one superior, healthwise? Consider the facts:

Fact 1: Some B and C vitamins are water soluble and will be lost if subjected to extended water contact. But if the vegetable is put in a large amount of rapidly boiling water, taking less time to come back to a boil and thus less time to cook, the vitamin loss is minimized. With steaming, the vitamin loss is minimized because the bean doesn't come in contact with the water at all.

Fact 2: Covered green vegetables turn drab olive green because acids, present in the vegetable, combine with heat and denature the chlorophyll. If these acids are allowed to escape in the form of steam in an uncovered pot, they simply dissipate, causing no damage. If not allowed to escape, the vegetable turns an unappetizing yellow green. If you wish to steam beans, you may somewhat circumvent this discoloration by keeping the cooking time as short as possible and uncovering the pan immediately after cooking. Or you may boil vegetables, uncovered, in *large* amounts of water—maintaining color and minimizing vitamin loss.

The Lemon Butter Sauce (page 32) is very good on beans. For a change, consider the following recipe.

GREEN BEANS WITH TOMATO NUGGETS

Prepare the beans early in the day by partially cooking them. Drain and cover them with plastic wrap. Place the beans on a counter or in the refrigerator if you're holding them for more than 2 hours. The butter sauce may also be made ahead. Then reheat both the beans and the sauce and toss together at serving time.

1 pound green beans

1 tomato, blanched, peeled, and seeded

juice of half a lemon

1 small garlic clove, minced

1 tablespoon reduced-calorie margarine

$1/_8$ teaspoon salt

freshly ground pepper to taste

Yield: 4 servings

Calories per serving: 60

Protein per serving: 2g

Fat per serving: 2g

    Saturated fat per serving: trace

Cholesterol per serving: 0

Carbohydrates per serving: 11g

Sodium per serving: 107mg

Fiber per serving: 2g

1. Cook the beans according to preceding instructions. Set them aside.

2. Dice the tomato.

3. Add the lemon juice and garlic to the margarine. Cook over medium heat for 30 seconds. Add the cooked beans and toss them in the pan until heated through. Add the tomato, stir just to heat through, and season with salt and pepper.

BEETS

While beets are generally boiled, they are delicious baked as well. Choose medium-size, smooth, firm beets for baking. Those that look shriveled or very large are apt to be too woody. The tops may be cooked like spinach and served with a few drops of fruity vinegar. Beets are a good source of potassium, calcium, phosphorus, and magnesium and contain about 35 calories in a ½ cup.

To bake, prick the beets in several places with a fork. Bake in a 350-degree oven until easily pierced with a fork, about 1 hour. *Alternately, microwave the beets at high (100 percent power) until tender. Time will vary with the number of beets cooked, about 10 minutes for 1 beet, as long as 30 minutes for 8 large beets.* Peel the beets and serve with a bit of orange juice heated with reduced-calorie margarine. Garnish with grated orange zest if desired.

BROCCOLI

Another year-round vegetable, broccoli is the health addict's dream. One large cooked stalk fulfills your vitamin C requirement by half as much again, provides your need for vitamin A, and supplies goodly amounts of riboflavin, iron, calcium, potassium, and fiber.

When purchasing broccoli, look for unopened buds that are dark green, not yellow. Store broccoli in a plastic bag in the refrigerator or in the vegetable crisper for not more than four days; 1½ to 2 pounds will serve 4.

Peeling and slicing the broccoli stalks is a wonderful way to get full value from this vegetable. Cut the stalks an inch below the buds. Separate the flower stems. Remove the leaves. If they look fresh, plan to cook them, for they are rich in vitamin A. Cut the branches from the stalks and peel the stalks using a vegetable peeler or a small, sharp knife. Slice the stalks into rounds on the diagonal.

Boil or steam broccoli as you would green beans (see page 240); 6–8 minutes is about right for crisp broccoli. This vegetable also takes well to stir-frying, but watch that oil!

Thinking Thin Tip

Ice water is far more appealing with a slice of lemon or orange.

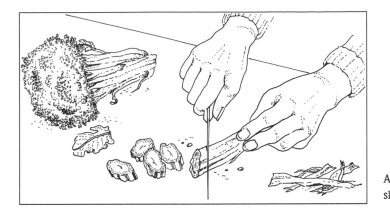

A peeled broccoli stalk is delicious to eat when it is sliced on the diagonal into thin rounds.

Very good hot with just a touch of reduced-calorie margarine and lemon (see the Lemon Butter Sauce, page 32), broccoli also takes well to dressing up with a cloak of Hollandaise or Mexican Cream Sauce, both in Chapter 2. And don't overlook it as a cold salad tossed with a light vinaigrette.

SESAME BROCCOLI

This recipe is a nice change from the norm. Cook the broccoli ahead and reheat in the sesame oil at serving time if desired.

1½ pounds broccoli (1 bunch of 2 to 3 stalks)
1 tablespoon sesame oil, available at specialty or oriental food shops
1 tablespoon sesame seeds
1 tablespoon reduced-sodium soy sauce

1. Prepare the broccoli for cooking. Boil or steam the broccoli, and drain it.

2. Heat the sesame oil in a skillet or wok for 15 seconds over high heat. Add the sesame seeds and the broccoli. Stir-fry until heated through. Transfer from the pan to a serving dish, and pour soy sauce on top.

Yield: 4–6 servings

Calories per serving: 55

Protein per serving: 3g

Fat per serving: 3g

  Saturated fat per serving: trace

Cholesterol per serving: 0

Carbohydrates per serving: 5g

Sodium per serving: 123mg

Fiber per serving: 4g

CARROTS

When purchasing carrots, for the sweetest flavor, buy those that have the greens attached. Although those sold in cellophane bags might have grown up in the same field, the green-topped ones will be much sweeter because they're probably fresher. Look to the stem end of the carrot for signs of age; if it is blackened, try another bunch. Remove the greens before storing or they will sap moisture from the carrot, causing the root to shrivel. Very fresh carrots need nothing more than a good scrubbing; older ones will be more tender if peeled.

One carrot supplies you with more than the recommended daily requirement of vitamin A. Carrots are also a rich source of cancer-combative beta-carotene. Carrots are one of the few vegetables more nutritious when cooked than eaten raw; cooking breaks down the tough cell walls, making the nutrients more available.

The following recipes are uncommon ways to serve the common carrot.

Thinking Thin Tip

The body converts only as much beta-carotene into vitamin A as it needs; any leftover is harmless. Excessive amounts of vitamin A, however, can cause toxic reactions.

LEMON GLAZED CARROTS

This vegetable is easily reheated.

1 pound carrots

juice of one lemon

$1/2$ teaspoon grated ginger root

1 teaspoon honey

1 tablespoon reduced-calorie margarine

freshly grated nutmeg

$1/8$ teaspoon salt

freshly ground pepper to taste

1 tablespoon minced fresh parsley

Yield: 4 servings

Calories per serving: 63

Protein per serving: 1g

Fat per serving: 2g

   Saturated fat per serving: trace

Cholesterol per serving: 0

Carbohydrates per serving: 12g

Sodium per serving: 164mg

Fiber per serving: 1g

1. Prepare the carrots for cooking by peeling if desired. Bring a $2^1/2$-quart saucepan $3/4$ full of water to a boil. Meanwhile, slice the carrots thinly into

rounds or matchsticks. Immerse the carrots and boil until tender, which will depend on how they are cut. Remove one every minute after five to test. When tender, drain.

2. In the carrot saucepan, combine the lemon juice, ginger, honey, and reduced-calorie margarine. Heat and stir until mixed. Add the carrots and cook over high heat, shaking the pan all the while for 1 minute.

3. Turn onto a serving platter. Season with nutmeg, salt, and pepper. Garnish with the parsley.

ORANGE-CARROT PUREE

This combination of carrot and orange gives purees a good name. It is very nice with lamb and excellent for parties because it easily reheats in a microwave.

> *1 pound carrots*
> *juice of 2 oranges*
> *grated zest of 1 orange*
> *1 teaspoon sugar*
> *1 tablespoon reduced-calorie margarine*
> *¹/₂ teaspoon salt*
> *freshly ground pepper to taste*
> *a few gratings fresh nutmeg*

Yield: 4–6 servings

Calories per serving: 48

Protein per serving: 1g

Fat per serving: 1g
    Saturated fat per serving: trace

Cholesterol per serving: 0

Carbohydrates per serving: 9g

Sodium per serving: 236mg

Fiber per serving: 1g

1. Scrape or peel the carrots as you desire. Roughly chop them.

2. Bring a 2¹/₂-quart saucepan ³/₄ full of water to a boil. Immerse the carrots, cover the pan, and boil until carrots are easily pierced with a fork, about 10 minutes.

3. Put the cooked carrots in a food processor or a food mill and puree. Add the orange juice, zest, sugar, margarine, salt, pepper, and nutmeg. Mix well.

CARROT AND SQUASH PUREE

This may also be made ahead and reheated in a microwave. It is delicious with turkey or other poultry. To vary, add a few tablespoons crème blanc (page 34) with the other seasonings.

1 small butternut squash, peeled and chopped

1 pound carrots, scrubbed, peeled, and roughly chopped

1 tablespoon reduced-calorie margarine

2 teaspoons dark rum

a few gratings fresh nutmeg

¹/₄ teaspoon salt

freshly ground pepper to taste

Yield: 6–8 servings

Calories per serving: 49

Protein per serving: 1g

Fat per serving: 1g
   Saturated fat per serving: trace

Cholesterol per serving: 0

Carbohydrates per serving: 9g

Sodium per serving: 114mg

Fiber per serving: 2g

1. Bring a 4-quart saucepan half full of water to a boil. Add the squash, cover, and cook 8 minutes. Add the carrots, cover, and cook until both are tender, about 12 minutes more.

2. Drain and mash the vegetables either in a food mill, food processor, or by hand. Add the margarine, rum, and nutmeg. Season to taste with salt and pepper.

CELERY

Celery is more than mere rabbit food. Cooked, it takes on a whole new personality, but with little alteration to its naturally skinny self.

One rib of this member of the parsley family (sometimes called a stalk, although technically the whole bunch is one stalk) supplies just 7 calories. It is a good source of potassium and supplies vitamins A and C as well as fiber.

When purchasing celery, avoid stalks that appear to be pithy or woody, or have limp and yellowing leaves. It needs to be kept both cold and moist to maintain its crispy snap and to protect it from becoming a limp throwaway.

NUTTED BRAISED CELERY

Try this recipe to disperse the ho-hums.

8 large ribs celery, strings pared
1/3 cup chicken broth or canned consomme
1/3 cup dry white wine
freshly ground pepper to taste
1 teaspoon reduced-calorie margarine
2 tablespoons finely chopped shallots
1 1/2 tablespoons chopped walnuts or sliced water chestnuts

Yield: 4 servings
Calories per serving: 64
Protein per serving: 2g
Fat per serving: 4g
  Saturated fat per serving: trace
Cholesterol per serving: trace
Carbohydrates per serving: 5g
Sodium per serving: 83mg
Fiber per serving: 2g

1. Slice the celery thin on the diagonal, or julienne it. Place it in a 10-inch glass pie plate or other microwave-safe dish.

2. Pour the broth and wine over the celery. Season with the pepper. Put the margarine on top and sprinkle with the shallots. Cover with plastic wrap.

3. Microwave at high (100 percent power) for 7 minutes. Sprinkle with walnuts. Microwave, uncovered, an additional minute.

DELICIOUS "CREAMED" CORN

4 ears corn

1¹/₄–1¹/₂ cups skim milk

2 tablespoons cornstarch

¹/₂ teaspoon salt

freshly ground pepper to taste

a few gratings fresh nutmeg

paprika for garnish (optional)

Yield: 4 servings

Calories per serving: 127

Protein per serving: 5g

Fat per serving: 1g

   Saturated fat per serving: trace

Cholesterol per serving: 1mg

Carbohydrates per serving: 27g

Sodium per serving: 321mg

Fiber per serving: 3g

1. Cut the corn from the cob.

2. Spray a nonstick 10-inch skillet with cooking spray. Add half the corn and saute over medium-high heat about 3 minutes or until kernels are tender and beginning to brown lightly.

3. Meanwhile, combine the remaining corn with the milk and cornstarch in the bowl of a food processor. Puree.

4. Add the pureed corn to the skillet. Stir to combine. Turn heat to low, add the seasonings, and simmer about 5 minutes. Add more milk if necessary. Garnish with paprika before serving, if desired.

MUSHROOMS

There's more to mushrooms than the bland, pale specimens commonly available. A whole new world of exotic mushrooms has come to market, with flavors that whisper of earth and woods. Some are dried and imported such as cepes (rhyme with step), chanterelles, and morels; others are being cultivated and marketed fresh such as shiitake and enoki. All are expensive but worth a pretty penny for those special occasions when you'd like to treat your guests, or yourself. The dried mushrooms are available at specialty food stores.

Although one would have to eat a lot of mushrooms to benefit from them, they are higher in minerals such as iron and copper than many other vegetables, and contain about 20 calories a cup. And few foods add such a touch of class for such little caloric expense.

Because mushrooms have a high water content and porosity, it's better to wipe them clean rather than washing them. This is particularly true if they are coupled with a sauce that would be diluted by excess moisture.

The recipes that follow use both the readily available supermarket mushroom and the very–in vogue cepe.

FETTUCCINE WITH CEPES

This wonderful pasta dish makes a great first course for a dinner party or a delicious main dish for a casual supper. The sauce may be easily made ahead and reheated just before tossing with freshly cooked fettuccine.

1 ounce dried cepes, also called porcini, or other dried mushrooms

boiling water

2 tablespoons minced shallots

1 clove garlic, minced

1¹/₂ cups beef stock or canned beef broth

1 cup tomato sauce (see page 33) or canned sauce

lots of freshly ground pepper to taste

8 ounces fresh fettuccine noodles

1 tablespoon reduced-calorie margarine, at room temperature

1 tablespoon minced fresh parsley

freshly grated Parmesan cheese

Yield: 4 servings

Calories per serving: 237

Protein per serving: 10g

Fat per serving: 5g
    Saturated fat per serving: 2g

Cholesterol per serving: 48mg

Carbohydrates per serving: 39g

Sodium per serving: 237mg

Fiber per serving: 3g

1. Cover the dried mushrooms with boiling water and soak for 20 minutes.

2. Spray a 10- or 12-inch nonstick skillet with cooking spray and saute the shallots over medium-low heat until limp. Add the garlic and cook another 30 seconds.

3. Add the beef stock and boil over high heat until reduced to 1 cup. Add the tomato sauce and boil until reduced to 1½ cups.

4. Drain the mushrooms and chop them. The juice may only be used if strained twice through a coffee filter. Add mushrooms to sauce base. Stir to combine. Season with freshly ground pepper.

5. Cook the fettuccine noodles according to package instructions. Drain the noodles and toss with the margarine. Toss the fettuccine with cepe sauce. Sprinkle minced parsley on top. Pass cheese at the table.

SHERRIED MUSHROOMS

This recipe is very nice with beef dishes and a treat when you add half an ounce to an ounce of dried mushrooms such as cepes. Soak the dried mushrooms for 20 minutes, drain and rinse, adding them at the end of Step 2. If made ahead, reheat the dish over very low heat or the crème blanc will curdle.

12 ounces mushrooms

2 teaspoons reduced-calorie margarine

2 tablespoons sherry or Madeira

3 tablespoons crème blanc (page 34) or plain nonfat yogurt

a few fresh gratings nutmeg

⅛ teaspoon salt

freshly ground pepper to taste

1 tablespoon minced fresh parsley

Yield: 4 servings

Calories per serving: 50

Protein per serving: 4g

Fat per serving: 1g

   Saturated fat per serving: trace

Cholesterol per serving: 1mg

Carbohydrates per serving: 6g

Sodium per serving: 120mg

Fiber per serving: 1g

1. Wipe the mushrooms clean and slice them, removing a sliver off the stem end if hardened.

2. Melt the margarine in a 10- or 12-inch nonstick skillet. When the foaming subsides, add the mushrooms and cook over medium-high heat, shaking the pan often until the mushrooms are lightly browned and all their moisture has evaporated.

3. Add the sherry and shake the pan while the wine evaporates. Remove the pan from heat and let it cool for 2 minutes.

4. Stir in the crème blanc, and season with nutmeg, salt, and pepper. To serve, garnish with the parsley.

ONIONS

Onions are to the larder as shoes are to the wardrobe; you won't get far without them. While not exactly nutritional powerhouses, they do contribute lots of flavor for a minimal calorie cost.

Members of the onion family that you are likely to use include:

"Yellow" onions: The yellow onion is the most common variety of onions. Actually brown-skinned, they are available year-round and are dried before being brought to market. They are generally sold in fishnet bags.

Spanish, Bermuda, and Red onions: With skins ranging from yellow to red, these milder varieties of onions are often eaten raw.

Pearl onions: These small onions with white skins are often served boiled as a vegetable side course. The slightly larger variety is called a boiling onion.

Scallions: Also called spring onions or green onions, these pencil-shaped onions are generally used raw.

Leeks: Leeks are to the French what a yellow cooking onion is to us—an all-purpose flavor enhancer. In this country, however, leeks are expensive, probably a compensation for low sales volume and spoilage. This is unfortunate because leeks are more subtle than the onion. Their mild flavor is prized for soups, stews, and vegetable side courses. They look like very thick, overgrown scallions.

Shallots: Looking like garlic bulbs, but with brown skins, shallots taste like a cross between garlic and onion. They are much used in French cooking.

Chives: A variety of onion in which the top rather than the bulb is used, chives look like thick grass. If chives are unavailable, use the minced green of scallions.

Dry onions (the all-purpose cooking onions, Spanish, Bermuda, and red onions, pearl onions, and shallots) should be stored in a cool, dry place where they are fine until they sprout (about 3 to 4 weeks). Never store onions near potatoes, because they will sprout quickly due to the moisture the potato gives off. Leeks and scallions will keep up to 3 weeks if closed in a plastic bag in the refrigerator.

SCOTCH ONIONS

This deliciously simple vegetable goes very well with roasted poultry or a beef dish. It may be made as much as a day ahead and gently reheated.

1 pound pearl or small white boiling onions

1 cup chicken broth

1/2 cup water

1/2 teaspoon salt

freshly ground pepper to taste

2 teaspoons reduced-calorie margarine

2 tablespoons Scotch

1 tablespoon minced fresh parsley (optional)

Yield: 4 servings

Calories per serving: 43

Protein per serving: 1g

Fat per serving: 1g

   Saturated fat per serving: trace

Cholesterol per serving: 1mg

Carbohydrates per serving: 6g

Sodium per serving: 301mg

Fiber per serving: 1g

1. Slice the ends from the onions and put a cross in the root end to prevent them from exploding.

2. Cover the onions with water in a 2 1/2-quart heavy-bottom saucepan and bring to a boil. Boil onions for 2 minutes, drain, and cool under running water. Slip and discard skins from the onions.

3. Return onions to the saucepan with the broth, water, salt, pepper, and margarine. Cover and boil gently until the liquid is almost absorbed and the onions are tender. Onions that are 1 1/2 inches in diameter will be done in about 12 minutes. If the onions are easily pierced with a fork before the liquid is absorbed, lift them from the pot with a slotted spoon and boil liquid at

high heat, uncovered, until only 2–3 tablespoons remain. Alternately, add more broth or water and extend cooking time if needed.

4. Remove the cover from the pan. Add Scotch with heat turned high. Boil, uncovered, until a semi-syrupy liquid remains. To serve, dribble a spoonful of sauce over onions. Sprinkle with the parsley if desired.

PEA AND LEEK PUREE

Leeks are very low in calories, a good source of potassium, and a fair source of vitamin C. Here they are perfectly paired with peas for a do-ahead dinner party dish worthy of the most sophisticated occasion.

Although "fresh" is today's culinary password, here I feel frozen peas will pass the test. Frozen peas, however, are higher in sodium than fresh peas; the sodium content for this recipe is for fresh peas.

1 bunch leeks (about 3 stalks)
³/₄ cup chicken broth
1 cup fresh or frozen peas
¹/₃ cup chicken broth
1 teaspoon reduced-calorie margarine
1 teaspoon freshly snipped tarragon leaves or ¹/₂ teaspoon dried tarragon
¹/₄ teaspoon salt
lots of freshly ground black pepper to taste

1. Cut and discard the green stalks from the leeks. Slice the white of the leek in half the long way, then dice. Rinse very thoroughly in a colander.

2. Put the leeks and the broth in a 1-quart saucepan. Cover and cook over high heat until tender, about 20 minutes. When the liquid is evaporated and the leeks are limp, empty into a food processor.

Yield: 4 servings
Calories per serving: 63
Protein per serving: 3g
Fat per serving: 1g
    Saturated fat per serving: trace
Cholesterol per serving: 1mg
Carbohydrates per serving: 12g
Sodium per serving: 191mg
Fiber per serving: 2g

3. Put the peas and the broth into the now-empty saucepan. Cover and cook for 2 minutes at high heat (a little longer for fresh peas). Empty into the food processor, unevaporated liquid and all.

4. Add the margarine, tarragon, salt, and pepper. Puree. The vegetable is ready to eat or may be reheated in the microwave before serving time.

Note: Without a food processor, you may puree the vegetables in a food mill, or in batches by hand, but you will have some difficulty pureeing it in a blender.

LEEK AND THREE-CHEESE PIE

Serve this pie with a salad and creamy risotto flecked with zucchini or asparagus for a vegetarian meal that will please even the staunchest meat and potato lovers. Leftovers heat very nicely in the microwave.

1 bunch leeks (about 4), whites only, chopped and well rinsed

1 cup chicken broth

1/2 cup egg substitute

3/4 cup skimmed evaporated milk

3/4 cup skim milk

*1 teaspoon Adobo seasoning (available in Spanish section of markets),
    regular salt, or seasoned salt*

freshly ground pepper to taste

1/2 teaspoon Dijon-style or stone-ground mustard

several gratings fresh nutmeg or a few shakes of ground nutmeg

2 ounces fat-free Swiss cheese, diced

2 ounces goat cheese, crumbled

3 tablespoons grated Parmesan cheese

Yield: 4–6 servings

Calories per serving: 146

Protein per serving: 12g

Fat per serving: 3g

   Saturated fat per serving: 2g

Cholesterol per serving: 9mg

Carbohydrates per serving: 18g

Sodium per serving: 598mg

Fiber per serving: 1g

1. Combine the leeks and broth in a 4-cup glass measure or other microwave-safe container. Cover with plastic wrap. Microwave on high (100 percent power) for 8 minutes. Stir. Cover again and microwave another 2 minutes on high. Drain while mixing eggs and milk.

2. Turn oven to 325 degrees. Combine the egg substitute, both milks, Adobo seasoning or salt, pepper, mustard, and nutmeg in the bowl of a food processor. Mix at full power about 30 seconds.

3. Layer the leeks in a glass 10-inch pie pan or other oven-safe dish. Cover with egg-milk mixture. Dot with cheeses and sprinkle with Parmesan.

4. Cook in the upper third of the oven for 45 minutes. Let rest 5–10 minutes before slicing into wedges.

POTATOES

Shopping for a plain old potato poses a surprisingly large amount of choices. There are many varieties, from round white to long russet, from new potatoes to old (mature). There are waxy spuds and mealy ones, some sold loose and others in bags. What's a body to do? Short of memorizing every variety and its particular use, let this be a simple guide. Purchase new potatoes, those that look like they're suffering from bad sunburn with chafed and peeling skin, for salads, boiling, and steaming. New potatoes are less likely to break in tossing because their high-moisture/low-starch ratio means they absorb less of the cooking liquid. Happily, new potatoes will absorb less of the dressing, too. Choose the old (mature) potatoes for mashing and baking. Their low-moisture content makes for fluffier mashed and baked potatoes.

Purchase only as many potatoes as you can use within 2 weeks, and don't store them in the refrigerator, if possible. Excessive cold converts the potato's starch to sugar, affecting the flavor. Store potatoes in a cool, dark spot. At room temperature they should keep 2–3 weeks. If kept in the light, green spots develop that give the tuber a bitter taste.

Thinking Thin Tip

Make dinner an occasion by setting the table with your best dishes and eating by candlelight.

As has been widely reported, a plain baked potato has about the same number of calories as a banana. Nutritionally and economically the humble potato is an excellent buy. It's high in energy-sustaining carbohydrates, yet low in fat. With a good amount of iron and potassium, some calcium, phosphorus, and vitamins B1, C, and niacin, it seems sensible to enjoy potatoes. The trick is to enhance the flavor without inflating the calorie count. The following recipes are such an attempt.

POTATO AND ARTICHOKE GRATIN

A "flash-y" dish, quick to do but a step above the ordinary.

1 teaspoon reduced-calorie margarine

3 potatoes, scrubbed, skins left on

1 9-ounce package frozen artichoke hearts, thawed, or 5 fresh artichoke hearts, sliced thinly

1½ cups skim milk

¾ cup skimmed evaporated milk

2 ounces goat cheese

1 teaspoon minced fresh tarragon

1 teaspoon salt

freshly ground pepper to taste

a few gratings nutmeg

2 tablespoons bread crumbs

1 tablespoon grated Parmesan cheese

Yield: 4–6 servings

Calories per serving: 163

Protein per serving: 9g

Fat per serving: 3g

  Saturated fat per serving: 2g

Cholesterol per serving: 7mg

Carbohydrates per serving: 25g

Sodium per serving: 510mg

Fiber per serving: 3g

1. Smear an 8x10-inch baking dish with the margarine.

2. Slice the potatoes thinly in a food processor or by hand.

3. *Combine the potatoes with 1 cup water in a microwave-safe container and microwave at high (100 percent power) for 8 minutes.* Alternately, bring the potatoes and water to cover to a boil on the stove top and simmer

until crisp-tender, about 15–20 minutes. Drain. Spread the potatoes and artichokes in the baking dish.

4. Add skim milk and skimmed evaporated milk to the potatoes. Crumble the goat cheese on top.

5. Add tarragon, salt, pepper, and nutmeg. Sprinkle with bread crumbs and Parmesan cheese.

6. Place in the upper third of the oven. Turn heat to 425 degrees (no need to preheat) and bake 30 minutes or until top is browned and milk is bubbly.

RED BLISS POTATO SALAD

Red Bliss potatoes are sometimes simply called red-skinned potatoes. This salad is quick to prepare because the potatoes don't need to be peeled. It is very good with a simple grilled fish or the Parchment Chicken with Tomato Vinaigrette on page 173.

1 pound Red Bliss potatoes
3 tablespoons sherry vinegar or red wine vinegar
1 teaspoon sugar
5 tablespoons plain nonfat yogurt
4 tablespoons reduced-fat and -calorie mayonnaise
2 tablespoons freshly chopped dill
½ teaspoon Dijon-style mustard
½ teaspoon salt
freshly ground pepper to taste
½ teaspoon capers, drained

Yield: 6 servings
Calories per serving: 99
Protein per serving: 2g
Fat per serving: 2g
   Saturated fat per serving: trace
Cholesterol per serving: trace
Carbohydrates per serving: 18g
Sodium per serving: 252mg
Fiber per serving: 3g

1. Cover the potatoes with water by a generous inch and boil them until easily pierced with a fork, about 25 minutes. Drain, cool under running water, and let potatoes rest 10–15 minutes before slicing.

2. Pour the vinegar over sliced potatoes, and sprinkle with sugar. Set aside while mixing sauce.

3. Combine yogurt, mayonnaise, dill, mustard, salt, and pepper in a bowl. Mix. Toss the sauce gently with potatoes. Taste for seasoning adjustment. Serve just slightly chilled with capers sprinkled over.

RED PEPPERS

Some years ago, French chefs began experimenting with roasting red peppers, turning them into wonderful sauces or delicious salads or combining them with herbs such as basil to create subtle but distinctive compound butters. Today it's almost impossible to open any cooking magazine without seeing at least one recipe using roasted red peppers.

Roasting a pepper, red or green, is actually to broil it, then allow it to cool in a tightly closed bag. The steam loosens the charred skin, which then pulls off as easily as old paint—if you've broiled it sufficiently but not overdone it. The broiling process cooks the flesh, turning it yet a deeper scarlet. It has a mild, sweet taste quite unsurpassed by other vegetables. It may then be marinated and served at room temperature as a salad; sauteed with any combination of vegetables; or pureed with herbs and a touch of vinegar. As a sauce it is delicious over other vegetables such as green beans, broccoli, and the like, or over fish or even poultry. It is wonderful on spinach fettuccine as a fine first course or as a casual dinner.

A red pepper is nothing more than a green pepper allowed to mature and ripen on the vine. Yet because most peppers are harvested when green, red peppers are somewhat scarce and often expensive. Although you can sometimes ripen a green pepper that has begun to blush by putting it with a cut apple in a paper bag for a day or two, it is likely to decay before becoming scarlet. When they are available, take advantage of their high vitamins A and C content by making up the following puree and freezing it.

To Roast Peppers

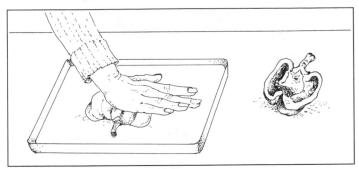

1. Place a seeded, halved pepper, skin side up, on a flat surface. Flatten pepper with the heel of your hand.

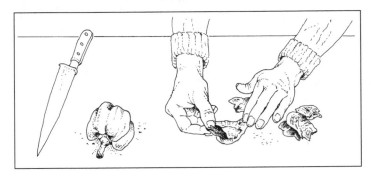

2. Broil pepper until it is completely blackened, cool in a tightly closed bag, then peel away and discard the charred skin.

To Julienne Peppers

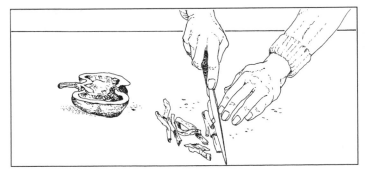

A roasted or raw pepper is often sliced into julienned strips for use in cooking.

Red Pepper Puree

This delicious sauce may be made ahead and reheated at serving time.

4 large red bell peppers
1 tablespoon extra-virgin olive oil
2 tablespoons minced fresh parsley
8–10 fresh basil leaves, snipped, or 1 teaspoon dried basil
1 clove garlic, minced
1/2 teaspoon salt
freshly ground pepper to taste

Yield: 6 servings
Calories per serving: 37
Protein per serving: 1g
Fat per serving: 2g
  Saturated fat per serving: trace
Cholesterol per serving: 0
Carbohydrates per serving: 4g
Sodium per serving: 174mg
Fiber per serving: 1g

1. Cut the peppers in half. Remove and discard the seeds and inner membranes. Flatten a pepper with the heel of your hand and place it, skin side up, on a baking sheet. Repeat. Broil the peppers until they're completely blackened and charred. The skin will not peel off easily unless it's burned, so don't be shy about doing so. Don't let the peppers dry out, however. Remove the burned peppers to a plastic or paper bag, roll the bag tightly closed, and place in the freezer until the peppers are cool enough to handle, about 10 minutes.

2. With your fingers, peel and discard the loosened skin from the peppers. Rinse the flesh under running water.

3. Roughly chop the peppers and combine them with the oil, parsley, basil, garlic, salt, and pepper in a food processor. Puree. If using a food mill or blender, puree the peppers first, then combine them with the other ingredients.

Pasta with Red Pepper Puree

Use the above recipe to coat 12 ounces fresh linguine. Cook and drain noodles according to package directions. Toss with the puree. Delicious as a side dish with lamb or as a first course for a dinner party. Remember to heat the plates when serving pasta. Pass grated cheese at the table if desired. Serves 4–6.

Green Beans with Red Pepper Puree

Use the above puree to sauce 1 pound cooked green beans tossed with 1 tablespoon reduced-calorie margarine. Serves 6.

MARINATED ROASTED PEPPERS

Roasted red peppers are also delicious when marinated in oil (tiny amounts, of course!), vinegar, and herbs and served at room temperature as a vegetable side dish. This dish is best made a day ahead.

2 red bell peppers

2 green bell peppers

1 tablespoon oil (walnut oil recommended)

1 tablespoon balsamic or malt vinegar, available at specialty food stores

2 tablespoons beef stock or canned consomme

1 clove garlic, minced

8 fresh basil leaves, snipped, or 1 teaspoon dried basil

⅛ teaspoon salt

freshly ground pepper to taste

1 tablespoon minced fresh parsley

Yield: 4 servings

Calories per serving: 56

Protein per serving: 1g

Fat per serving: 4g

   Saturated fat per serving: trace

Cholesterol per serving: trace

Carbohydrates per serving: 6g

Sodium per serving: 69mg

Fiber per serving: 1g

1. Cut the peppers in half. Discard the seeds and inner membranes. Place the peppers, skin side up, on a baking sheet. Broil them until they're blackened and charred. Put the peppers in a plastic or paper bag, roll bag tightly closed, and chill them until cool enough to handle.

2. Peel and discard the skin. Lay the peppers in a glass or ceramic dish.

3. Combine the oil, vinegar, stock, garlic, and basil. Pour the mixture over peppers. Sprinkle the peppers with salt, pepper, and parsley just before serving.

WOK SAUTE
OF PEPPERS AND BROCCOLI

This is a basic method for sauteing any combination of vegetables with roasted red peppers. Likely combinations are sliced Chinese celery, pea pods, zucchini, and so forth. Strips of cooked lean ham are very good, too, when served with vegetable dinners. The use of a wok cuts down on the amount of fat needed and also allows you to push the quicker-cooking vegetables up on the rim out of heat's way. If you're using a traditional flat skillet, just add the slowest-cooking vegetable first. These vegetables may be readied for cooking ahead of time, but stir-fry them at the last moment. Their freshness will be compromised if reheated.

Yield: 4 servings

Calories per serving: 44

Protein per serving: 2g

Fat per serving: 1g

   Saturated fat per serving: trace

Cholesterol per serving: trace

Carbohydrates per serving: 7g

Sodium per serving: 149mg

Fiber per serving: 2g

4 tablespoons chicken broth or canned consomme

1 small clove garlic, minced

1 cup broccoli flowerets sliced, and stems, peeled and julienned

1 teaspoon oil, possibly more if using a skillet instead of a wok

1 cup mushrooms, sliced

3 red bell peppers, roasted, peeled (see Steps 1 and 2, page 260), and julienned

¹/₄ teaspoon salt

freshly ground pepper to taste

1 tablespoon minced fresh parsley

1. Heat the wok over high heat. Add the broth and garlic and cook, stirring constantly, for 30 seconds.

2. Add the broccoli and cook over high heat, stirring until crisp-tender, about 1 minute. Push the broccoli up onto the sides of wok (or remove from the wok and keep warm).

3. Add the oil and mushrooms. Cook, stirring over high heat, about 1 minute. Push the mushrooms up onto the sides of wok.

4. Add the red peppers. Cook over high heat, stirring constantly until heated through, about 30 seconds longer.

5. Push all the vegetables down to the bottom of wok to heat through. Season with salt and pepper. Sprinkle with parsley and serve.

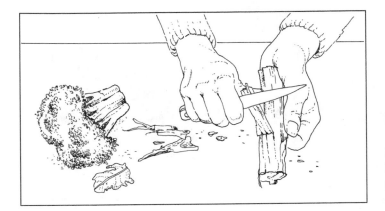

Peeling the tough outer skin from the broccoli stalk before cooking the broccoli will make the whole stalk more tender to eat.

SPINACH

This versatile vegetable might not have made Popeye's muscles bulge, but it certainly contributed to his general well-being. A mere half-cup of cooked spinach supplies an adult with twice the daily requirement of vitamin A, half the vitamin C, and one-fifth the RDA of iron. It is also a good source of folic acid, a B vitamin. All this for just 28 calories! You might have also heard that it is rich in calcium, but because of the presence of oxalic acid, the calcium is not available to the body.

When purchasing spinach, avoid spinach with yellowing or mushy leaves. Spinach sold in bulk (that is, by the pound) requires very thorough washing to remove the inevitable sand and grit. You'll also want to strip off the stems, as they are both tough and slightly bitter. After stemming, soak the leaves in a sinkful of tepid water for a few minutes. Lift the leaves from the water, drain, rinse the sand from the sink, and repeat, this time with cold water.

Spinach sold in cellophane bags is generally sand-free, but you still may wish to remove the stems and backbones and rinse the leaves in cold water, especially if serving them raw in a salad.

Stored in a plastic bag in the refrigerator, spinach will keep 4 to 5 days.

SPINACH-RICOTTA TART

This simply made tart is quick to put together, easy to trek to a picnic, and a treat to eat hot or at room temperature. It makes a nice lunch, light dinner, or out-of-the-ordinary vegetable side dish. Alternate slices of summer squash with the tomato for a colorful change. Make as much as a day in advance, but for best results, do not freeze. Phyllo is available in the frozen food section of most supermarkets. Leftover phyllo dough will keep in the refrigerator up to 4 weeks; if refrozen it tends to get crumbly.

Yield: 6–8 servings

Calories per serving: 163

Protein per serving: 14g

Fat per serving: 6g

  Saturated fat per serving: 3g

Cholesterol per serving: 20mg

Carbohydrates per serving: 16g

Sodium per serving: 515mg

Fiber per serving: 3g

2 pounds fresh or frozen spinach

1 16-ounce container part-skim ricotta cheese

1 onion, diced

¾ cup egg substitute

10 fresh basil leaves, snipped, or 1 teaspoon dried basil

1 teaspoon salt

freshly ground pepper

a few gratings nutmeg

2 sheets phyllo dough

2–3 medium tomatoes

black olive (optional)

2 tablespoons grated Parmesan cheese

1. Wash the spinach very thoroughly. Pack into a 2½-quart saucepan with the water that clings to its leaves. Cover and cook over high heat until the leaves are wilted, about 30 seconds to one minute. Drain in a colander, pressing the spinach with the pan bottom to extract as much water as possible. If using frozen spinach, simply thaw and squeeze to remove excess moisture.

2. Put the spinach in a food processor (or chop finely and place in a bowl), add the ricotta cheese, onion, egg substitute, basil, salt, lots of pepper, and nutmeg. Mix well.

3. In a 9-inch quiche pan, crisscross the two sheets of phyllo. Pour in the spinach-cheese mixture. Trim the corners of the phyllo so just 2 inches remain, and roll the edges in to create a rim of pastry. Don't be alarmed when the dough tears, that will make it appear flaky when cooked.

4. Preheat oven to 400 degrees.

5. Slice the tomatoes. Cut each slice in half. Arrange slices to resemble a flower by overlapping them in a circle on top of the tart. Put a black olive at center if desired. Season with more pepper. Spray the edges of the pastry with cooking spray.

6. Bake the tart in the lower third of the preheated oven. Sprinkle the Parmesan cheese over the top after 25 minutes. Cook about 15 minutes more. The tart is done when the center no longer shakes when wiggled, and a knife inserted slightly off center comes out cleanly. Let the tart rest 10 minutes before slicing.

Thinking Thin Tip

Parmesan and goat cheese are among the lowest-fat cheeses available.

SUMMER SQUASH

Soft-shelled summer squash (though many varieties are available year round) is a good supplier of vitamins A and C with a virtually free calorie count— about 15 calories in a half cup. And—joy of joys!—it tastes good, too.

A rundown on the most popular varieties:

Zucchini and cocozelle: both pale green; best harvested about 5 inches long and 2–3 inches in diameter.

Yellow crookneck and straightneck: pale yellow that deepens as the squash reaches maturity; sometimes has bumpy skin. Best harvested when about 6 inches in length and 3–4 inches in diameter.

Scallop, pattypan, or cymling: dish-shaped squash with a scalloped edge; pale green changing to white as the vegetable matures. Best 3–4 inches across.

Purchase summer squash when the skin is soft enough not to need peeling. Refrigerate it for up to a week. If you garden or have ever been the dubious recipient of those baseball bat–sized zucchini, don't give it to your kids for batting practice. Peeled and seeded, just as you would a cucumber, it makes a fine soup (page 85). You also may prepare it as outlined here with the addition of a little chopped onion and a sprinkling of dried bread crumbs, then freeze it. Bake it in a 350-degree oven until heated through.

ZUCCHINI SAUTE

This recipe works well with any of the summer squash. While it may be readied for cooking in advance, saute it just before serving. Don't be put off by the amount of salt (it's washed out).

3 small zucchini

2 teaspoons salt

1 tablespoon reduced-calorie margarine

1 whole clove garlic, peeled

a few gratings fresh nutmeg

lots of freshly ground pepper to taste

Yield: 4 servings

Calories per serving: 22

Protein per serving: 1g

Fat per serving: 2g

   Saturated fat per serving: trace

Cholesterol per serving: 0

Carbohydrates per serving: 2g

Sodium per serving: 75mg

Fiber per serving: 1g

1. Cut the ends from the zucchini and grate either by hand or in a food processor. Place the squash in a sieve and toss with the salt. Let the vegetable rest at least 20 minutes. The salt draws excess moisture from the vegetable.

2. Rinse the salted zucchini very thoroughly under running water, tossing and squeezing the vegetable in your fingers to rinse out the salt. Squeeze the zucchini against the sieve to remove the water. Taste to be sure the salt is removed.

3. Melt the margarine in a 10-inch nonstick skillet over medium-high heat. Spear the garlic clove on a toothpick and add it to the margarine. When margarine is foamy, add the squeezed zucchini and saute, stirring constantly, until just heated through, about 2 minutes. Season with nutmeg and pepper. Remove the garlic.

ZUCCHINI BOATS WITH EGGPLANT CAVIAR

Make the eggplant caviar for this dish a day or two before serving, and pre-pare and assemble the boats early in the day. Bake or reheat at dinnertime. Or pile the eggplant caviar into hollowed, salted, and drained tomatoes for cool dining on sun-sweltering days. Leftover eggplant caviar can have another life as an hors d'oeuvre mounded on cucumber slices, stuffed in blanched mushroom caps for broiling, or spread on *croustades* and sprinkled with Parmesan cheese.

Yield: 6 servings
Calories per serving: 55
Protein per serving: 2g
Fat per serving: 4g
  Saturated fat per serving: 1g
Cholesterol per serving: 1mg
Carbohydrates per serving: 5g
Sodium per serving: 380mg
Fiber per serving: 1g

For the Eggplant Caviar

1 medium eggplant, a little over a pound

1 tomato, blanched, peeled, seeded, and chopped

1 clove garlic, minced

1 tablespoon red wine or raspberry vinegar

1 tablespoon extra-virgin olive oil

1 tablespoon minced fresh parsley

1 tablespoon pine nuts or blanched almonds

a few drops hot pepper sauce

¹/₂ teaspoon salt

freshly ground pepper to taste

For the Zucchini Boats

3 small zucchini or 1 overgrown one

¹/₂ teaspoon salt

2 tablespoons grated Parmesan cheese

To Prepare the Eggplant Caviar

1. Preheat oven to 400 degrees. Cut off the ends of the eggplant and pierce it in several places with a fork. Bake eggplant until soft, about 30 minutes. Cool slightly. *Alternately, microwave at high (100 percent power) for 12 minutes or until soft.*

2. Skin the eggplant, cut it into quarters, and scoop out seeds. Put the pulp in a food processor or blender.

3. Add the tomato, garlic, vinegar, oil, parsley, pine nuts, pepper sauce, salt, and pepper. Blend but leave the mixture chunky. Taste for seasoning.

4. Refrigerate the eggplant caviar at least 2 hours to marry flavors. May be frozen without flavor loss up to 2 months.

To Prepare the Zucchini Boats

1. Cut the zucchini in half lengthwise. Scoop out a hollow with a teaspoon. Repeat. Seed and cut each half in thirds if using 1 overgrown squash.

2. Bring a 2½-quart saucepan half full of water to a boil. Add the halved zucchini and blanch 3 minutes (10 minutes if using a very large one). Drain. *Alternately, wrap zucchini in plastic wrap. Microwave at high (100 percent power) for 4 minutes.*

3. Preheat oven to 350 degrees. Place the zucchini boats in an oven-safe serving dish just large enough to hold them. Season with salt. Mound 3 tablespoons of eggplant caviar into each small half, or divide the mixture to fill the larger zucchini boats. Sprinkle with cheese. Bake in the 350-degree oven about 30 minutes or until bubbly and cheese is browned.

Note: Boats may be held for several hours, even a day, before cooking.

RATATOUILLE

Ratatouille is a medley of eggplant, zucchini, onions, peppers, and tomatoes heady with the perfume of sweet basil. It takes a bit of time to prepare but is best made a day ahead. It also freezes well. Make it when summer's produce is at its peak, and serve it beside a cold poached salmon or a simple roasted chicken. All by itself it makes for a most satisfying lunch. For an all-vegetable meal, serve it with rice.

1 small eggplant, about ¹/₂ pound

3 teaspoons extra-virgin olive oil

1 medium zucchini

4 tablespoons chicken broth or canned consomme

2 green peppers, diced

2 medium onions, diced, about 1³/₄ cups

1 clove garlic, minced

1 pound tomatoes, blanched, peeled, and seeded

10 fresh basil leaves, snipped, or 1 teaspoon dried basil

1 teaspoon salt

freshly ground pepper to taste

1 tablespoon minced fresh parsley

Yield: 6 servings

Calories per serving: 74

Protein per serving: 2g

Fat per serving: 3g

  Saturated fat per serving: trace

Cholesterol per serving: trace

Carbohydrates per serving: 12g

Sodium per serving: 355mg

Fiber per serving: 3g

1. Cut the ends from the eggplant and slice it into rounds ¹/₂-inch thick. Stack the slices and cut the rounds into 6 or 8 wedges.

2. With cooking spray, spray a nonstick skillet large enough to hold the eggplant in one layer. Add 2 teaspoons of the oil and turn the heat to high. When hot, add the eggplant and cook over high heat until tender and lightly browned, about 8 minutes. Lower heat if eggplant starts to burn. Shake pan vigorously by the handle during cooking to keep the eggplant from sticking, and to turn it. Transfer to a casserole.

3. While the eggplant cooks, cut the ends from the zucchini, slice it into rounds, stack the slices, and cut them into wedges.

4. Spray the skillet again, add the rest of the oil, along with the zucchini, and cook over high heat until lightly browned. Shake the pan often during cooking. Transfer zucchini to the casserole with the eggplant.

5. Add the broth to the now-empty skillet, add the peppers, onions, and garlic, cover the skillet, and cook over medium-low heat until the vegetables are limp. If there is visible liquid after cooking, raise the heat to high to evaporate. Add these to the eggplant mixture.

6. Bring a 2½-quart saucepan half full of water to a boil. Core the tomatoes and make a cross in each one's bottom. Immerse in the boiling water until the skins loosen, about 40 seconds. Cool under running water. Skin the tomatoes. Holding a tomato over a strainer within a bowl, squeeze the seeds from each one. Hold the strainer over the casserole and press the seeds with a wooden spoon to extract the juice. Discard the seeds. Chop the tomato pulp and add it to the casserole.

7. Snip the basil into the eggplant-tomato mixture. Season with salt and lots of freshly ground pepper. Toss to mix well. Sprinkle parsley on top.

8. Casserole may be baked, covered, at 350 degrees for about 35 minutes or until heated through, or cooked over low heat, covered, on top of the stove. Be careful the vegetables don't burn on the bottom. *Alternately, it may be microwaved at high (100 percent power) for 15 minutes, covered with plastic wrap.* Serve warm, at room temperature, or cold.

TOMATOES

While genetic engineering promises vine-ripened tomatoes will arrive at your supermarket any day now, right now the only good tomato is still a local tomato. It doesn't matter where "local" is—though New Jerseyites will disagree—it only matters that the tomato is allowed to ripen on the vine to develop peak flavor. Don't be misled by the current "vine-ripened" label. Vine ripened does mean the fruit was picked at maturity, but possibly while still green. The reddening is accomplished by spraying the shipment with ethylene gas. Other vine-ripened tomatoes are picked when just pink. These need no booster of ethylene gas, but they do need, in my opinion, Mother Nature to raise them right. Only the sun can impart the sweet, rich flavor of a truly vine-ripened tomato, the sort you buy at a local farmstand.

Another tomato you may have seen is the greenhouse or hydroponic tomato. This is grown in water and is amazingly good, though quite expensive.

Although tomatoes, or a not-so-reasonable facsimile, can be purchased all year long, the season for most local tomatoes is from May to September, depending on your location. "Seconds," bruised or misshapen tomatoes, are perfect for many uses at about half the price of the perfect specimens.

An uncooked tomato supplies a little over half an adult's daily need for vitamin C, for a meager 35 calories.

The recipes that follow are for those sun-dappled months when local tomatoes abound.

CHEESE-FROSTED TOMATOES

Select small- to medium-size local tomatoes for this quick vegetable dish. To cook on a covered grill, place them on a sheet of aluminum foil. Tomatoes may be prepared for cooking hours before baking.

6 ripe tomatoes
¹/₄ teaspoon salt
freshly ground pepper to taste
1 tablespoon olive oil
6 teaspoons Basil Salsa, page 31, or 15 leaves fresh basil, snipped, or
    3 teaspoons dried basil
6 tablespoons grated Parmesan cheese

1. Core the tomatoes and make a cross on each one's bottom. Bring a 4-quart saucepan half full of water to a boil. Immerse the tomatoes for 30 seconds, or just long enough to loosen the skins. Remove them, cool under running water, and peel off the skins.

2. With a melon baller, make a well where the core was. Place the tomatoes in a baking dish.

3. Preheat oven to 325 degrees. Season tomatoes with salt and pepper. Drizzle with oil. Place a teaspoon of Basil Salsa or the basil in each tomato well. Divide the cheese over the top and bake in a 325-degree oven for 20 minutes. If desired, broil until the cheese is lightly browned.

Yield: 6 servings
Calories per serving: 68
Protein per serving: 3g
Fat per serving: 4g
   Saturated fat per serving: 1g
Cholesterol per serving: 4mg
Carbohydrates per serving: 5g
Sodium per serving: 190mg
Fiber per serving: 1g

Tomato and Chèvre Tart

Tomatoes and cheese, a standard coupling of age-proven compatibility, are updated here with the introduction of chèvre. The production of chèvre, essentially a cottage industry, has caught on in this country, although most chèvre is imported. For your pleasure, here's a tart that travels well and, like most vegetable tarts, is as tempting at room temperature as it is hot from the oven.

Yield: 6 servings

Calories per serving: 144

Protein per serving: 10g

Fat per serving: 3g

  Saturated fat per serving: 2g

Cholesterol per serving: 6mg

Carbohydrates per serving: 20g

Sodium per serving: 322mg

Fiber per serving: 3g

3 pounds tomatoes

3 tablespoons chicken broth

2 medium onions, chopped (preferably mild)

1 clove garlic, minced

8–10 fresh basil leaves, snipped, or 1 teaspoon dried basil

1/8 teaspoon fennel seed

1 teaspoon sugar

1/2 teaspoon salt

freshly ground pepper to taste

3/4 cup egg substitute

1/2 cup crème blanc (page 34) or nonfat sour cream

a few gratings fresh nutmeg

2 ounces chèvre cheese, such as Montrachet or Banon (if a milder
*   taste is preferred)*

2 sheets phyllo dough

1. Bring a 4-quart saucepan ¾ full of water to a boil. Blanch the tomatoes, peel the skins, and seed the tomatoes into a strainer supported over a bowl. Press the seeds with a spoon to extract the juices, then discard seeds. Chop the tomatoes roughly and set aside with reserved juices.

2. Put the broth in a 10-inch skillet over high heat. Add the onion, cover, and cook over medium-high heat until limp, about 6–8 minutes. Add the garlic the last few minutes of cooking.

3. Add the reserved juice, tomatoes, basil, fennel seed, sugar, salt, and pepper. Cook over medium-low heat, stirring occasionally, for 5 minutes. If there is more than $\frac{1}{4}$ cup liquid left, raise the heat to high to evaporate. Set the mixture aside.

4. In a bowl or a food processor, beat together the egg substitute, crème blanc, and nutmeg. Set it aside.

5. Crisscross the 2 sheets of phyllo in a 9-inch removable-bottom tart ring or in a 9-inch quiche pan. Trim the overhanging pastry with scissors to $1\frac{1}{2}$ inches.

6. Preheat oven to 350 degrees. Pour the tomato-onion mixture into the pan. Add the egg mixture. Crumble the chèvre on top. Roll and crumple the pastry edges in to create a rim. Don't worry if the pastry tears. Spray the pastry edge with cooking spray to help it brown. Place in the bottom third of the preheated 350-degree oven and bake 45 minutes or until the center no longer wiggles when shaken. Let it rest 10 minutes before slicing.

Note: Never spray cooking spray into the oven; an explosive fire could result.

WINTER SQUASH

Hard-shelled squash, commonly called winter squash, is available much of the year. Some varieties such as acorn and buttercup are marketed throughout the year.

Squash is indigenous to the New World and was unknown in Europe until explorers returned home with the new vegetable. When North American Indians introduced the English settlers to "askootasquash," meaning eaten raw, the Europeans shortened the name to squash and proceeded to cook it. Cooking is still the norm.

The common varieties include:

Acorn: ribbed dark-green skin.

Buttercup: dark green with stripes of gray; blossom end is turban shaped.

Butternut: smooth buff-colored skin with a bulbous end.

Hubbard: warty skin with maybe blue-gray, green, or an orange tint.

Turban: two-toned with the top knot blue-gray, and the remainder an orange with stripes.

Spaghetti squash: a recently popular hard-shelled squash. It is a gourd of oriental origin that is becoming increasingly available. When cooked, its bland but pleasantly crunchy strands resemble thin spaghetti, but with far fewer calories.

Most varieties of winter squash provide a tasty source of beta-carotene, along with significant amounts of riboflavin and iron. They supply approximately 35 to 70 calories a half-cup.

Winter squashes are long-keeping vegetables. They do best in a cool, dry, well-ventilated spot where they will keep one to four weeks.

SPAGHETTI SQUASH PRIMAVERA

Spaghetti squash may be tossed with just a hint of reduced-calorie margarine and seasoned with salt and pepper, or you can gussy it up, as it is here. It is delicious with either the Basil Salsa (page 31), or the Lemon Parsley Sauce (page 30). It may be baked, boiled, microwaved, or steamed.

This casserole will satisfy some appetites as a complete meal, though others may want a little something else. It may be assembled early in the day or at the last minute.

1 2-pound spaghetti squash

1 tablespoon reduced-calorie margarine, at room temperature

2 ounces grated Parmesan

¹/₂ bunch broccoli flowerets, sliced

1 cup shelled fresh peas (about 1 pound in the pod)

1 small zucchini, julienned

3 ounces cooked lean ham, cut into strips

³/₄ cup sliced mushrooms

1 teaspoon salt

freshly ground pepper to taste

Yield: 4–6 servings

Calories per serving: 141

Protein per serving: 10g

Fat per serving: 5g

   Saturated fat per serving: 2g

Cholesterol per serving: 15mg

Carbohydrates per serving: 13g

Sodium per serving: 746mg

Fiber per serving: 4g

1. Cut the squash in half the short way. Place it, cut side down, with 1 inch of water in a baking dish just large enough to hold it.

2. Bake at 350 degrees until the shell is easily pierced with a fork and the flesh shreds when pulled with a fork, about 45 minutes. *Alternately, wrap the halves in plastic wrap and microwave at high (100 percent power) for 15 minutes or until tender.* Cool, scoop out, and discard the seeds. Pull the strands from the squash into a bowl. Discard the tough skin. Toss the squash strands with the margarine and the cheese.

3. While the squash is baking, prepare the vegetables. Bring a 2¹/₂-quart saucepan ³/₄ full of water to a boil. Add the broccoli, boil 1 minute; add the

peas, cook 1 minute more; add the zucchini and cook 30 seconds more. Drain and cool all the vegetables under running water. Set vegetables aside.

4. Spray an 8-inch nonstick skillet with cooking spray, add the ham strips, and stir-fry them until they're lightly browned. Transfer strips from the pan to a paper towel.

5. In the same pan, sprayed again if necessary, stir-fry the mushrooms until lightly browned.

6. In a large bowl, combine the cooked spaghetti squash, drained vegetables, mushrooms, and ham. Season with salt and pepper and toss well to combine. Spoon into a casserole. Casserole is ready to eat, or set aside. Reheat, covered, in a 350-degree oven for 30–35 minutes. Uncover the last 10 minutes of cooking. *Alternately, heat in the microwave at high (100 percent power) 5–8 minutes or until warmed through.*

BOURBON SQUASH SOUFFLÉ

A puffy presentation of pureed butternut squash combined with bourbon and a hint of maple syrup, this soufflé is just the thing when you want a vegetable dish of distinction. Everything except beating the egg whites may be readied far in advance of the actual cooking, making it an easy-to-make party dish. If you prefer, you can make the soufflé in its entirety and freeze it, uncooked. Turn the freezer to its coldest setting. Cover the soufflé with aluminum foil or plastic wrap and freeze solidly. If the soufflé was frozen in a freezer-to-oven dish, bake it frozen, and double the cooking time. In a more fragile dish, thaw for 30 minutes, then bake, again doubling the cooking time. Some of the dramatic puff is sacrificed in this method, but it is convenient.

Yield: 6 servings

Calories per serving: 115

Protein per serving: 6g

Fat per serving: 1g

   Saturated fat per serving: trace

Cholesterol per serving: 2mg

Carbohydrates per serving: 20g

Sodium per serving: 272mg

Fiber per serving: 2g

1 medium butternut squash, about 1¼ pounds

2 tablespoons bourbon

3 tablespoons maple syrup

½ teaspoon salt

freshly ground pepper to taste

a few gratings nutmeg

3 tablespoons cornstarch

1½ cups skim milk

¼ cup egg substitute

1 tablespoon grated Parmesan cheese or dried bread crumbs

4 egg whites

a pinch cream of tartar

1. Preheat the oven to 400 degrees. Peel the squash, chop into eighths, and discard the seeds. Bring a 2½-quart saucepan ⅔ full of water to a boil, immerse the squash, and cook it until tender, about 20 minutes. Drain.

2. Mash the squash with the bourbon, maple syrup, salt, pepper, and nutmeg. Set the mixture aside.

3. Dissolve the cornstarch in the milk. Set it over medium-high heat and whisk until thickened, about 3 minutes. Set aside.

4. In a food processor or a bowl with a hand-held mixer, beat the egg substitute into the squash puree. Beat in the thickened milk. Set aside or refrigerate.

5. Spray a 1-quart soufflé dish or other straight-sided baking dish (preferably with a 6-inch diameter) with cooking spray. Sprinkle in cheeses or bread crumbs. Shake the dish to evenly distribute. Make a collar for the dish by folding a length of aluminum foil, long enough to encircle the dish with a 2-inch overlap, into thirds. Spray the nonseamed side of the foil with cooking spray, or butter it heavily. Wrap this collar seam side out, tightly around the dish, secure it with a straight pin or paper clip.

6. When you're ready to complete this soufflé, beat the egg whites until foamy. Add the cream of tartar. Beat until soft peaks form. Scoop the egg whites on top of the squash mixture. Fold them in gently. Ladle (pouring can deflate the whites) the soufflé mixture into the soufflé dish.

7. Put 1 inch water in an 8-inch square baking dish. Put the soufflé dish in the baking dish on top of the stove. Turn heat to high, simmer for 5 minutes. Baking pan and all, slide soufflé into the bottom third of a preheated oven. Check the soufflé after 35 minutes. If the top is browning too fast, cover loosely with foil. Cook 15 to 25 minutes more. Soufflé is done when a skewer inserted slightly off center comes out dry. Remove collar and serve immediately.

WHOLE WHEAT VEGETABLE TORTILLAS

Speed your prep time by picking up prechopped vegetables from the supermarket salad bar. Be sure to check the label when purchasing tortillas; buy those made without lard, which is high in saturated fat.

1 stalk broccoli, flowerets only, chopped

2 small carrots, thinly sliced

1/2 green pepper, thinly sliced

1/2 zucchini, thinly sliced

1 cup thinly sliced mushrooms

4 tablespoons chopped Spanish onion

1/2 teaspoon seasoned or regular salt

1/2 teaspoon dried oregano

1 tablespoon reduced-calorie margarine

4 whole wheat taco-size tortillas

1 medium tomato, chopped

2 scallions, chopped

2 ounces fat-free cheddar cheese, shredded

Blackened Tomato Salsa (page 165) to pass at the table

Yield: 4 tortillas

Calories per tortilla: 186

Protein per tortilla: 10g

Fat per tortilla: 5g

   Saturated fat per tortilla: 1g

Cholesterol per tortilla: 3mg

Carbohydrates per tortilla: 30g

Sodium per tortilla: 628mg

Fiber per tortilla: 4g

1. Combine the broccoli, carrots, green pepper, zucchini, mushrooms, onion, salt, and oregano in a 4-cup glass measure or other microwave-safe container. Add 3 tablespoons water, cover with plastic wrap, and microwave at high (100 percent power) for 5 minutes or until vegetables are tender but crisp. Drain.

2. While the vegetables cook, spread the margarine on one side of each tortilla. Spray a 12-inch nonstick skillet with nonstick cooking spray. Lay the tortillas, two at a time, buttered side down, in the skillet.

3. Cover one half of each tortilla with the mixed vegetables. Divide the tomatoes, scallions, and cheese among them. Fold the top half of the tortilla over the filling. Saute at medium-high heat until one side is lightly browned, about 4 minutes. Flip and cook on the other side until lightly browned, about 3 minutes. Pass salsa at the table.

RISOTTO

A creamy risotto is a wonderful side dish. When embellished with summer squash, zucchini, diced tomato, and a bit of Parmesan cheese, it's a deliciously satisfying main dish as well. For proper results, check the Italian section of your market for arborio, a short-grain rice.

1 small onion, minced

1 cup arborio rice

2 teaspoons reduced-calorie margarine

1 13¾-ounce can chicken broth

1 cup water

1 chicken bouillon cube

1 small summer squash, diced (optional)

3 tablespoons grated Parmesan (optional)

Yield: 6 servings

Calories per serving: 142

Protein per serving: 3g

Fat per serving: 1g

   Saturated fat per serving: trace

Cholesterol per serving: trace

Carbohydrates per serving: 29g

Sodium per serving: 226mg

Fiber per serving: 1g

1. Combine the onion, rice, and margarine in a 2-quart heavy-bottom saucepan. Lightly toast the rice mixture over medium-low heat about 3 minutes, stirring often.

2. *To microwave, combine toasted rice and all remaining ingredients except squash and Parmesan in a microwave safe 2½-quart dish. Stir, cover, and microwave on high (100 percent power) for 10 minutes. Add squash, stir, cover, and microwave on high for an additional 7 to 8 minutes. Stir in Parmesan; let stand 5 minutes before serving.* To cook conventionally, while the rice toasts, bring the chicken broth, water, and bouillon cube to a boil in a 1-quart saucepan.

3. Add about ½ cup of broth to the rice. Stir, cover, and adjust heat so rice just simmers in the hot broth.

4. Continue to add the broth, gradually, stirring after each addition. The rice should absorb the liquid before more is added. When about ¾ of the liquid has been added, stir in the summer squash, if desired. When all the liquid is absorbed, stir in the Parmesan. Let the risotto sit about 2 minutes before serving.

VEGGIE MADNESS

Why not? After all, there's "Chocolate Madness" on every dessert cart. So, vegetables aren't quite as addicting as chocolate, and few people actually crave a good, juicy carrot, but this is still a pretty good recipe for those vegetable addicts among us. Go ahead, go mad. Your hips will never regret it, which is more than I can say for "Chocolate Madness." Hint: Fresh herbs make an important difference in this dish.

Yield: 4 veggie addict or 6 nonaddict
   servings
Calories per serving: 49
Protein per serving: 2g
Fat per serving: 1g
   Saturated fat per serving: trace
Cholesterol per serving: trace
Carbohydrates per serving: 9g
Sodium per serving: 399mg
Fiber per serving: 3g

1 stalk broccoli, stems peeled and thinly sliced, flowerets chopped
½ cup chopped cauliflower
1½ carrots, cut in thin sticks
4 tablespoons chicken broth
½ zucchini, sliced in thin sticks
½ red bell pepper, sliced in thin strips
½ summer squash, sliced in thin sticks
4 ounces mushrooms, sliced
¼ cup Spanish onion, chopped
⅓ cup minced fresh parsley
1 teaspoon Adobo seasoning (available in Spanish section of many
      markets), seasoned salt, or regular salt
freshly ground pepper to taste
1 tablespoon fresh minced tarragon or 1 teaspoon dried tarragon
1 clove garlic, minced
1 shallot, minced
1 tablespoon lemon juice
1 tablespoon reduced-calorie margarine
3 tablespoons chicken broth

1. In a microwave-safe bowl, combine the broccoli, cauliflower, carrots, and 4 tablespoons chicken broth. Cover with plastic wrap and microwave at high (100 percent power) for 8 minutes.

2. Uncover and add the zucchini, red pepper, summer squash, mushrooms, and onion. Stir to combine. Sprinkle with parsley. Season with Adobo seasoning or salt and pepper.

3. Combine the tarragon, garlic, shallot, lemon juice, margarine, and 3 tablespoons broth in a 1-cup glass measure or other microwave-safe container. Heat at high (100 percent power) for 1 minute or until margarine is melted. Pour mixture over the veggies.

4. Cover again with plastic wrap and cook at high (100 percent power) for 7 minutes more.

FOUR-VEGETABLE PIE
WITH FRESH MOZZARELLA CHEESE

Whether served as an elegant side dish or as the star of an all-vegetable meal, this dish will garner much-deserved raves. It may be prepared through step 5 early in the day. Adobo seasoning is available in the Mexican and/or Spanish section of many markets.

Yield: 4–6 servings

Calories per serving: 129

Protein per serving: 7g

Fat per serving: 7g

  Saturated fat per serving: 3g

Cholesterol per serving: 12mg

Carbohydrates per serving: 12g

Sodium per serving: 558mg

Fiber per serving: 2g

1 medium eggplant, cut in half lengthwise, then sliced thinly crosswise

8 plum tomatoes, sliced thinly lengthwise

¹/₂ bulb fennel, diced

¹/₂ cup diced Spanish onion

3 tablespoons chopped fresh basil

¹/₂ teaspoon seasoned or regular salt

freshly ground pepper to taste

1 tablespoon lemon juice

1 teaspoon reduced-calorie margarine

2 tablespoons bread crumbs

2 tablespoons grated Parmesan cheese

1 teaspoon dried oregano

¹/₂ teaspoon salt, seasoned salt, or Adobo seasoning

freshly ground pepper to taste

4 ounces fresh mozzarella or part-skim mozzarella cheese, sliced thinly

1 tablespoon excellent-quality oil, such as olive or walnut

1. Lay the eggplant in a single layer on cotton or paper towels. Sprinkle with salt and let rest 10–15 minutes.

2. Turn eggplant over, salt the other side, and let rest another 5 to 10 minutes. Rinse and pat dry.

3. Form a ring of eggplant slices up along the sloped edge of a 10-inch glass pie plate or other microwave-safe dish. Leave the center of the dish empty. Intersperse the tomato slices between the eggplant slices.

4. Combine the fennel and onion. Fill the center with this mixture; some will spill onto the eggplant as well.

5. Sprinkle basil on top. Season with salt and pepper and sprinkle with lemon juice.

6. Cover with plastic wrap. Microwave at high (100 percent power) for 18 minutes.

7. While the vegetable pie cooks, melt the margarine in an 8-inch nonstick skillet. Combine the bread crumbs, Parmesan, oregano, salt or Adobo season-ing, and pepper. Stir to brown lightly over medium-low heat, for about 1 minute.

8. Remove plastic wrap from pie. Make a ring with the cheese slices, leaving a small circle empty in the middle of the pie. Divide the bread crumbs between this center and the outside perimeter of the pie. Drizzle oil over all.

9. Place pie in the upper third of an oven, turn heat to 425 degrees, and bake until lightly browned, about 5–8 minutes, or broil until crumbs are browned. Let rest 5–10 minutes before slicing in wedges.

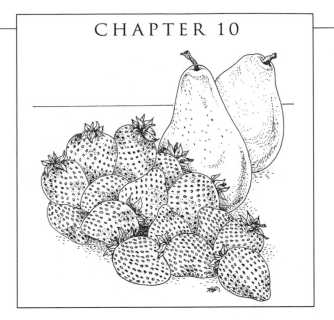

Sweets and Treats

THE RECIPES

SWEETS AND TREATS

Because the premise of *Gourmet Light* rests on fine foods skillfully prepared, there is no room for ersatz, make-do ingredients. This restriction (but certainly no limitation) excludes the use of saccharin or other artificial sweeteners. Thus most of the desserts here capitalize on the naturally occurring sugars (fructose) in fruits and/or rely on reduced amounts of cane sugar.

Most desserts are based, in some combination, on sugar, flour, and fat, either butter and/or cream. These key ingredients are among the most caloric of all foods, while contributing few nutrients. Sugar, white or brown, contains about 873 calories a cup. White sugar is virtually nutrient empty, while 3½ ounces of brown sugar supplies almost as much potassium as does a banana and a small amount of calcium—but at a terrific calorie toll. The second key ingredient in sweets is cream at 838 calories and 80 grams of fat a cup. And flour is another 800 calories a cup, to say nothing of butter at 1,600 calories and 200 grams of fat a cup, an important component of the dessert cart, however in hidden form. The body tallies these calories more accurately than the bank does your checks.

This small collection of dessert recipes, in keeping with the *Gourmet Light* theme, limits the use of sugar, fats, and flours. But by its mere existence, this section acknowledges that one cannot live by fish and green beans alone, nor even the ideal dessert of unadorned fresh fruit. It is hoped, particularly if weight loss rather than maintenance is your goal, that portion sizes are closely watched.

BERRIES AND ALMOND CREAM

Fresh strawberries, blueberries, or raspberries smothered in cream—sweet heaven that can be yours given the *Gourmet Light* touch. This custard sauce, with the texture of clotted cream and the fragrance of vanilla or almond, is wonderful over fresh, ripe fruits or as a dipping sauce for a fruit fondue, all for a meager 55 calories and 1 gram of fat. It is also delightful spooned over slices of Almond Angel Cake, page 313. Perhaps the best endorsement is from a friend who mused, "Mmmmmmmmm, it tastes fattening!"

Yield: 6 servings

Calories per serving: 104

Protein per serving: 6g

Fat per serving: 1g

  Saturated fat per serving: trace

Cholesterol per serving: 37mg

Carbohydrates per serving: 18g

Sodium per serving: 71mg

Fiber per serving: 3g

For the Almond Cream

1 1/2 cups skim milk

3 egg whites

1 egg

3 tablespoons sugar

1 teaspoon almond extract

a few gratings fresh nutmeg

For the Berries

1 quart fresh strawberries or other berries, stemmed and rinsed

1 tablespoon sugar

1. *In a microwave oven at high (100 percent power), heat the milk in a 4-cup measuring cup or other microwave-safe container for 5 minutes or until scalded.* Alternately, scald the milk in a heavy-bottom 1-quart saucepan on the stove over high heat.

2. While the milk heats, process the egg whites and egg in the bowl of a food processor at high for 1 minute.

3. With the food processor on high, dribble the scalded milk into the eggs. Add the sugar. Continue to process for an additional 2–3 minutes.

4. Pour the egg-milk mixture into a 2½-quart heavy bottom saucepan. Place over medium-high heat, stirring constantly in a figure-eight pattern with a wooden spoon. As mixture begins to emit steam wisps, lower heat to medium. Continue to stir until custard doubles in volume and begins to thicken. Reduce heat if sauce nears the boiling point. The custard will condense, thicken to the consistency of melted ice cream, and coat a metal spoon. This happens when the sauce reaches about 175 degrees, in a total cooking time of about 6 minutes.

5. Strain the sauce into a bowl. Stir in the extract and nutmeg. The sauce can be served warm, at room temperature, or chilled.

6. Clean the berries. Cut strawberries in half if desired. Toss with the tablespoon sugar. Divide berries among serving dishes and spoon on almond cream.

Note: Some chefs like to toss fresh strawberries with just a touch of black pepper on the premise that it heightens their flavor.

BURGUNDY POACHED PEARS WITH CRÈME ANGLAISE

For this variation on a classic dessert, poached pears perched atop a puddle of custard sauce are gently broiled until lightly browned. The components of the dish may be readied a day before, then assembled up to 4 hours before serving. The poaching liquid may be frozen and reused over and over again.

4 pears, peeled, halved, and cored
2 tablespoons lemon juice

Yield: 4 servings

Calories per serving: 185

Protein per serving: 6g

Fat per serving: 1g

   Saturated fat per serving: trace

Cholesterol per serving: 1mg

Carbohydrates per serving: 41g

Sodium per serving: 226mg

Fiber per serving: 4g

For the Poaching Liquid

1 liter burgundy wine

1/2 cup sugar

1 vanilla bean

juice of a half a lemon

a cinnamon stick

3 whole cloves

For the Crème Anglaise

3/4 cup egg substitute

3 tablespoons sugar

1/4 teaspoon salt

1 cup skim milk, scalded

1 teaspoon vanilla extract

To Prepare the Pears

1. As you peel the pears, slip them into a bowl with the lemon juice to keep them from turning brown.

2. Bring the poaching ingredients to a boil in a 4-quart saucepan. Reduce to a simmer, immerse the pears, cover, and poach until a skewer easily pierces the fruit. Turn the pears during cooking, as they will not be completely covered. Do not cook until mushy. The cooking time will depend entirely on the ripeness of the fruit, anywhere from 10 to 25 minutes or even longer.

3. Drain the pears when tender on a rack over a sheet of waxed paper (to collect drippings). Freeze liquid for future poachings (you can leave the spices in the wine).

To Prepare the Crème Anglaise

1. In a heavy 2½-quart saucepan, beat together the egg substitute, sugar, and salt. Do not ribbon the mixture.

2. Slowly add the scalded milk, whisking all the while.

3. Insert a thermometer at the side of the pan if you like. Stirring with a wooden spoon over medium heat, notice the changes that occur. At 140 degrees, steam rises from the custard. At 155 degrees, the foam starts getting lighter, and at 165 degrees, the surface is smooth and the custard is ready.

You may heat the custard to 180 degrees, but not higher, or the eggs will curdle. Without a thermometer, stir the custard over medium heat until it is thick enough to coat a metal spoon, about 3–4 minutes.

4. Strain the custard into a bowl and stir in vanilla extract.

To Finish the Dessert

1. Preheat broiler. Spread the custard sauce on an ovenproof serving dish such as a quiche dish, or on 4 ovenproof serving dishes such as baking shells.

2. Place the poached pear half, flat side down, on a cutting surface. Cut into 5–6 segments, but leave stem end uncut so the pear becomes "fanned." Repeat with remaining pears. Place the pear fan on the custard sauce and broil until heated through.

Note: A few drops of red food coloring added to the poaching liquid will heighten the color of the poached pears.

Making a Pear Fan

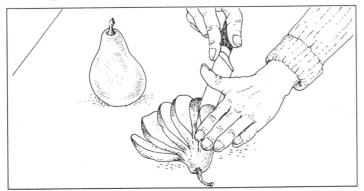

Place a poached pear half, flat side down, on a flat surface. Cut it into five or six segments, leaving them attached at the stem end.

CANDIED ORANGES WITH MELBA SAUCE

The simplicity of this classic dessert I find very appealing—juicy seedless oranges enhanced with a sugar syrup and drizzled with ruby red raspberry sauce. It may be prepared a day in advance.

8 small navel oranges

³/₄ cup sugar

1¹/₂ cups water

juice of ¹/₂ lemon

2 kiwis

2 tablespoons orange-flavored liqueur, such as Triple Sec or
*   Grand Marnier*

a 10-ounce package frozen raspberries, thawed

Yield: 8 servings

Calories per serving: 178

Protein per serving: 1g

Fat per serving: trace
    Saturated fat per serving: trace

Cholesterol per serving: 0

Carbohydrates per serving: 44g

Sodium per serving: 3mg

Fiber per serving: 4g

1. With a vegetable peeler, remove the zest (no white) from 2 of the oranges. Julienne the rind and set aside.

2. In a heavy 2¹/₂-quart saucepan, dissolve the sugar in ¹/₂ cup of the water over very low heat. The solution must not boil until the sugar is thoroughly dissolved or it will crystallize. Do not stir the sugar as it dissolves, but swirl the pan by its handle.

3. When all the sugar is dissolved, add the remaining cup of water, the lemon juice, and julienned orange peel. Bring to a boil for 30 seconds, then lower the heat so solution simmers. Cover and simmer 1 hour.

4. Meanwhile, peel the oranges over a bowl to catch the juices. Peel the kiwis. Slice both the oranges and kiwis thinly horizontally. Reshape the oranges into their original form, interspersing the kiwi slices between the orange slices. Hold together with toothpicks. Pile into a deep glass bowl and chill until serving time.

5. Remove the sugar syrup from heat. Stir in the orange-flavored liqueur. Pour it over the oranges.

6.Place the berries in a food processor or blender and puree. Force the puree through a strainer. Discard the seeds. Stir in the orange juice from peeling the oranges in Step 4. Drizzle half of the sauce over oranges and pass remaining sauce at the table.

Note: The oranges may be sauced with the sugar syrup and held at room temperature up to 6 hours before serving.

GRAND MARNIER MOUSSE

This cool, cloudlike mousse literally melts in your mouth. It needs at least 2 hours chilling time to set before serving; yet it should be served within 24 hours, as the egg whites break down with time.

1 envelope unflavored gelatin

¹/₄ cup cold water

¹/₂ cup sugar

¹/₂ cup cold water

4 eggs

¹/₄ teaspoon salt

²/₃ cup freshly squeezed orange juice

zest of 1 orange

3 tablespoons orange-flavored liqueur, such as Grand Marnier or
*   Triple Sec*

2 tablespoons rum

2 tablespoons sugar

Yield: 8 servings

Calories per serving: 128

Protein per serving: 4g

Fat per serving: 3g
    Saturated fat per serving: 1g

Cholesterol per serving: 106mg

Carbohydrates per serving: 19g

Sodium per serving: 101mg

Fiber per serving: trace

1. Soften the gelatin in the ¼ cup water in a glass measuring cup for about 2 minutes. Place the cup in a small saucepan ⅓ full of water and warm over medium heat, stirring occasionally, until gelatin is dissolved and clear, about 3 minutes. Set aside.

2. Meanwhile, combine the sugar with ½ cup water in a 1-quart saucepan. Dissolve the sugar over very low heat, swirling the pan by the handle. Do not stir with a spoon. When the solution is clear, turn the heat to high and boil 1 minute. Do not let sugar syrup begin to brown. Set it aside.

3. Separate the eggs. Break the egg yolks into the top part of a double boiler, the whites into a glass, ceramic, or copper bowl. Set the bottom of the double boiler with 1 inch of water over high heat. Insert the top half of double boiler. Beat the yolks over the simmering water until thickened and very pale in color, about 2 minutes. Regulating heat so the water just simmers, continue beating while dribbling in the hot sugar syrup from Step 2. Beat until the mixture doubles in volume, thickens, and feels warm to the touch, about 6–8 minutes. Remove from heat and continue beating until mixture ribbons (falls from beaters in a wide band that lies on top of the mass for a moment before sinking in).

4. Stir the dissolved gelatin, salt, orange juice, zest, orange liqueur, and rum into the yolks.

5. Wash the beaters thoroughly and beat the egg whites until stiff. Gradually beat in the sugar.

6. Fold the whites into gelatin-yolk mixture.

7. Pour the mousse into individual glasses or a 6-cup mold sprayed with cooking spray. Chill at least 2 hours to set. Unmold if desired.

CREPES SUZETTE

Crepes Suzette were invented by the Franco-American cook Henri Charpentier. Quite by accident, the butter sauce he was preparing caught on fire, with results that thousands of cooks have since plagiarized. Here is my reduced-calorie version. The crepes and sauce may be readied early in the day, then assembled and flamed before serving to appreciative guests.

Yield: 6 servings

Calories per serving: 127

Protein per serving: 3g

Fat per serving: 3g

Saturated fat per serving: trace

Cholesterol per serving: 1mg

Carbohydrates per serving: 21g

Sodium per serving: 106mg

Fiber per serving: trace

For the Crepes

1/3 cup egg substitute

3/4 cup skim milk

6 tablespoons flour

pinch salt

1 tablespoon reduced-fat margarine

For the Sauce

1 1/2 tablespoons reduced-fat margarine

2 tablespoons sugar

2 tablespoons orange marmalade

1 tablespoon each orange and lemon zest

*juice and pulp of 3 fresh oranges (reserve 2 tablespoons for dissolving
    cornstarch)*

2 teaspoons cornstarch

*1 tablespoon orange-flavored liqueur, such as Grand Marnier, Curaçao,
    or Triple Sec*

1 tablespoon kirsch (or use 2 tablespoons orange liqueur)

To Prepare the Crepes

(May be done as much as 1 day in advance.)

1. Beat the egg substitute and milk together, add the flour sifted with the salt, and stir just to combine. Chill 2 hours.

2. Melt ½ teaspoon of the margarine in a nonstick 8-inch skillet until foamy. Ladle just enough batter into the pan to film bottom. Pour excess batter back into bowl when bottom sets. Cook a crepe over medium-high heat until browned on one side. Flip, cooking on underside just to firm (this will be the inside, unseen part), and slide onto a plate. Continue cooking, adding margarine as necessary and placing a sheet of wax paper between the crepes. Crepes may now be used or chilled up to 12 hours or frozen until needed. The recipe makes ten to twelve 12-inch crepes.

To Prepare the Sauce

1. Combine margarine, sugar, marmalade, orange and lemon zest, and juice and pulp of oranges in a 1-quart saucepan over medium heat until heated through.

2. Dissolve the cornstarch in the reserved juice. Stir into the hot orange sauce and stir over medium heat until thickened, about 4 minutes.

To Assemble the Crepes and Serve

1. Fold the crepes in triangle shapes with the unbrowned side facing in, by folding first in halves and then into quarters. Arrange on a flameproof serving dish with sides, such as a quiche dish or a chafing dish. Overlap the crepes by ½ inch. If preparing early in the day, cover with aluminum foil. Before serving sprinkle very lightly with water and heat in a 350-degree oven for about 15 minutes, covered, until warmed through.

2. Pour the warmed sauce over the heated crepes. Keep them warm in the oven or over hot water in a chafing dish while preparing the liqueur for flaming.

3. Heat the liqueurs in a long-handled butter warmer, one with a lip is preferred. When bubbles appear at the pan's edge, remove from the heat. Place dish of warmed crepes on the table. Ignite liqueur with a fireplace match or other long taper. Pour the flaming liqueur over the crepes. Use a spoon to lift sauces as it flames. Serve when flames die out.

MIRACLE CHEESECAKE

This is incredibly good and contains absolutely minimal (read no) fat. Drain the yogurt a day or two before you want to serve this delicious cheesecake, and budget at least 4 hours chilling time. The cheesecake is most successful baked in a 7-inch pan with 3-inch sides. You may find such a springform pan in specialty kitchen stores, or scrub out the aluminum tray of those dimensions from a frozen pot pie.

Yield: 8 servings
Calories per serving: 118
Protein per serving: 11g
Fat per serving: trace
   Saturated fat per serving: trace
Cholesterol per serving: 11mg
Carbohydrates per serving: 16g
Sodium per serving: 401mg
Fiber per serving: trace

16 ounces nonfat vanilla yogurt, drained (see page 54 for yogurt
   cheese instructions)
1 pound nonfat cream cheese
1/2 cup egg substitute
6 tablespoons sugar
1 tablespoon cornstarch
1 teaspoon vanilla extract
the zest of 1 lemon
several gratings fresh nutmeg
a dash salt
cinnamon sugar (optional)
1 pint fresh strawberries, hulled (optional)
1/4 cup "fruit only" strawberry preserves, melted (optional)

1. Preheat the oven to 325 degrees. Combine the drained yogurt cheese (you'll have about 1/2 cup) with all the remaining ingredients except the optional items in the bowl of a food processor. Turn the machine on full power and process 4 full minutes.

2. Meanwhile, spray the baking pan with nonstick cooking spray. Sprinkle with cinnamon sugar if desired. Place the dish on a cookie sheet.

3. Pour the cheesecake mixture into the prepared pan. Bake in the upper third of the oven for about 50–55 minutes or until the mixture no longer jiggles when the cookie sheet is nudged. A toothpick inserted in the center will be slightly tacky. Chill the cake for at least 4 hours.

4. If you wish to add a strawberry topping, cover the cheesecake with the berries with what was the hull side down and tips pointing up. Dab melted preserves on top, concentrating on the edges.

Flaming

Recipes frequently call for igniting liquor, sometimes for effect, sometimes to mellow the sharp alcohol taste. For success with flaming liquors, remember the following tips:

- The liquor must be heated just to the point where small bubbles appear at the edges of the pan.
- If it boils longer than about 10–20 seconds, add more liquor.
- Add a pinch of sugar to ensure long burning.
- Select a long-handled, small pot, preferably with a spout, to heat the liquor. Butter warmers are ideal.

PORT WINE SORBET

A cool finish, perfect for a warm summer meal, this port wine sorbet is ideal with melon. To serve, fill a fluted champagne glass two-thirds full of melon balls that have been marinated in a bit of port wine. Top with a scoop of this sorbet. A tiny dollop would also make a refreshing intermezzo for a formal meal. An ice cream maker is necessary to produce the needed texture. The ginger is available at specialty markets and some general food stores.

¹/₃ cup sugar
¹/₂ cup port wine
1 teaspoon minced crystallized ginger
1 cantaloupe
juice of 1 lemon
seedless red grapes (optional)

Yield: 4 servings
Calories per serving: 129
Protein per serving: 1g
Fat per serving: trace
    Saturated fat per serving: trace
Cholesterol per serving: 0
Carbohydrates per serving: 29g
Sodium per serving: 13mg
Fiber per serving: 1g

1. Combine the sugar, wine, and ginger in a small saucepan over very low heat. Swirl handle until the sugar dissolves. Raise heat to high and boil 5 minutes, without stirring. Remove from heat and chill until cool to the touch.

2. Cut the cantaloupe in half and discard the seeds. Cut off and discard the rind. Puree the flesh in a food processor or food mill.

3. Combine the puree in the cream can of an ice cream maker with the chilled wine syrup and the lemon juice. Process according to manufacturer's instructions, then harden in the freezer.

4. Serve garnished with red grapes, if desired.

FRUIT FONDUE

This is more of an idea than an actual recipe, because proportions and ingredients are strictly up to the cook and the pantry. Assemble a variety of fruits. Cut them into bite-size pieces. Arrange them around a pot or chafing dish of raspberry dipping sauce. Include, if you like, a batch of Almond Cream (page 290) and squares of Almond Angel Cake (page 313). Diners can dip the fruits and cake into either the almond cream or the raspberry sauce. If you prefer, you may film the bottom of a small saucer with 2 to 3 tablespoons of raspberry sauce, place a skewer of fruit over the sauce, and drizzle almond cream on top—a light and pretty summertime dessert.

Yield of sauce: approximately 1 cup
Calories per tablespoon: 23
Protein per tablespoon: trace
Fat per tablespoon: trace
  Saturated fat per tablespoon: trace
Cholesterol per serving: 0
Carbohydrates per serving: 5g
Sodium per serving: trace
Fiber per serving: trace

For the Raspberry Dipping Sauce

1 10-ounce package frozen raspberries or strawberries, thawed

1 tablespoon cornstarch

1 tablespoon orange-flavored liqueur, such as Grand Marnier or Triple Sec

1 tablespoon kirsch (optional)

1. Puree the berries in a food processor or blender. Strain and discard the seeds.

2. Dissolve the cornstarch in the liqueurs.

3. Stir the dissolved cornstarch in the raspberry puree over medium-high heat in a 1-quart saucepan until slightly thickened. Serve hot or chilled.

HOT APPLE TART

Personally, I find any recipe that calls for a half cup of something from some other recipe immediately unappealing. After all, gearing up for one recipe doesn't mean I'm willing to make another. But I urge you to make an exception in this case, or you'll miss perhaps one of the best desserts in this modest collection. This thin apple tart, with its crust of phyllo and icing of Almond Cream (page 290) is best served hot. All components may be readied up to 4 hours in advance, then assembled and baked just prior to serving time. Poached pears may be used in addition to or instead of the apples. Leftovers may be gently reheated in a 300-degree oven for 10 minutes.

Yield: 4 servings

Calories per serving: 144

Protein per serving: 3g

Fat per serving: 6g

   Saturated fat per serving: 1g

Cholesterol per serving: 7mg

Carbohydrates per serving: 18g

Sodium per serving: 152mg

Fiber per serving: 1g

> *¹/₂ ounce sliced or slivered almonds*
>
> *2 tablespoons dried bread crumbs*
>
> *1 tablespoon sugar*
>
> *dash cinnamon*
>
> *2 sheets phyllo dough*
>
> *2 tablespoons reduced-calorie margarine, melted*
>
> *1 apple, Granny Smith or Yellow Delicious recommended*
>
> *1 tablespoon brown sugar*
>
> *4 tablespoons Almond Cream (page 290)*

1. Spray a 7½-inch removable-bottom tart ring with cooking spray. You may use a slightly larger pan, but results won't be as pleasing.

2. In a food processor or blender, combine the almonds, bread crumbs, sugar, and cinnamon. Pulverize until they're fine crumbs. Set aside.

3. Lay a sheet of phyllo into the tart ring, vertically, overlapping it in the middle as you would a sheet of tissue paper in a box. Butter sparingly with a pastry brush dipped in the melted margarine. Sprinkle with half the nut-crumb mixture.

4. Now lay another sheet in the pan, horizontally, also overlapping in the center. Butter very slightly and sprinkle with the remaining crumbs.

5. Fold the overhang inside the rim of the pan.

6. Slice the apple in half the long way, then into quarters. Core it. Slice the quarters very thinly. Arrange the apple slices over the tart ring in circles, with pieces of the apple resting on the phyllo dough rim. Brush all with the remaining margarine. Sprinkle brown sugar over the apples. Set aside, if you wish.

7. When you're ready to complete the tart, preheat the oven to 425 degrees.

8. Place the tart in the lower third of a preheated oven for 20 minutes or until the apples are softened.

9. Spread almond cream over the apple tart and broil for 4–5 minutes or until the almond cream is bubbly and golden. Let the tart rest 5 minutes and serve. It also can be held up to 1 hour on a serving tray.

Thinking Thin Tip

If you're trying to wean yourself from cream and/or sugar in coffee, try adding a 3-inch piece of vanilla bean or a cinnamon stick to the grounds when you make it. The added flavor will help.

MIMOSA SHERBET

Celebrate your success with this champagne-based sherbet. While it may be made without an ice cream freezer simply by hardening in a conventional freezer, it will have a smoother texture if processed in an ice cream freezer.

1 scant cup sugar
⁷/₈ cup water
juice of 1 orange
1 cup Brut champagne
1 tablespoon orange-flavored liqueur, such as Triple Sec or
    Grand Marnier
2 egg whites
mint leaves (optional)

Yield: 6 servings
Calories per serving: 158
Protein per serving: 1g
Fat per serving: trace
    Saturated fat per serving: trace
Cholesterol per serving: 0
Carbohydrates per serving: 32g
Sodium per serving: 22mg
Fiber per serving: trace

1. Combine sugar and water in a 2½-quart saucepan. Swirl the pan by the handle over very low heat until the sugar is dissolved. Do not stir. When the solution is perfectly clear and the sugar is dissolved, raise heat to high and boil without stirring for 7 minutes.

2. Remove the sugar water from heat, pour it into a bowl, and place in the freezer for 15 minutes.

3. Remove from freezer and stir in orange juice, champagne, and orange liqueur.

4. Beat egg whites until stiff, then fold them into champagne mixture. Freeze in an ice cream freezer according to the manufacturer's instructions. Sherbet will be soft after processing. Place in freezer to harden. Garnish with a mint leaf if available.

MANGO MOUSSE

This is a very light, refreshing dessert. Because its color is so pale, you might like to garnish the serving dish or individual servings with a few slices of fresh, colorful fruit—more mango or perhaps oranges. Use only very ripe fruit for this mold.

1 ripe mango, peeled and pitted
1 envelope unflavored gelatin
1 tablespoon cold water
juice of 2 limes
2 egg whites
a tiny pinch salt
¹/₄ teaspoon cream of tartar
¹/₃ cup sugar or 4 tablespoons fructose

Yield: 4 servings

Calories per serving: 111

Protein per serving: 4g

Fat per serving: trace

   Saturated fat per serving: trace

Cholesterol per serving: 0

Carbohydrates per serving: 26g

Sodium per serving: 64mg

Fiber per serving: 1g

1. Peel and puree the mango in a food processor or blender.

2. Soften the gelatin in the cold water until it's spongy.

3. Heat the lime juice in a 1-quart saucepan. When steaming, stir in the gelatin and stir until dissolved, about 1–2 minutes, over medium-low heat.

4. Stir the dissolved gelatin into the fruit puree.

5. Beat the egg whites and salt until foamy. Add the cream of tartar and continue beating until soft peaks form. Gradually add the sugar while beating until stiff.

6. Gently fold the whites into the puree-gelatin mixture.

7. Spray a 2-cup mold with cooking spray. Spoon mousse into mold, tap on kitchen counter to knock out air bubbles, and chill for 4 hours. Unmold and garnish with fresh fruits before serving, if desired.

MAPLE-WALNUT CHIFFON PARFAIT

Frothy and airy, this light dessert smacking of walnuts and maple syrup is a most pleasant way to end a meal. Plan on 3 to 4 hours for the dessert to chill and set.

1 envelope unflavored gelatin	$1/2$ teaspoon salt
$1/2$ cup skim milk	1 tablespoon rum
$1/2$ cup egg substitute	1 teaspoon walnut extract
$1/2$ cup reduced-sugar maple syrup	3 egg whites, beaten until stiff
4 ounces nonfat cream cheese	$1/4$ cup chopped walnuts
several gratings nutmeg	3 tablespoons fat-free granola

1. Soften the gelatin in $1/4$ cup of the milk. Set aside.

2. Beat the egg substitute with the remaining milk, $1/4$ cup of the maple syrup, and the cream cheese, nutmeg, and salt in the bowl of a food processor. Scrape mixture into a heavy-bottomed 2-quart saucepan.

3. Whisk the egg mixture over medium heat until it becomes frothy and swells, about 4 minutes. Remove from heat and whisk until somewhat cooled, about 30 seconds.

4. Stir in the gelatin, rum, and walnut extract. Set aside.

5. Fold the remaining $1/4$ cup maple syrup into the egg whites. Fold the whites into the gelatin mixture. Fold in the walnuts.

6. Divide the mixture among 6 parfait glasses. Sprinkle tops with the granola. Chill 3 to 4 hours. Serve with reduced-fat whipped cream or nondairy topping if desired.

Yield: 6 servings

Calories per serving: 100

Protein per serving: 9g

Fat per serving: 3g

   Saturated fat per serving: trace

Cholesterol per serving: 4mg

Carbohydrates per serving: 7g

Sodium per serving: 355mg

Fiber per serving: trace

RASPBERRY CREPES SOUFFLÉ

This showy dessert—a raspberry meringue folded inside a thin crepe, which is in turn doused with more raspberry—waits for no man, woman, or child. It needs to be served immediately from the oven, or a slumped collection of crepes will be all you will have to show for your efforts. The crepes and the meringue soufflé mixture, however, may be readied and assembled days in advance, frozen, and baked without thawing, making a light and lovely dessert that takes just 20 minutes from freezer to table.

Yield: 6–8 servings

Calories per serving: 107

Protein per serving: 4g

Fat per serving: 1g

   Saturated fat per serving: trace

Cholesterol per serving: 28mg

Carbohydrates per serving: 21g

Sodium per serving: 64mg

Fiber per serving: 1g

For the Crepes

1 egg, beaten, or ¼ cup egg substitute

½ cup nonfat milk

¼ cup flour

pinch salt

1 tablespoon sugar

1 tablespoon orange zest

For the Soufflé

1 10-ounce package frozen unsweetened raspberries, thawed (fresh, of course, would be wonderful)

4 egg whites

½ teaspoon cream of tartar

4 tablespoons sugar (slightly more for fresh berries)

1 teaspoon cornstarch or arrowroot

1 tablespoon orange flavored liqueur, such as Grand Marnier or Triple Sec

To Prepare the Crepes

(May be done as much as 1 day in advance.)

1. Beat the egg and milk together, add the flour (sifted with the pinch of salt) and remaining ingredients, and stir just to combine. Chill for 2 hours.

2. Spray a nonstick 8-inch skillet with nonstick cooking spray. Place skillet over high heat. Ladle just enough batter into the pan to film bottom. Pour excess batter back into bowl after bottom has set. Cook crepe over medium-high heat until browned on one side. Flip, cook on underside just to firm (this will be the inside, unseen part of the crepe), and slide onto a plate. Continue cooking, spraying skillet as necessary. Place a sheet of waxed paper between the cooked crepes. Crepes may now be used or chilled or frozen until needed. The recipe makes six to eight 6-inch crepes.

To Prepare the Soufflé

1. Preheat oven to 350 degrees. With cooking spray, spray an ovenproof serving dish large enough to hold 8 folded crepes.

2. Puree the raspberries in a food processor or blender. Strain and discard the seeds.

3. Measure 1/3 cup raspberry puree and set it aside.

4. Beat egg whites until foamy. Add cream of tartar, gradually beat in sugar, and beat until just shy of stiff peaks.

5. Fold the 1/3 cup raspberry puree into the beaten egg whites. Divide soufflé mixture among the crepes, placing about 3 heaping tablespoons on the unbrowned side of each crepe. (Discard or cook separately any leftover soufflé.) Fold crepe ends to middle. Place crepes seam-side down in prepared ovenproof dish. Crepes can now be frozen, or they must be baked immediately. Bake unfrozen crepes soufflés 12 to 15 minutes (bake frozen crepes soufflés 15 to 20 minutes) or until puffed and golden. Serve with confectioners' sugar sifted on top or the following sauce.

6. Combine the remaining raspberry puree with cornstarch dissolved in the orange liqueur. Cook, whisking over medium-low heat, until slightly thickened, about 2 minutes. Film serving plates with thickened raspberry puree, place puffed crepe soufflé on top, or drizzle raspberry puree over the crepe soufflé.

Vanilla Ice Milk

This basic recipe is far better than any store-bought version you might buy. And, with additions, it can be flavored with coffee, maple walnut, pumpkin rum, ginger, or any other concoction you might devise. It does require an ice cream maker to develop the proper texture, however.

4 cups skim milk

1 cup sugar

1 1/2 teaspoons good-quality vanilla extract

1/8 teaspoon salt

1. Pour the milk, sugar, vanilla, and salt directly into the cream can of the ice cream maker. Stir with a wooden spoon until sugar dissolves. Process in an ice cream maker according to the manufacturer's instructions.

Yield: 12 1/2-cup servings

Calories per serving: 89

Protein per serving: 3g

Fat per serving: trace

  Saturated fat per serving: trace

Cholesterol per serving: 1mg

Carbohydrates per serving: 20g

Sodium per serving: 55mg

Fiber per serving: 0

Coffee Ice Milk

Dissolve 4 tablespoons instant powdered coffee in the milk. Continue with the recipe.

Yield: 12 1/2-cup servings

Calories per serving: 93

Protein per serving: 3g

Fat per serving: trace

  Saturated fat per serving: trace

Cholesterol per serving: 1mg

Carbohydrates per serving: 21g

Sodium per serving: 56mg

Fiber per serving: 0

MAPLE WALNUT ICE MILK

Use ¾ cup sugar and ¼ cup maple syrup. Substitute 1 tablespoon maple extract for the vanilla extract. Fold ⅓ cup nuts into the processed ice cream before hardening in freezer.

Yield: 12 ½-cup servings
Calories per serving: 111
Protein per serving: 3g
Fat per serving: 2g
   Saturated fat per serving: trace
Cholesterol per serving: 1mg
Carbohydrates per serving: 21g
Sodium per serving: 56mg
Fiber per serving: trace

PUMPKIN RUM ICE MILK

Substitute 1 tablespoon rum for the vanilla extract. Add several gratings fresh nutmeg and ½ teaspoon ground cinnamon to the milk-sugar mixture. Stir ½ cup canned or homemade unsweetened pumpkin puree into the ice milk after processing and before hardening in the freezer.

Yield: 12 ½-cup servings
Calories per serving: 95
Protein per serving: 3g
Fat per serving: trace
   Saturated fat per serving: trace
Cholesterol per serving: 1mg
Carbohydrates per serving: 21g
Sodium per serving: 55mg
Fiber per serving: trace

GINGER ICE MILK

Simmer the milk with a 3-inch piece of peeled ginger root for 20 minutes. Discard the ginger. Cool. Stir 1 tablespoon finely minced crystallized ginger into the ice milk just before hardening in freezer.

Yield: 12 ½-cup servings
Calories per serving: 92
Protein per serving: 3g
Fat per serving: trace
   Saturated fat per serving: trace
Cholesterol per serving: 1mg
Carbohydrates per serving: 21g
Sodium per serving: 55mg
Fiber per serving: trace

RASPBERRY ICE
WITH CASSIS SAUCE

Tart raspberry tempered with a sweet sauce of vanilla and cassis—a seasonless dessert thanks to the year-round availability of frozen berries. An ice cream maker is necessary to produce the fine texture. Like most homemade ice creams and sherbets, it is best made no more than 24 hours before serving.

1/2 cup sugar

1/2 cup water

2 10-ounce packages frozen raspberries (in light syrup) or 1 pint fresh raspberries

1 teaspoon lemon juice

1 tablespoon crème de cassis

For the Sauce

3 tablespoons crème de cassis

1/2 cup vanilla ice milk, softened

Yield: 7 3-ounce servings

Calories per serving: 180

Protein per serving: 3g

Fat per serving: trace

    Saturated fat per serving: trace

Cholesterol per serving: 1mg

Carbohydrates per serving: 40g

Sodium per serving: 56mg

Fiber per serving: 1g

To Prepare the Ice

1. Combine the sugar and water in a 1-quart saucepan over low heat. Swirl the pan by the handle until the sugar is dissolved. Do not stir. Raise heat to high and boil 5 minutes. Chill.

2. If using fresh berries add sugar, sparingly, to taste. Puree the berries in a food processor or blender. Strain and discard the seeds.

3. Combine chilled syrup with raspberry puree, lemon juice, and cassis. Freeze in ice cream maker according to the manufacturer's instructions.

To Prepare the Sauce

1. Stir the crème de cassis into the softened ice milk. Serve 2 tablespoons over each serving.

ALMOND ANGEL FOOD CAKE

This quickly made cake pairs the lightness of beaten egg whites with the crunch of almonds. Baked in a ring mold, it can be served with a mound of fresh sliced fruit in the center, and the whole napped with Almond Cream (page 290). It would also make a nice addition to a fruit fondue tray, and it is very tempting all by itself.

1 ounce slivered or sliced almonds
1/2 cup sugar
6 tablespoons cake flour
1/2 cup egg whites (about 5–6)
a pinch salt
1/2 teaspoon cream of tartar
1 teaspoon vanilla extract
1/2 teaspoon almond extract

Yield: 8 servings
Calories per serving: 100
Protein per serving: 4g
Fat per serving: 2g
   Saturated fat per serving: trace
Cholesterol per serving: 0
Carbohydrates per serving: 17g
Sodium per serving: 59mg
Fiber per serving: 1g

1. Spray a 4-cup ring mold with cooking spray or butter and flour. Preheat oven to 300 degrees.

2. Pulverize the almonds in a food processor or blender. Do not allow them to get mushy. Set aside in a bowl.

3. Sift together the sugar and flour; mix with the almonds.

4. Beat the egg whites until foamy, add salt, and continue to beat until soft peaks form. Add the cream of tartar and continue to beat until stiff but not dry.

5. Fold the flour-sugar-nut mixture into the egg whites along with the extracts. Do not overbeat. Spoon into the prepared ring mold and place in the bottom third of the 300-degree oven. Turn heat off after 30 minutes but leave the cake in oven for another 10 minutes. Then cool, inverted on a rack, for 30 minutes. Run a flexible-bladed spatula around the rim and center of the mold to release the cake. If it doesn't come free, let it cool a while longer.

PUMPKIN-APRICOT-WALNUT MUFFINS

Mini-muffins are a wonderful way to satisfy a sweet tooth without sacrificing good nutrition. My attempts to create a fat-free muffin were dismal; these have just enough oil (the kind with the lowest saturated fat) to produce a cake-crumbly texture. I've also included a touch of chopped nuts to lend a pleasing flavor and crunch. Enjoy them plain or with orange-flecked nonfat cream cheese.

Yield: 36 mini-muffins

Calories per muffin: 47

Protein per muffin: 1g

Fat per muffin: 2g

   Saturated fat per muffin: trace

Cholesterol per muffin: trace

Carbohydrates per muffin: 6g

Sodium per muffin: 102mg

Fiber per muffin: 1g

1 ¹/₄ cups all-purpose white flour

¹/₂ cup unprocessed bran (wheat, or oat)

1 teaspoon baking powder

¹/₂ teaspoon baking soda

1 teaspoon ground cinnamon

¹/₂ teaspoon ground ginger

¹/₂ teaspoon ground allspice

¹/₂ teaspoon ground cloves

1 teaspoon salt

2 egg whites, lightly beaten

³/₄ cup canned pumpkin

¹/₄ cup canola oil

¹/₃ cup molasses or brown sugar

¹/₃ cup skim milk

¹/₄ cup nonfat plain yogurt

1 teaspoon vanilla extract

¹/₄ cup diced dried apricots

2 tablespoons chopped walnuts

1. Spray 3 mini-muffin tins (each with 12 muffin cups) with cooking spray. Preheat oven to 400 degrees.

2. Sift together the flour, bran, baking powder, baking soda, spices, and salt.

3. Mix together the egg whites, pumpkin, oil, molasses, milk, yogurt, and vanilla.

4. Stir the wet ingredients into the dry ingredients with as few strokes as possible. Overbeating makes a tough muffin, because the gluten in the flour becomes activated.

5. Stir in the apricots and walnuts. Divide the mixture among the muffin cups. Bake in the middle of the oven for 15–18 minutes or until the muffins spring back when pressed.

Vanilla

Vanilla beans come from a variety of orchid. When fresh, the pods are green and oddly odorless, but when dried, they become incredibly fragrant. To make your own vanilla extract, split a vanilla bean in half and make a slit along its length to expose the minute tiny beans inside. Place the beans in a 2-ounce jar (an old vanilla extract bottle is perfect), fill it with vodka, cap the jar tightly, and let it rest 1 month in a cool, dark place. The resulting extract is wonderful in many desserts. Add 2 drops to the ground coffee beans in your next pot for a delicious cup of coffee. The bean may be reused.

RAISIN-OATMEAL-CARROT COOKIES

These toothsome high-fiber morsels are chock-full of goodies—pineapple, raisins, granola, oatmeal, and spices—but they are not terribly sweet. Sprinkling the cookies with cinnamon sugar, rather than incorporating the sugar in the dough, makes them taste a little sweeter. If you'd like them sweeter still, you may add up to 4 tablespoons brown sugar without adjusting any other ingredients.

Yield: 36 cookies

Calories per cookie: 50

Protein per cookie: 1g

Fat per cookie: 1g

   Saturated fat per cookie: trace

Cholesterol per cookie: 0

Carbohydrates per cookie: 9g

Sodium per cookie: 89mg

Fiber per cookie: 1g

3 tablespoons canola oil

1/4 cup honey (if heated a moment in the microwave, it will be easier to measure)

1/2 cup egg substitute or 2 eggs

2 medium carrots, grated (about 1 packed cup)

1/2 cup crushed pineapple

1 teaspoon prechopped ginger (available at specialty food stores) or 1/2 teaspoon ground ginger added with dry ingredients

1 teaspoon vanilla extract

1 1/2 cups whole wheat flour

1 teaspoon baking soda

1 teaspoon salt

2 teaspoons ground cinnamon

1/2 teaspoon ground cloves

about 1/4 teaspoon freshly grated nutmeg

2/3 cup oatmeal, not instant

1/3 cup fat-free granola cereal (raisin cinnamon recommended)

2 tablespoons unprocessed bran

2 tablespoons raisins

cinnamon sugar

1. Cream together the oil and honey in the bowl of a food processor. (Add the brown sugar now, if desired.) With the machine on full power, mix in the eggs, carrots, pineapple, ginger, and vanilla extract. Set aside.

2. Sift the flour, baking soda, salt, cinnamon, cloves, and nutmeg into a medium-size bowl.

3. Preheat the oven to 350 degrees. Spray 2 or 3 cookie sheets with nonstick cooking spray.

4. Stir the carrot-honey mixture into the flour. Stir in the oatmeal, granola, bran, and raisins. Stir the dough only enough to just combine, or cookies will be tough.

5. Scoop rounded tablespoons of dough onto cookie sheets. Sprinkle lightly with cinnamon sugar. If sweeter cookies are desired, put a pinch of granola on each cookie top before baking. Bake until cookies are lightly browned and firm when touched, about 15 minutes. Sprinkle again with cinnamon sugar, if desired.

GOURMET LIGHT
MENUS

INFORMAL DINNER MENUS

Fettuccine with Cepes
Veal Chops with Red Pepper Butter
Pea and Leek Puree
Japanese Dressing on Snow Peas
Candied Oranges with Melba Sauce

Pear and Havarti Salad with Pine Nuts
Chicken Paillards with Blackened Tomato Salsa
Asparagus
Boiled New Potatoes with Parsley*
Mimosa Sherbet

Pasta Salad with Basil Salsa
Veal Scallops with Sun-Dried Tomatoes and Shiitake Mushrooms
Julienned Summer Squash
Grand Marnier Mousse

Grilled Corn and Tomato Chowder with Fresh Herb Salsa
Fire and Ice Salad
Fresh Fruit Macerated in Champagne*

Entertaining Menus

Mushrooms à la Grecque
Duxelle Melba (with cocktails)
Two-Mushroom Consomme
Breadsticks*
Roasted Tenderloin of Beef
Gourmet Light Béarnaise Sauce
Scotch Onions
Green Beans with Red Pepper Puree
Crepes Suzette

Seviche
Poached Chicken Breast with Mustard Hollandaise
Wild Rice with Golden Raisins*
Sauteed Young Spinach*
Pea Pod and Water Chestnut Salad
Sherry Ginger Dressing
Raspberry Crepes Soufflé

Chèvre-Stuffed Artichokes
Rolls*
Sedona Shrimp with Coconut and Coriander
Bibb, Red Leaf, and Watercress Salad
Herbed French Vinaigrette
Burgundy Poached Pears
Crème Anglaise

GRILL MENUS

Seared Ginger Tuna with Wasabi Butter
Red Bliss Potato Salad
Zucchini Saute
Fresh Fruit in Season*

Clam and Ham Appetizers
Grilled Shrimp on White Beans
Mixed Greens with Oak Creek Orange-Walnut Dressing
Miracle Cheesecake

DINNERS FOR A SUMMER EVENING

Chilled Tomato Soup with Basil-Walnut Cream
Sole, Scallop, and Pea Pod Salad
Berries and Almond Cream

Crudités with Curried Cream Dip
Santa Fe Seafood Salad with Cilantro Cream
Breadsticks*
Raspberry Ice with Cassis Sauce

MIDWEEK DINNER MENUS

Pork Cutlet in Cider Cream Sauce
Risotto
Green Beans with Lemon Butter Sauce

Warm Seafood Salad with Chinese Noodles
Almond Angel Food Cake

Whole Wheat Vegetable Tortilla
Brown Rice*
Vanilla Ice Milk

Fish in a Flash
Sesame Broccoli
Steamed Rice*

Red Pepper and Goat Cheese Pizzetta
Tossed Salad with Sesame Seed Dressing

SUNDAY SUPPER MENUS

Bouillabaisse of Scallops
Rolls*
Caesar Salad
Raisin-Oatmeal-Carrot Cookies

Pasta with Red Pepper Puree
Mixed Greens with Balsamic-Walnut Oil Vinaigrette
Hot Apple Tart

HOME FROM VACATION POUND-CHASER

Lemon-Lime Fish Fillets in Parchment Paper Hearts
Orange Carrot Puree
Tossed Salad
Fresh Herb Vinaigrette
Fresh Melon with Port Wine Sorbet

PICNICS IN THE PARK

Black Bean and Corn Salad
Pita Bread*
Strawberries to dip in Almond Cream

Ratatouille
Chèvre-Stuffed Artichokes
Pumpkin-Apricot-Walnut Muffins

Chicken and Pasta Salad with Golden Raisins and Capers
Wilted Cucumber Salad
Raisin-Oatmeal-Carrot Cookies

* The asterisk means the recipe is not in this cookbook.

Index

M

ABOUT THE AUTHOR

For several years GREER UNDERWOOD has been a cooking teacher specializing in reduced-calorie gourmet dishes. Her love of cooking was sparked by two years in Europe during which she was exposed to and fascinated by the foods of many countries. Being small in size, however, Greer had to learn ways to combine her love of fine food with her knowledge of calories and nutrition.

Besides teaching, Greer has marketed a line of specialty sauces under the name, Foodstuff. She is a member of Boston's Women's Culinary Guild, and lives in Hingham, Massachusetts, with her husband and two teenage non–nutrition-minded sons.

Greer's food articles have appeared in *The Boston Globe, The Christian Science Monitor, Early American Life, Self, Creative Ideas for Living,* and other national magazines.